Be Happy or I'll Scream!

Also by Sheri Lynch

Hello, My Name Is Mommy

Be Happy
or
I'll Scream!

*My Deranged Quest
for the Perfect
Husband, Family, and Life*

Sheri Lynch

St. Martin's Press
New York

www.stmartins.com

Book design by Mary A. Wirth

LIBRARY OF CONGRESS CATALOGING-IN-PUBLICATION DATA

Lynch, Sheri.
   Be happy or I'll scream! : my deranged quest for the perfect husband, family, and life / Sheri Lynch.—1st ed.
      p. cm.
   ISBN 0-312-34233-0
   EAN 978-0-312-34233-3
   1. Lynch, Sheri.   2. Mothers—United States—Biography.   3. Wives—United States—Biography.   4. Motherhood.   5. Family.   6. Family on television   I. Title.

HQ759.L94 2006
306.85—dc22   2005044453

First Edition: February 2006

10 9 8 7 6 5 4 3 2 1

For my family

Contents

Acknowledgments

I'm indebted to my agent, Marc Gerald, without whose encouragement, enthusiasm, and consistent prodding, I might never have begun, much less completed, this project. Elizabeth Beier, my editor at St. Martin's, for her trust, wisdom, ideas, and input—and for renting a pirate and pirate ship for her son's fourth birthday party. It's a joy to work with such a kindred spirit. Marsha Ferebee, who listened patiently to all of my frustrated ravings as I worked—and then offered exactly the right advice, every single time. My mother-in-law, Joanne Nolan, who has no idea what she gave me when she said, years ago, "You're a *writer*." It was the first time I'd ever heard those words out loud. I can't think of a better or more wonderful compliment to try and live up to.

Thanks also to Leslie Vandenherik, for the gift of guilt-free afternoons in which to write. The very accommodating crew at Port City Java in Charlotte, where I spent many productive Tuesday afternoons working away at my favorite window table. (The one Tuesday I skipped, Dave Matthews dropped by for a cappuccino. He chatted and signed autographs for an hour. Probably at *my* table. Go figure.) And to Bob Lacey, Max Sweeten, Todd Haller, Angela Snider, Tony Garcia, Rick Jackson, and all of my coworkers at Jefferson-Pilot for your unconditional support—and for looking the other way every time I sneak off to write.

To every person who appears in these pages, thank you for your patience and good humor. I've changed only a few names, to protect the unwitting from embarrassment.

Finally, my heartfelt gratitude to the people who inspired this whole crazy undertaking: my husband, Mark, and our children, Eric, Olivia, and Caramia. You are the best fellow adventurers anyone could wish for. I love you.

Introduction

My destiny was set at age six when I accepted Timmy Bonafiglia's earnest proposal of marriage. Timmy promised me a split-level house, matching his-and-hers Chevy Vegas, and a lifestyle fueled by the exorbitant salary he expected to earn as a manager at JCPenney. What can I say? I was dazzled. Even the first-grader I was could see that Timmy was a catch. His family lived in the nicest house on our block, a perfectly maintained Cape Cod complete with an enormous aboveground swimming pool and a barbeque pit. Timmy's mom dressed almost exclusively in citrus-colored culottes, white Keds, and pink frosted lipstick. Timmy's dad was himself a JCPenney store manager, thus paving the way for a Bonafiglia dynasty in reasonably priced retail. Theirs was the good life, suburban style, and I wanted a taste. Plus, the Bonafiglias seemed happy and wholesome in a way that my own family did not; marriage to Timmy represented more than a step up on the social ladder. It offered an escape as well. Timmy would be my white knight, the rescuer who would sweep me off to my very own happily ever after of cookouts, car pools, and casseroles. And so, while other little girls spent their childish daydreams on visions of faraway kingdoms and castles and unicorns, I set my sights squarely on suburbia. How pathetic is that?

I'd love to be someone whose dearest ambition is to scale Mount Everest. I've met some of those people, and they do seem more powerfully alive than the rest of us, though I suppose it's possible that the extra gleam in their eyes is due to complete madness. But having seen the IMAX movie, I know full well that it's a really brutal climb to that famed summit, wickedly cold, and ends at an altitude I've only experienced from the cramped seat of a commercial airliner. If there's one thing I've figured out, it's my limitations: any sport that requires supplemental oxygen is one my body wasn't designed to tackle. Also, the prospect of plummeting to a lonely death in a bottomless, icy crevasse is pretty much all the incentive I've needed to avoid accidentally hiring a Sherpa and turning up at base camp.

It's not that I'm totally averse to thrills. I've been hang gliding (nightmares about falling for months afterward), parasailing (one poorly fastened buckle and you'll be lucky to ever walk again), mountain biking (three years' worth of orthodonture potentially wiped out by a single wayward tree root), and even to Minneapolis in January (not that bad; you can actually shop downtown all day without once having to step outdoors). My thrills have always come instead from simpler things: home, family, special moments with the ones I love. At least I thought they were simple—until I tried to create the perfect family of my own.

When you consider that *real* families are thrown together by genes and circumstance, not writers and casting directors, it's nuts to try to build a fantasy family out of whatever materials you've got lying around. It's nuts to even want to. But is it impossible? I wanted to know—and for purely personal, entirely selfish, not-at-all-scientific reasons. It hit me one afternoon as I was decorating gingerbread cookies with my then-two-year-old daughter. Flour, sugar, and gobs of rapidly drying batter adhered to every surface of the kitchen, including our arms, clothes, and hair. Even the dog was filthy. (Don't be fooled: no matter how bright they act, two-year-olds actually make lousy hand-mixer operators.) We'd finally reached the best part of the whole process and were lustily spackling our misshapen cookies with icing and sprinkles when my husband strolled in. Swallowing a gingerbread man in two bites, he glanced around at the demolished kitchen, rolled his eyes, and said, "What a disaster. Who'd ever want to just buy some cookies at the store? Not *your* mommy. *Your* mommy thinks she's living in a TV show."

It was a delicious moment of epiphany. Because he was almost right. I didn't think I was living in a TV show; that would be completely crazy, and we'd have to get doctors involved. But I sure *wanted* to live in a TV show. I wanted the kind of life where cookies were baked and bonding was accomplished and Valuable Life Lessons were learned. I wanted laughter, mixed with a few tears, of course, and some frustrations of the kind that led to growth, maybe a handful of challenges and difficulties to build character (without eroding the soul), and mostly, loads of fun, joyful, wonderful memories. What I yearned for, in other words, was an entire life made up of Very Special Episodes.

Suddenly, all of my efforts, dreams, and poorly thought-out domestic endeavors made sense. I wasn't just some random Type A wackjob whose home-ec gene periodically ran amok. I was a woman on a mission! It was a nutty mission, to be sure, but a quixotic one, too. If life really is the nasty, brutish, short ordeal that Thomas Hobbes so famously warned us about, then why not make the time you've got as heartwarming and amusing as possible? And what better place to start than with your very own family?

I love the idea of family. I also love the phrase *nuclear family*, the way it sounds vaguely thrilling, and dangerous, and futuristic. Growing up in the murky shadow of the Cold War, back in the days when

Sting could get massive airplay on MTV with a cheerless ditty warning us about atomic annihilation at the hands of the Russians, I couldn't help noticing that the word *nuclear* was very frequently attached not just to *family* but also to *weapon, war, winter,* and *power.* Coincidence? Or was it because nuclear families rely upon the same threat of mutually assured destruction to maintain the delicate balance of power as our government does? The split atom is plenty scary, but the family is really the most potent force in the Universe. Our families drive us to do great things, noble things, to establish dynasties, whether in politics or in dry cleaning. Our families also drive us to despair, to drink, and straight into therapy. We may criticize them or lionize them; we may hate them while unconsciously re-creating them; but we almost never manage to escape them.

My obsession with family is regrettably complicated by the fact that I am completely warped from too many years spent watching other people's families on television. And I'm not talking about those poor souls on *COPS,* either. Sitcom families are the ones most to blame for screwing me up. Growing up with these grinning and guffawing television clans for neighbors made me take a hard look at the family I'd been born into. We were nuclear, all right, if by that you mean unstable and potentially noxious. We couldn't even manage to get the suburban props right. There may have been a swing set in our backyard, but dead deer were as likely to be swinging on it as we were. That way, our father could more comfortably gut each carcass in full view of the neighbors. We had virtually nothing in common with the charming, attractive, stable, and happy folk on the small screen. Unless you count the Munsters. We were a little bit like them, minus that cool car, the big house, and the regularly employed dad.

Thirty-minute bursts of shiny, happy, smiling prosperity—who wouldn't be entranced? I lapped it up. I wanted what I saw on television. This meant I had to give up on my family of origin pretty quickly. The two most critical characteristics of all TV moms and dads, patience and predictability, were precisely the traits my parents were most deficient in. They refused to conform to the television model—they wouldn't even consider joining the Rotary or the PTA, much less pack our whole brood off to Hawaii or Disneyland during a ratings sweep. Also, they were far more inclined to smack us in the head for bad behavior than sit us down for a meaningful heart-to-heart. Their other crimes included smoking, cursing, arguing loudly, and, shockingly, sleeping in the nude. They couldn't be bothered with our shoe-box dioramas, our school art contest posters, or our annoying insistence on regular meals. When our father troubled himself to impart an important life lesson, it usually involved making us memorize the quickest route to the corner store so that we could fetch him a Pepsi and a pack of Pall Malls.

Perhaps we kids were to blame for their parental shortcomings. Maybe we just weren't cute enough. Perhaps if my brothers and I hadn't been such crushing disappointments, our parents might not have been so terribly hopeless. Quite possibly we had brought a life that played like an R-rated version of an after-school special entirely on ourselves. With this in mind, I vowed to do things differently once I had a family of my own.

My first challenge in creating my own perfect family was to figure out exactly what the essential features of the perfect television family were. It wasn't wealth or class status; poor families were just as rich in love and harmony as rich families. Poverty, it seemed, could actually be unifying, encouraging the family members to rely on each other even more. Look at the Waltons! Or almost any episode of *Good Times*. To be poor and struggling was apparently not the dreadful handicap for my TV friends that it was for those of us on the other side of the screen. A traditional, intact family was also optional; any division created by divorce—or, better yet, death—wasn't a tragedy but a rich comic opportunity. Thanks to the untimely demise of Mrs. Tanner, the girls on *Full House* got to have all sorts of wholesome fun with Dad, Uncle Jessie, and Joey. Like I

xvi   **Introduction**

wouldn't have *happily* traded my own mother for John Stamos, mullet haircut and all?

It appeared that you could strip almost any family-themed television program down to its very core and find exactly two common points: reasonably enthusiastic kids and a thoroughly agreeable father/husband. So critically important is the agreeable husband to the mix that there are almost no family sitcoms without one. Even Shirley Partridge, raising her musical brood on that garishly painted school bus, had the long-suffering Reuben Kinkaid standing in for the missing and necessary Mr. Agreeable.

Think how much of the comedy in a family sitcom is driven not by the silly antics of children but by the constant struggle on the part of the husband/father to reconcile himself to being hapless, harmless, and put-upon. Since Mr. Agreeable must at all times remain a good sport no matter how foolish or annoying the scenario, he's forever waging a fierce internal battle with his own inner alpha butch.

Go all the way back to *I Love Lucy* and you'll find the beleaguered and blustery but ultimately pliable Ricky Ricardo. Zip forward four decades and there's the always-game Dan Conner of *Roseanne*. With his tubby physique and spotty employment, Dan may have seemed as real as it gets—but even he was forever good to go, no matter how tough the going got. In the world of TV families, Mr. Agreeable might holler and stomp, but at the end of each episode he's usually cheerfully bemused and resigned to his fate. What he's not is cranky, mean, sullen, or scary. Forget male models and movie stars—these guys are the *real* female fantasy. Clearly, if I wanted a TV kind of family, I'd have to be married to a TV kind of man.

Next requirement: reasonably enthusiastic kids. Kids are integral to the whole television family concept. Without them you might be forced to house a dotty in-law in your basement just to have something to talk about with your spouse. There's no getting around

it: if you're going to have the ideal TV family, you're going to need
some kids. The more the better, which is why it's helpful to have lots
of neighbors. That way, you can borrow their kids when the occasion calls for a crowd, then send them home when they get too loud
or smelly. Which they do, and more swiftly than you think, believe
me.

As obnoxious as real kids can be, they're a big improvement on
their TV counterparts, most of whom are weirdly—almost
creepily—precocious, annoying, full of snotty comebacks, and entirely too much the center of attention. Naturally, that's just what we
loved about them when we were kids, and not only identified with
these pint-size egomaniacs, but actually rooted for them against the
chowderheads they were stuck with for parents. Now that *we're* the
adults, however, that sort of thing simply won't stand. We want our
kids to instead be smart, adorable, and hugely appreciative of our
every gesture and sacrifice. The rest of the time we just want them to
be quiet. And, with a little luck, spending the night at someone else's
house.

Once Mr. Agreeable and a brood of spunky youngsters are
firmly onboard, the perfect family is finally ready to tackle the next
critical component: a series of Wholesome Adventures. Exotic vacations are always good, but as we've learned on television, every day
can and should be filled with laughter and new discoveries. Even
mundane chores are made fun when the family joins together to do
them. The important element to focus on is togetherness, whether
while washing the dog or visiting the Empire State Building. TV families actually want to be together; even TV teenagers aren't nearly as
repulsed and mortified by their parents as you probably were by
yours.

And TV siblings are often close, if not best, friends. You never
once saw Greg Brady tie little Bobby to a chair and drool saliva on
him in a grotesque parody of Chinese water torture. The older Tanner girls on *Full House* made it all the way to adulthood without even

trying to trick Michelle into letting them give her a buzz cut. Was there some secret—setting aside the fact that every bit of it is make-believe—to achieving this level of family harmony?

The answer, hiding in plain sight in countless hours of canned camaraderie, had to be communication. Members of the TV families talk but, even more important, listen to each other. Communication is the single driving catalyst that can turn any Wholesome Adventure into a Valuable Life Lesson. After much careful analysis, I decided that I had hit upon the recipe to remake my family into an ideal family:

1. Mr. Agreeable
2. Enthusiastic brood
3. Wholesome Adventures
4. Communication

This was a thrilling discovery. Only four ingredients! Maybe this was easier than anyone had ever realized. Maybe TV had something good to teach us after all. I was anxious to get started. I felt reasonably confident about the material I had to work with, too. By cleverly marrying a mechanical engineer, I guaranteed myself a husband who could construct and operate all of the many toys, tools, and Christmas decorations that were necessary to create a smoothly running and perfect home. Though not exactly what you'd call agreeable, he was at least very handy. Then there was his upbringing in a particularly wholesome midwestern suburb—perhaps his stubborn lack of jolly initiative might be overcome by the forces of genetics and environment, if not by sheer wifely coercion. Kids were plentiful: Eric, Mark's son from his first marriage, and two daughters of our own, Olivia and Caramia. As a bonus, we also have Eric's friend Alex, whose mother died when he was six, leaving him to weather his father's subsequent parade of wildly unsuitable girlfriends. Between my job in syndicated radio and my husband's decision to stay home with the children, we were a network TV exec's pitch meeting dream:

"She's a wacky morning deejay! He's an anal-retentive stay-at-home dad! Can a couple with three divorces between them, a sullen preadolescent son, a prickly ex-wife, two preschool daughters, and a senile French bulldog really achieve Mom's dream of becoming the perfect television-style family?"

I knew from the start that it wouldn't be easy. It would require extraordinary patience and planning. I'd have to begin by persuading my husband to go along. The kids would be another matter, armed as they always are with a whiny litany of complaints ranging from hot and tired to bored and hungry. I hoped to just tune them out; practically speaking, how much resistance could three children under the age of twelve, none of whom has any money or better prospects, successfully mount against me? I gave myself a year to pull off the transformation. Twelve months of weekends, holidays, vacations, dinners, chores, and errands. For twelve months of daily life, breakfast to bedtime, I would make a superhuman effort to consciously treat each and every single day as an episode in our ongoing story. That meant not only deliberately structuring loads of memorable moments but also searching for any that might be buried in our mundane routines. I'd ferret out the heartwarming, pin down the meaningful, and mercilessly stalk any and all Valuable Lessons to be had. At the end of it, I hoped we'd be one of those freakishly happy and close families that make you wonder just what exactly everyone is on. It was the challenge I'd been ready for since I was six years old and first entranced by the promise of true suburban paradise. Okay, so the Chevy Vega turned out to be a lemon and Timmy Bonafiglia turned out to be gay. These developments were merely minor roadblocks on the path to glory, not dream killers. It would take a whole lot more than that to dim the luster of the nuclear family for me. Blame it on the Brady Bunch.

"Just give me a year," I pleaded with my husband. "Act like a happy TV kind of person, become a happy TV kind of person. Mind over matter. It's that simple."

His response indicated that Mr. Long-Suffering had quite a bit of work to do in the area of character development: "You're nuts. Why do all of your ideas make me feel so tired?" Like any true sit-com wife, I interpreted that grumbling to mean a "yes" and pressed forward, filled with optimism and enthusiasm and good intentions.

Armed with nothing more than the ecstatic vision of prime-time picket fence perfection, I set out to transform our lives. Given enough time and practice, I firmly believed, everyone would come to see it my way. After all, this is America, and surely here, if nowhere else, it's possible for one determined woman to transform her entire life into one long Very Special Episode.

Or so I thought.

Be Happy or I'll Scream!

1

T.R.A.P.

I knew I was beaten on the day I finally admitted to myself that I was using the dog as a vacuum cleaner. "Get on over here, Champ!" I'd wearily bellow, hardly pausing to watch as our elderly and almost completely daft French bulldog lapped up whatever rice, peas, Cheerios, or raisins the baby had flung around the kitchen. It was a job that required some supervision, though far less effort than reaching for the Hoover: "You missed a spot right here, buddy." Sometimes I'd even help him halfway up onto the baby's seat so that he could pry loose any morsel that might have wedged itself between the bottom of her booster and the chair. It was slovenly and gross, and I knew it. Of course I knew it. I could even feel my clean-freak mother's disapproval clear across two thousand miles and three time zones. But I was tired, so tired, too tired to care, much less worry about some dog saliva and a few stray elbow noodles. Three kids, a husband, and a full-time career had lowered my standards to depths I never thought possible. In the span of a few short years, I'd been transformed from an anal-retentive, obsessive nutcase into a who-cares-as-long-as-we-don't-have-bugs obsessive nutcase. Which I guess counts as progress, or will have to, since there's no going back.

I've poured my energy—the energy I might have used for cleaning, serious volunteering, learning a new craft, or at least doing Pilates—into a crazy experiment. One that I realized probably wasn't working out all too well on the evening I caught a glimpse of myself looking haggard and crazy-woman sloppy in the sunglasses department at Wal-Mart. While my husband tried on new shades, I stood clutching a package of *Dora the Explorer* underpants for our three-year-old, and numbly watched as our one-year-old gnawed on the metal arm of a tipsy display rack. Part of my brain screamed, Germs! Oh my God! Germs! Exposed metal! Danger! Danger! Danger! But the rest of that soggy organ slyly whispered, Ah. She's not crying. Excellent. Why not enjoy a minute here to yourself? . . . Which is precisely what I did, staring bug-eyed off into the middle distance, half-listening to the chatter of my family and the murmurs of my passing fellow Wal-Martians. That's when my husband's righteously disbelieving voice sliced into my dazed reverie like a knife. "WHAT are you chewing? Mommy! Hello? Hello? Do you see what your baby is doing? THAT'S not too disgusting! Here!" *Thwomp!* He dumped the baby into my arms, her face screwed up in rage and disappointment. I knew that we had only seconds before the now-building scream would tear loose from her throat—shrill, deafening, insane. Whipping a colorful, trendy, pediatrician-approved teething device from my bag, I waved it at her, a gesture rich in both hope and futility. Furious, she knocked it out of my hand. More screaming.

Sensing an opportunity, our three-year-old sidled up. "Mommy, can I please have some Skittles?" She nodded her head "yes" while asking, hoping to hypnotize me into granting her request.

"No Skittles," I answered firmly, still convinced that I might yet pull off the whole calm, reasonable, I'm-in-charge-here parenting charade. "You've already had a treat."

My husband was now swabbing out the baby's mouth with a Wet One, an indignity that only slightly muffled her roaring.

"But I want some Skittles!" Olivia barked. "You have to give me some Skittles!" Furious that her demands were being ignored, Olivia then upped the ante to full-blown hysteria. Inspired, the baby lustily joined in. Stereo shrieking.

Shooting me a look of pure aggravation, Mark hissed, "Let's just pay and get out of here."

As we hustled our little treasures out the door, both grimy-faced and wailing, it hit me: What I wanted was a family just like the families on television. What we actually became, however, was Those People. The family no one wants to be anywhere near on an airplane or in a restaurant. We were loud, we were grubby, we were bickering—and we were at Wal-Mart on a Friday night. How on earth had we gotten so far off course?

It began as a New Year's resolution. After a frantic holiday season of too much shopping and too many toys, of juggled schedules and events, of expectations reaching too high and energy levels hovering too low, I wanted a break. No, that's not quite strong enough. I wanted a different life—for all of us. I couldn't understand why everything always felt so rushed and crazy. Everyone was healthy. We weren't starving or cold. Nothing was on fire, leaking, or ready to explode. So why did we exist in a state of constant, chronic chaos? I flirted briefly with the idea of quitting everything and moving the whole family to a modest cabin out west, but my parents did that, and believe me, it created far more problems than it solved. Our approach to making a new life in rural Wyoming was so half-assed that compared to us, the Unabomber in his ratty shed looked like a responsible guy with a bright future. When it comes to experiencing the raw thrill of an isolated, poverty-stricken, sub-zero winter or two, I've been there and done it, thank you. You can keep it. I like my creature comforts, i.e., electricity, flush toilets, and central heating, way too much to willingly surrender them.

Besides, what I wanted wasn't exactly a simpler life; I wanted a television life. A fantasy, in other words, made up of rollicking, wholesome, happy, zany fun. I knew such a thing was an unattainable goal, of course, in much the same way that I knew getting a body like a swimsuit model's was an unattainable goal. But that didn't stop me from hitting the gym every February. All that was needed was a plan and a bit of willpower. Compared to the impossible task of morphing my five-foot-six-inch dependably sturdy frame into that of a willowy bikini mannequin, transforming my beautiful family into an idealized little band of adventurers seemed just about ridiculously easy. We'd simply have to commit to living our lives to the absolute fullest, seizing every moment, instead of just schlepping from place to place, mess to mess.

Phase One of my plan consisted of getting every member of the family to buy into the whole notion. The baby, Caramia, and the three-year-old, Olivia, were easy. Not only were they both already my loyal followers; they were easily bribed with balloons, key rings, or a fistful of Pepperidge Farm Goldfish. The eleven-year-old, Eric, was easy, too—I just didn't mention it to him, knowing that he'd go along with pretty much anything that didn't conflict with PlayStation, Gameboy, or whatever he was watching on TV at the moment. My husband, Mark, was another story altogether. It was a classic case of differing priorities. My idea of the perfect day included a family outing, a shopping trip, and a fabulous meal. His perfect day began with sex, followed by a dangerous and dirty ride on his mountain bike, followed by even more sex, and finished off with a gigantic bag of something really sugary and gross, like Mike and Ikes or cheap jelly beans. Suffice it to say, neither one of us was living our idea of perfect. Mark's initial response to my suggestion that we conquer the stresses of daily life by thinking and acting like a sitcom family was a disbelieving "What is *wrong* with you? That's nuts." It took some serious persuasion to bring him around. I designed my argument around four key points.

Think Yourself Happy

Research shows that perception is a powerful factor in determining state of mind. Of course, research can be made to show a lot of things. In this case, I counted on my husband being too busy and too distracted to try to prove me wrong. This approach, being very similar to *count your blessings*, was designed to emphasize all of the many fabulous aspects of our busy life, and to stress the importance of being grateful for each and every last one. Especially those aspects that were very soon to be inflicted in large numbers on us, by me.

Remember: They're Growing Up So Fast

What parent, gazing into the sullen adolescent face of their once-adorable spawn, hasn't felt the mortal sucker punch of time? Babies turn into kids, then teens, then adults, in the blink of an eye. Better get in all the balloon animals and beach trips you can while the kids are still cute and enamored of you. Someday you'll be scrounging together their bail money and wondering if maybe you should have taken them to play mini-golf more often. Why not do it now, while you still can?

Adapt to the Challenges

Argue with Darwin all you want, but there's a lot of truth in that whole survival-of-the-fittest business. With kids, someone or something will always be broken, off-schedule, or horribly expensive. Only those parental organisms that can adapt to hardship and somehow manage to thrive despite deprivation of sleep, privacy, and cash will survive. And don't think you can save yourself from any of it. Cowering in the house in front of the television offers no protection from the aggravation, expense, and sheer fatigue of having a family. Accept that you're probably going to wind up old, broke, and exhausted, and just fling yourself into it with everything you've got. Then, when you're old, broke, and exhausted, at least you'll have some good stories to tell.

Plan for Adventure

If you just sit around waiting for something amazing to happen, chances are excellent that absolutely nothing will ever come your way. Fun is something you generally have to seek out. Fun that finds you is usually someone else's fun. That's not always a bad thing, but after a while it feels unsatisfying at best, downright abusive at worst. Remember all those great ideas you had about what your life would be like one of these days? The scary truth is, these days are here— and not only here but flying by and gone. It's past time to get busy. Think basic physics: A body at rest tends to remain at rest. A body in motion tends to remain in motion. Maybe you dozed through that class in high school, but it means, very simply, a person sacked out on the couch like a big, lazy, bloated hog will stay sacked out on the couch, possibly forever. Start living now, *really* living, before you drop dead and leave your kids with a houseful of pointless crap and clutter to sort through, argue over, then dump into Hefty bags for the garbage collectors.

To make it easy for everyone to remember, I condensed it all into four words: *Think, Remember, Adapt, and Plan*—or T.R.A.P., for short. And Mark *was* trapped. Given the choice between being a man who really seizes life by the throat and being a joyless lump of couch-riding livestock, what self-respecting human being would proudly opt to be pork? Mark was in—he just didn't know for what.

With everyone safely snared in my T.R.A.P., the next step was to figure out which areas of our family life most needed the television treatment. Interesting casting wasn't the problem. We're a blended family, with a few extra Hollywood touches thrown in to boost the overall level of wackiness, misunderstanding, and melodrama. The Mommy (that's me) does a syndicated radio show heard in towns all over the country. Not only does that lend a bit of showbiz glamour to the whole enterprise, it all but guarantees weekends full of events featuring stilt-walkers and free hot dogs—pure gold for any adventure-seeking American family. Mark (aka The Daddy) left his engineering career to be a full-time stay-at-home father. How much more Sensitive New Man can you get? Eric, my stepson, lives with his mom in another state during the school year, spending summers, holidays, and every other weekend with us. His mother, my husband's first wife, is gay, which explains pretty efficiently how I came to be in the picture in the first place. Mark and I have two daughters, a three-year-old dinosaur maniac who never stops talking and a one-year-old who never stops bellowing.

Thanks to the clan-expanding metrics of divorce, Mark and I also have a huge extended family. Between us, we've got four sets of parents, five sisters, three brothers, six stepbrothers, and an entire army of aunts, uncles, cousins, nieces, and nephews. That amounts to dozens of birthdays to keep track of and remember—a task at which I consistently fail. Like many women trying to juggle family and career in a world that apparently expects us to earn like a CEO, keep house like Donna Reed, and look like a barely legal porn star, overwhelming guilt and anxiety push everything else out of my mind. So I throw pizza at my family three nights per week and constantly shuffle back and forth to the Hallmark store to buy ridiculously overpriced cards for my swollen horde of relations, not one of whom is considerate enough to live within reasonable babysitting distance. Not that we'd have taken advantage of them if they did— we were both too paralyzed by guilt to even seriously contemplate finding a sitter. Mark because he was a stay-at-home dad and, by golly, the kids were his *job*. And me because I had to go to work every day and wasn't that already too much time spent away from my babies? Clearly, Mark and I were nuts. Changes needed to be made.

The problem, I thought, wasn't that our family was idly bored, but that we had far too many of the wrong sorts of things to do. Granted, a lot of that involved laundry and meals. But shouldn't life be more than endlessly pretreating garments for stains and barking, "Swallow that bite right this minute!" over and over again? No one had warned Mark and me that having multiple small children was akin to being placed under house arrest. No sooner did one wake up than the other wanted a nap. Whole days passed by while we waited for everyone in the house to be simultaneously awake, fed, dry, and not sobbing. On the rare occasions that the stars aligned to permit an outing, it would invariably rain, or snow, or hail. Or one of the babies would suddenly throw up, just to keep us off-balance. (This phenomenon, known as *decoy barfing,* is a purely random event, neither preceded nor followed by any other symptoms or disability. It's done strictly for laughs—the child's, not yours.) Back we'd trudge into the house, our hopes dashed, another Sunday afternoon shot. Next thing you know it's Monday morning, then Friday night again, then Halloween, Christmas, and the Fourth of July. Where did all of those days go?

There's an interesting theory floating around that tries to address the mystery of why time seems to fly as we get older. It has to do with routine, with falling into a behavioral rut. When we're young, every day is packed with new experiences, new things to discover, explore, and learn. The days feel long and full, dense with meaning. As we age, we have fewer new experiences. We try new things less frequently. We follow the same patterns, day after day— often eating the same foods, driving the same routes, having the same conversations over and over. This tiresome drudge, also known as having a job and paying the bills, requires less mental engagement than learning how to tie one's shoes or do long division, for example. As a result, each day blends into the next, with few landmarks to distinguish one from the other. Until the day you look up and say, "Whoa there! Where the hell did my twenties/thirties/ forties go?" It's depressing, isn't it? But it's not hopeless.

If it's routine that literally makes our minds numb and our lives zip by too quickly, then it only stands to reason that shaking up those routines could make life feel longer, fuller, and infinitely more fabulous. That was exactly what I wanted for my family. And in the cold light of a January morning, it seemed perfectly reasonable. New people, new adventures, new places, new habits. We'd swap the daily grind for something fresh and different, something with a purpose, a plan, a plot. All I'd have to do to beat the mundane was turn every possible opportunity into an episode. And I felt more than qualified for the job. After all, I'd been called a drama queen my whole life. Now I was finally ready to embrace the title and ascend to the throne. No longer would we be ruled by chores and obligations. Surveying my cluttered little kingdom, I announced, "This year, everything is going to be different around here." No one was listening, of course. For all the reaction I got, I might as well have uttered the words "There is a lobster growing out of my head." But no matter. Know those signs sold at truck stops that declare, "If Mama ain't happy, ain't nobody happy"? I was Mama. And it was time to make me happy.

2

The Long Good Morning

6:47 A.M. The first day of our brand-new, infinitely happier life starts exactly the same way as our old, infinitely too frantic life: with a three-year-old crashing through our bedroom door and shrieking, "Mommy! You have to wipe me!"

"Daddy wants to do that, sweetie. Let Daddy," I mumble, pulling a pillow over my head in a doomed attempt at hiding

"No! Not Daddy! Only you can wipe me, Mommy! Not Daddy! *Ever* Mommy!" She bursts into the full-blown torrent of agonized sobs that she keeps simmering and ready at all times. When it comes to a hair-trigger defense system designed to swiftly and efficiently annihilate all opposition, NORAD doesn't have anything on this kid.

I stagger out of bed and follow my daughter, naked from the waist down, an eight-foot-long plume of toilet paper trailing in her wake. "Hey," my husband groggily calls. I turn back and stick my head into our bedroom.

"See if you can get her back to sleep," he says with a hopeful leer. "And then come back to bed."

Olivia prances back into the room and tugs on my arm. "Mommy! I want waffles! And juice! Can I go outside? Can I? Just for one minute, Mommy? Can I?" She's hopping from foot to foot, already so charged up that the only way she's going back to her bed is if we shackle her to it. It's tempting. But then I remember that today is the first day of our new life, and that it simply wouldn't do to begin with a bout of toddler bondage. So I force my sleep-puffy face into what I hope is a wry but dazzling grin and say to my husband, "Well, it looks like the only thing that's going to be hot around here this morning is breakfast. So why don't you get up and I'll have yours ready!"

And then I march Olivia out of the room, ignoring my husband calling after me, "What the *hell* has gotten into you?"

The breakfasts of my childhood were composed largely of Cheerios and secondhand cigarette smoke. Sometimes, if we were good, we'd get to have Tang—a sickly-tasting orange drink made from a powdered mix and, at our house anyway, room-temperature tap water. Tang, advertised as the drink of orbiting American astronauts, was an expensive brand-name product and, as such, a real luxury for us. So thrilled were we to have it that we never questioned why we even *wanted* the drink of the astronauts, who, floating in space, didn't have the easy access to real oranges that we, living two miles from a supermarket right here on earth, were lucky to enjoy. Spooning enough sugar onto our Cheerios to make a grainy mud in the bottom of the cereal bowl, swirling glasses of gritty Tang, squinting at each other through clouds of bluish Pall Mall smoke— that was the breakfast of champions at our house. If my mother was feeling particularly ambitious and we hadn't been too obnoxious, she might even fling a slice or two of cinnamon toast our way. This was your basic Wonder bread, slathered in butter, sprinkled with cinnamon, and heaped with yet more sugar. After a high-octane meal like that, we'd be careening around the living room, chattering like rabid monkeys, and pinching, poking, grabbing, slapping, yanking, and tripping each other. "Jesus Christ!" my father would rage. "Can't these damn kids sit still for a minute?"

I decided to take breakfast a little more seriously once I had children of my own. I'd heard the whole argument about breakfast being the most important meal of the day, the solid foundation for everything from excellence in school to more skillful social interaction to staying out of jail. A careful examination of my family's academic and prison records indicated that perhaps there might be a shred of truth in all of that fancy nutritional research. Apparently, refined sugar and tobacco were poor choices for the first meal of the day. According to the picture on the side of pretty much every cereal box ever manufactured, a balanced breakfast would more ideally consist of: a bowl of cereal with milk, an egg, a strip of bacon, a piece of toast, and a glass of orange juice. So wholesome and varied was this parade of food groups that I wondered how the venerable Pop-Tart, with its frosted slab of flavorless Sheetrock-dry cookie wrapped around a gluey smear of quasi-fruit jam, had ever made the breakfast-table cut. Isn't a Pop-Tart nothing more than an oversized cookie dressed up in a fancy foil bag? If that qualified as breakfast, then Fig Newtons and chocolate milk must rate as a meal that any parent could feel proud to serve before sending the kids off to school, right?

The cereal-eggs-bacon-toast-juice extravaganza always struck me as an awfully large pile of food to shove in front of any child, especially first thing in the morning. And eggs were a tricky proposition. Maybe it began as an evolutionary strategy back in the hunter-gatherer days when choosing the wrong thing to eat could result in sickness or death, but most of the kids I've known would run screaming in horror at the sight of a poached egg. Compare its rubbery, sinister weirdness to the reassuringly friendly colors of a bowl of Fruity Pebbles. To the average eight-year-old, the Fruity Pebbles are going to appear a far less risky choice. Then there's the laziness factor. Given the option of cooking first thing in the morning or sleeping for an extra fifteen minutes, who doesn't want to chuck a bowl and spoon across the table and be done with it?

Clever TV advertising had almost tricked me into bridging the gap between cooking, symbolic of serious motherhood mojo, and just serving cereal, that icon of convenience, with instant oatmeal, the best of both worlds. Much as I yearned for what the commercials promised, a kitchen full of photogenic youngsters in flannel pajamas expressing ravenous delight over their steaming bowls of beige muck, I knew that was pure Hollywood. My mother convinced my brothers and me to eat instant oatmeal only by threatening us with a good beating. Since we never saw the actual package that it came in, we eventually reached the conclusion that she was saving a few bucks on groceries by forcing us to eat warmed-over wallpaper paste. Instant oatmeal was definitely out. If I was going to try to be the ultimate TV family kind of mom, it appeared I'd have no choice but to wield a spatula. It was a terrifying endeavor. Cooking breakfast every morning now seems almost like a quaint anachronism, the province of farmers, ranchers, and June Cleaver. What busy working mother in her right mind would even attempt such a crazy thing?

It turned out that there *was* a force stronger than my laziness, strong enough even to lure me to the stove: fear of carbohydrates. Thanks in part to the Atkins and South Beach diet books, I developed a phobia of pancakes, waffles, bagels, English muffins, toast, cereal, and oatmeal. Carbohydrates were the enemy and must be routed at all costs from the pantry. Breakfast for me was eggs, eggs, and more eggs. I bought an electric skillet and got into the habit of cooking those eggs every single morning, usually before dawn, like some turn-of-the-century bachelor farmer. Once the kids came along, I looked forward to many cheerful mornings in which I, in full Donna Reed mode, would serve heaping platters of nutritious scrambled eggs to my fresh-faced and docile family. Wrong. They didn't want heaping platters of eggs; they wanted Cap'n Crunch and doughnuts.

Each member expressed this in his or her own subtle way. Eric stared at the eggs on his plate as though he'd never before been presented with such a foul offering, wrinkled his nose, and informed me, "Actually, I just like these the way my mom makes them." My gentle investigation of her methods revealed that she alone on earth possessed the secret to properly scrambling an egg and would, in a grievous loss to mankind, be taking that information to her grave. (First Law of Stepparenting: Accept that you can do nothing well and try, just try—go ahead, I dare you—to not take it personally.)

For her part, when whining and bargaining proved futile, Olivia promptly crammed an entire plateful of scrambled egg into her mouth, and then refused to swallow any of it. She simply sat there, cheeks bulging, drooling saliva and bits of egg onto her pajamas. The baby tasted a single forkful and then smacked the plate containing the rest onto the floor, where, thank God, the dog was poised and ready for cleanup. My husband, the sugar addict, sighed heavily and pushed the eggs around with his fork as if to say, "Is there no end to the torment I must endure at the hands of this she-devil who insists on cooking for me?"

This wasn't going to be as easy as I'd hoped. Here it was Day One, we'd been awake for barely an hour, the inmates were rioting over the menu, and the kitchen looked like hell. Not an auspicious beginning for our new and improved family life. In my head I'd been picturing us seated around a spacious table in a sun-drenched kitchen, acres of gleaming countertops and cabinetry all around. Somehow I'd forgotten that we didn't actually live on a professionally designed and decorated make-believe movie set. Toys, books, and puzzles covered our kitchen floor—the result of one of my worst ideas ever: putting a toy box in the kitchen. This was intended to help the children occupy themselves for five minutes while I transformed take-out rotisserie chickens into dinner. This, like so many of my domestic brainstorms, backfired in every direction. For starters, the girls assumed that the whole point of the toy box was to

dump the contents on the floor as quickly and as often as possible. I
suspect they did this not out of naughtiness but out of a genuine desire to be helpful, to make Mark and me feel useful. From what I
could tell, they seemed to view us as kindly simpletons who liked
nothing better than to be given lots of mindless, repetitive tasks to
perform. Picking up blocks. Putting away puzzles. Stacking books.
Easy stuff, but things we could feel good about accomplishing. Now,
watching the dog twist his head sideways and nearly upside down in
pursuit of a chunk of egg that was slowly dripping into the triangle
hole of the baby's shape sorter, I began to grasp that our home was
quite possibly a pigsty.

The sink was full of dirty sippy cups. I could scrawl my name
in the dust on the stove. The answering machine was covered in
Post-it notes and blinked with unplayed messages—most of them
guilt-inducing bulletins from our leisure-addled retired parents.
Catalogs and magazines were piled on the counters. There was mail
everywhere. Incoming, outgoing, never opened, forgotten. Packets
of photographs waiting to be archived in albums teetered in stacks
next to books, boxes of crayons, and aluminum cans waiting to be
carted out to the recycling bin in the garage. There was a mostly
empty black purse and a overfull brown purse, a briefcase, a book
bag, and an assortment of mobile phones, car keys, and sunglasses
all jockeying for counter space with a toaster, a coffeemaker, a knife
block, a giant decorative candlestick topped by a dusty never-lit candle, three aging bananas, and one half-dead plant. It easily could
have been the movie set of my imagination, as long as the movie in
question was about a deranged shut-in who never threw anything
away. If chaos had a headquarters, my kitchen was it. Nothing
gleamed. Nothing shone. Nothing was in its proper place. Even the
blue sponge in the sink reproached me, grubby and tattered and
whispering, "E coli. E coli. E coli."

As I took inventory of the squalid surroundings in which we
were rearing our helpless young, I made the honest but strategically

fatal mistake of turning my back on my family. Seizing the opportunity, one of the little egg traitors had sneaked off to the pantry and dragged out not one but four boxes of cereal. Eric was covertly scarfing up a bowl of chocolate-and-peanut-butter-flavored puffs. Olivia was painstakingly picking the marshmallow treats out of a pile of Lucky Charms, leaving the cereal behind to swell and bloat in the milk like oats with a bad case of PMS. The baby appeared to be eating a paper napkin. And my husband, engrossed in the business section of the newspaper, said, around a mouthful of cinnamon graham nutty something-or-others, "You're just like an old woman over there with all the puttering. Just sit down and eat, why don't you."

Swallowing my now-cold and rigorously carb-free breakfast, I took comfort in the knowledge that true visionaries are often misunderstood. My family had failed to cooperate; so what? It was only the first morning of our brand-new life. Resistance was to be expected. I'd wear them down. Change would come slowly, but it would come. We'd begin by cleaning up this kitchen, blazing a trail through the clutter and mess—making a fresh start in a world of wide-open countertops, a place where a person could think. Or at least walk without impaling a foot on the surprisingly sharp horn of a plastic triceratops. With space being scarce, only essentials could remain. That meant finding a better home for dozens of tiny cars, balls, and stuffed animals, and boxing up unnecessary items, like cookbooks. After all, if they're balking at scrambled eggs, odds are good that they'll really rebel at anything from *Vegetarian Cuisine Behind the Iron Curtain*. Even the perfect TV family won't touch fried sauerkraut balls. Best to be realistic, right?

"I have an announcement to make," I began. "Things are going to change around here, starting immediately."

Eric was the first to react, sinking a little lower in his chair. His eyes darted toward the staircase. I watched him calculate the odds of making a successful escape: three steps to the stairs, run at top speed, barricade himself in the playroom, and crank up the volume on Cartoon Network. Then he slumped, almost imperceptibly. He knew that I'd probably outrun him and, if not, I had a key to every lock in the house. Resistance was futile and he knew it.

"First we're going to clean this place up. Then we're going to start having some adventures."

Mark rolled his eyes. Olivia experimented with pushing a marshmallow shamrock into her nostril. The baby gnawed on a plastic spoon.

"What do you mean by 'adventures'?" Eric asked suspiciously. "Does that include me?"

I beamed. "Of course it does. Adventure means lots of different things, fun things. Instead of working all the time or watching television or just sitting around—"

"Or going to school," Eric helpfully interrupted. "Because I don't go to work, and Olivia and Caramia don't even go to school. They just sit around here all day. Being lazy." Eric is the most literal-minded, rational child ever born. He's a genius at spotting flaws, especially mine. At age five, after I'd gone to unbelievable extremes of cheating and card swapping to let him beat me at yet another game of Candy Land, he gazed at me with sadness and declared, "You're not very smart, Sheri. And you don't have good luck. You're just a big loser."

"Yes, honey, but they're not lazy; they're babies," I replied impatiently. "We can't really expect them to have jobs, right? Who'd hire them? The point is, we're going to get out into the world and really *live*. That's what I mean by 'adventure.'"

Mark looked glum. "Oh boy, here we go. This sounds bad."

"No, it does not. It sounds great. It sounds like fun. Olivia, get your finger out of your nose."

"It sounds like work to me," Mark grumbled.

"Well, you have to work at having fun. Now, let's get this place cleaned up and we can have our first adventure." I had no idea what that first adventure might be; I'd never actually gotten this far in my daydreaming. Anything outdoors was out of the question; it was January. January in North Carolina meant a cold, dreary, rainy monsoon that turned into snow about once every three years. This wasn't one of those years. Our inaugural adventure would have to be indoors. Bowling? Too loud. The mall? Too crowded. A museum? Not wise, with toddlers grabbing at everything within reach. I was almost desperate. Then it came to me in a flash.

"We're going to the pet store to look at fish! Won't that be fun?"

"Uh," said Eric.

"Fish," said Mark.

"Nemo!" cried Olivia. "We are going to see Nemo! That is a good idea, Mommy! I like fishes!"

And so we began. Unfortunately, the pet store was closed on Sunday. With the baby fussing and ready for a nap, it made no sense to drive another ten miles to visit PetSmart. I refused to abandon my quest for adventure, so we ended up at the one place in suburbia that can be counted on for round-the-clock entertainment: Wal-Mart. Wal-Mart sells a few varieties of fish, none spectacular. Unimpressed, Eric wandered off to look at video game cartridges. Mark made up some story about our needing cleaning supplies and then bolted. The girls and I were left alone to stare at a tank of neon fish. They were sliverlike, fluorescent pink and blue and green. They didn't look real. "They're not," the boy standing next to us informed me. "Well, they are, but they're not really that color. They inject them with something or feed them some dye to make them look like that."

"Really?" I asked. I'd never heard of dyeing a fish before. It sounded like a pretty sick thing to do. But maybe human beings are so jaded now that even God's simplest creatures need an extreme makeover in order to amuse us. That was a depressing thought. Of course, this wasn't the first time that being at Wal-Mart bummed me out. But it was usually seeing some poor kid getting smacked around in the checkout lines by a wigged-out parent that made me feel sad, not the cosmic—and cosmetic—plight of an itty-bitty fish doomed to travel out of there in a small plastic bag to its ultimate, final destination: a flushed toilet.

"Yeah, it makes them glow in the dark. It's pretty cool." He stared at the tank, mesmerized. He was about thirteen, in a faded *South Park* T-shirt and baggy jeans.

"I just can't believe that they actually *dye* them to look like this. That's pretty sad for the fish, don't you think? To be dyed fluorescent?"

The boy shrugged. "Yeah. Maybe. But maybe nobody would buy them if they were just regular. Some people don't want a fish that's just a plain fish. They have to have, like, a superfish, you know?"

I did.

3

Chicago! Chicago!

In a last desperate attempt to stop the girls from screaming like the unappeasable maniacs they are, Mark and I were frantically staging our own airsickness-bag puppet show when the pilot finally announced, "Ladies and gentlemen, once again from the flight deck, we're beginning our descent into Chicago. Please return your seats and tray tables to the upright and locked position. We should have you on the ground in about fifteen minutes or so. Flight attendants, prepare the cabin for arrival."

Olivia kneeled on her car seat, nose pressed against the Plexiglas window.

Mark leaned over her, saying, "Look, Olivia; look at all of those big buildings. That's Chicago."

Olivia stared wide-eyed as the plane gently dipped one wing and made a banking turn toward the city. Then she shot to her feet, banging her head into the overhead storage compartment, and, teetering precariously on her car seat, shouted, "The plane is going down, Mommy! It's going down!"

Not surprisingly, many of our fellow passengers on that particular US Airways flight to the Windy City appeared a bit uneasy with our little prophet of doom's impromptu in-flight announcement. The woman on the aisle one row ahead turned around and stared at Olivia in genuine alarm. I had pretty much the same reaction—and the kid making the spooky declaration was mine.

"Don't fall, airplane!" Olivia yelled, as Mark and I struggled to wrestle her back into the straps and harnesses of her seat.

Caramia, wadded in blankets and stuffed haphazardly into her infant carrier, took advantage of our momentary inattention to gnaw vigorously on an orange crayon that had, perhaps by sorcery or some other dark and inexplicable magic, suddenly materialized in her fist. I snatched at the crayon with one hand and swiped at the bits of waxy orange slobber that dribbled out of her mouth as Mark tossed a sippy cup and a stuffed panda my way. Deprived of her crayon, Caramia howled in fury as the airplane swayed and jittered. While cooing at our increasingly unhinged baby, I failed to notice the bag full of toys, snacks, and books at my feet sliding into the aisle. The aircraft, making its final approach, was tilted just enough to dump the contents onto the floor, allowing a plush, musical, and deeply beloved toy ball to roll merrily into first class and disappear.

Meanwhile, Olivia remained glued to her window, squinting into the late-afternoon sun. The glass-fronted buildings along the city skyline blazed red-gold and shimmered like an image from a travel poster or a mirage. Mark reached across the aisle and squeezed my knee. "Maybe she wants to nurse?" he suggested helpfully, nodding at the flailing, angry, and now-beet red Caramia. "Or maybe you could just give her some gum to chew? Or something?" Since passing her a stick of Dentyne seemed unwise, I shot him a dirty look, then twisted around in my seat to try to nurse the baby. I was still buckled in and just about to contort myself into a position familiar to Cinemax subscribers but rarely attempted in mid-air when, thankfully, the plane lurched, then bumped down onto the runway.

The speakers overhead crackled: "Ladies and gentlemen, welcome to Chicago. The local time is five-oh-five."

Caramia abruptly stopped screaming and popped her thumb into her mouth. I unclenched my jaws, untangled my legs, and reached for the clasp on my seat belt as Olivia clapped her hands and hollered, "Chicago! Chicago! I love this place!" The entire plane erupted in applause.

When I was growing up, a family vacation to a big city, complete with a hotel stay and visits to historic sites or museums, was as foreign to me as the idea of loading my worldly belongings onto the hump of a camel and setting off with the Bedouins. I remember absolutely marveling at a television commercial for Holiday Inn, in which some lucky youngsters frolicked in a swimming pool while their parents beamed indulgently at them from the comfort of their poolside chaise lounges, and an unseen announcer extolled the virtues of clean rooms and roadside convenience. Even at age seven or eight I couldn't help but wonder, What the hell planet are *they* from? Vacations weren't something we took. I once worked up the nerve to ask my father why our family never went on fancy trips to places like Hawaii or Florida, like the Brady Bunch or the people in books did. He squinted, took a long drag on his cigarette, and answered, "You're a kid—your whole frigging life is a vacation." Given that philosophy, Disney World was obviously out of the question. He did pack all of us off to a cabin in the Pocono Mountains once, and apparently that experience was just grim and mildewy enough to warrant never repeating. As for museums, we crossed those elite thresholds only on school field trips. And hotels, well, hotels were simply too exotic and expensive to even consider. If we went anywhere, it was to a relative's home, where we sacked out in sleeping bags on the floor. Even on cross-country car trips between Wyoming and New Jersey, hotels were off-limits. My parents traded driving duties around-the-clock while my brothers and I dozed in a squirming, miserable pile in the backseat. "You lucky kids are seeing America," my mom would observe as the three of us shivered by the gas pumps at a Stuckey's Truck Stop in Nebraska, or Iowa, or the Dakotas. The America we saw from the backseat of that Chevy consisted of endless miles of dirty gray interstate highway cutting through a monotonous series of wintry, dead, middle-of-nowhere landscapes. But we didn't dare whine. We sensed that they were just itching for an excuse to kill us and dump our bodies—and we knew better than to give them one.

Our Windy City odyssey began with spam e-mail. "I found some incredibly cheap fares online for spring break," I declared. "What do you think about everyone going on a little trip?"

Mark's predictably wary response: "A little trip to where?"

"Well, how about Chicago?"

"Chicago. Hmmm."

I let it breathe for a moment. Mark went to college in Chicago, Northwestern University, and he loved the city. But like a stubborn old farm mule who balks at plowing unless he thinks it's *his* idea to get out in the sun for a spell, Mark had to be led to the harness with great care and cunning. I didn't resent this; on the contrary, I respected it, and frankly enjoyed the challenge. Coaxing him through the barn merely sharpened my wiles and improved my game. It was marital chess. I had my strategies, and I had learned to be patient. Like a spider.

"Yes, Chicago. You know—deep-dish pizza, museums, the aquarium, the zoo. Your dad could drive down for a day or two. He really misses you. And you know how much fun he and Olivia would have together at the aquarium. She adores her grandpa Dean." There—a favorite food, a little culture, an appeal to filial guilt, a warm Hallmark moment between the generations, and the specter of a blissful Olivia. The tickets were as good as bought.

Never doubt that an enthusiastic child is both a blessing and an accomplice. Olivia had single-handedly rescued many of my wacky schemes and plans from the maw of failure simply by being so completely delighted by anything in her path that no one could even hope to remain sour or negative in her company. She loved every idea I came up with, no matter how stupid, bothersome, or messy. She was always up for any activity, any adventure that was new and different. She embraced everything. She feared nothing. She was my biggest ally. I invoked her name whenever I felt Mark might need an extra push or incentive to get with the program.

"Are you sure you want to go anywhere? You don't want to just hang out here and do some stuff? Just not travel until the girls are a little older? Think how much easier that would be."

The obligatory token resistance—token, yes, but not to be taken lightly. Token resistance, like a burr beneath a saddle, can have dire consequences if overlooked. The best way to defuse token resistance to even the most half-baked or grandiose plan is to immediately acknowledge the wisdom of your opponent's position, and then swiftly annihilate their argument with an appeal to something bigger than both of you. In this case, I reached for two of the biggest of the big guns: money and mortality.

"It probably is easier just to stay home, but look at it this way: My job is so unreliable. Who knows if we'll even be able to afford to travel by the time the girls are a little older? And by then they'll be in school, and we'll have those schedules to deal with. You know how hard it is to coordinate stuff with Eric's school calendar. And besides, who even knows if your dad will be around by then? His health's not the greatest. I just feel like we ought to carpe diem while we can, you know? It'll be fun. Olivia's a good traveler, and Caramia is tiny enough still to go with the flow. Let's not be prisoners just because we have kids! Let's not be boring! Let's live!" It was scorched earth as far as the eye could see. We bought the tickets.

Now, having used them, we had to hunt down and haul off the

plane all of the junk we'd dragged onboard. With both girls fussy and grumbling, we waited until every other passenger had trudged down the jetway before we dared to disembark. As usual, this process took three times longer than it should have. If people had any sense, they'd be so grateful to be alive after shooting through the atmosphere in a metal tube at hundreds of miles per hour that they'd sprint off of the airplane and do cartwheels through the terminal. Instead, they shuffle off like drugged zombies. It's a mystery. I was more antsy than the kids by the time Mark edged into the aisle with the two car seats, the duffel bag full of toys—none of which had distracted either child for more than three consecutive minutes and all of which had, at one point or another, rolled all over the damn plane—and Caramia. I slung my handbag and the diaper bag over one shoulder, and Olivia over the other. Looking like weary refugees from Gymboree, we staggered into Midway Airport to begin our adventure.

Midway may be a smaller airport than Chicago O'Hare, but we still managed to find ourselves marooned at a gate situated roughly 3.2 miles distant from Baggage Claim. Hunched under the weight of car seats, bags, and babies, Mark and I made our slow pilgrimage to retrieve our luggage. What with the baby's Whoozit being clamped between my teeth and my being totally winded from the exertion, conversation was impossible. Which gave me plenty of time to think:

The law in many states, including the one we call home, now mandates that children eight years and younger who weigh less than eighty pounds must be restrained in booster seats in cars. This meant I could look forward to years and years of dragging car seats through airports, assuming that I ever agreed to leave the house again. With all of our parents choosing to live at least a thousand miles away from both us and each other, Mark and I seemed fated to spend the next ten or fifteen years dragging ourselves and our kids all over the country. Which struck me as completely insane. Effective immediately, Grandma could bloody well cross over the river and through the woods to get to our house for a change. She's retired now—what else does she have to do?

That new, nagging lower back pain severe enough to keep me awake at night was not merely an inevitable symptom of ageing but the clear result of forcing my spine to do the work of a Ryder truck. I'd tried stretching, and I'd tried chiropractic, but now, limping along past the airport Cinnabon, I wanted narcotics. I felt a sudden, unexpected wave of sympathy for Rush Limbaugh. Poor man was in pain. Back pain is awful, awful, awful. Then I remembered how he'd sent his housekeeper out, big wuss that he was, to score his pills, and I felt sorry for her. It was a classic case of the feudal lord oppressing his serfs, wasn't it? Where I come from, people bought their own illegal drugs and were happy to do it, thank you very much. Of course, Limbaugh's housekeeper did go along with the plan for a good long while, before ultimately turning fink. Hmmm. Even from the perspective of my own solidly criminal upbringing, it was hard to know exactly who—if anyone—deserved more pity in that tawdry melodrama. So, as the grinding pain knifed down my leg, I mostly felt sorry for myself. I used to be the kind of person able to travel light— I could go a whole week with just one carry-on bag. Now I seemingly couldn't leave the house without dragging at least seventy-five pounds' worth of crucial necessities along for the ride. Since I had kids, my new definition of traveling light was packing up every last thing we owned but the furniture and dishes. Wait—I take that back. We did take the dishes: a Hello Kitty fork, spoon, and bowl.

And finally, Mark was right about our just staying home. It would have been better. It would have been easier. Naturally, I would never, ever, under any circumstances, acknowledge this rightness. I would never confirm his suspicions, no matter how tempted by exhaustion and aggravation I might be. That would be our undoing. So being a madcap, adventurous family was hard work? That was fair. Anything in life worth having took hard work—or so I believed. Besides, if I told him that he'd been right about this, he'd want to be right about all sorts of other things, and that was a can of worms best left unopened. We'd never get anything accomplished that way.

"Everyone stop!" Mark suddenly yelled, veering into an alcove between a bank of pay phones and a restroom. "I think I left my mobile on the plane!" As I silently counted to ten and prayed, Lord, give me the strength to not bludgeon him with a LeapPad if we have to turn around and retrace even one of our steps, so help me God, the wayward phone turned up in a side pocket of the toy duffel and we were able to continue our painful trek to Baggage Claim. Our bags, the last to be retrieved, were patiently waiting, passing the time in lonely orbit on carousel number 13.

Things rapidly improved from there. We crammed ourselves and our three suitcases, three carry-on bags, and a baby stroller into a cab and headed for Embassy Suites. Embassy Suites has everything that the family on the move requires: an indoor pool, breakfast, and free booze. Throw in a little Nickelodeon and you're pretty well set for an outstanding weekend. After checking in, we headed downstairs to P.J. Clarke's for dinner. Olivia refused everything on her plate except for three french fries. Caramia fell asleep sitting up, cracker in hand. Mark and I carefully tiptoed back to our room, eased open the door, and laid her down in the crib. Her eyes snapped open—and the screaming began. There was no calming her down. And Olivia, who was overtired herself, got the squirrelly eyes and began jumping on the bed, shouting, "Look at me, Mommy! Look at me jump! Watch me! Watch me now!" More screaming from Caramia. Olivia ricocheted off the headboard and wailed, "I hurt myself! I hurt myself! You have to kiss it! Aaaaaagggghhhh!" Forced to compete, Caramia cranked up the volume on her desperate howl-o-meter.

Scooping up the baby in one arm and the diaper bag in the other, Mark shouted, "I'll take her out for a walk and find her some yogurt. You put Olivia to bed."

The instant the door closed behind them, Olivia's tears evaporated—gone, just like that. "Mommy, can you read me a story now? I will get my dinosaur. Wait right here, okay, Mommy?" And she hopped off the bed as happy as you please and began rummaging through the toy duffel, chattering busily to herself about meat eaters and plant eaters. It was as though I'd hallucinated the whole head-banging, heartrending, sob-laden episode of the past five minutes. Diabolical.

Hours later, I lay in bed and took deep, cleansing breaths. I chanted my new mantra: "We're on an adventure. We're on an adventure." We're on an adventure. I mapped out our plans in my head. Tomorrow, Grandma Jacque and Grandpa Dean would drive down from their home in northern Wisconsin and check in to the hotel for a visit. It'll be great to see them, I thought, and pawn the kids off on them for at least an afternoon—no! Stop that! Away, bad thoughts! Try another cleansing breath. Better. I resumed strategizing. Okay, we'll get together and have some lovely family time, then get Grandma to take the kids to the pool so Mark and I can sneak off to have sex and a nap—no! More wickedness! This is family time! We're on an adventure, remember? More cleansing breaths. Good. So, here's the plan: First lunch, and then the aquarium. We'll take lots of pictures, really make some memories. That's more like it. Yes. Pictures and memories. It was such a beautiful thought that I finally drifted off to sleep, full of happy plans—but not before calculating the odds of my nipping off to H&M while no one was looking to do a little shopping. Alone. Blessedly, blissfully alone. Bad, bad, selfish, shopaholic mommy.

A family trip is a learning experience. Not because you acquire knowledge of your chosen destination—face it: how much data can a three-year-old absorb about Lake Michigan, or the Sears Tower, or, for that matter, pretty much anything other than food and *Sesame Street*? No, a family trip is an opportunity to learn something about each other. For example, I like to have the right tools, equipment,

and clothing necessary to tackle the job at hand. My husband, however, thinks that I buy way too much crap. That's his pet word for
any and all merchandise: *crap*. At home, I'm able to buy that crap,
hide it, and then pretend that we've always had it and that he's just
simply never noticed it before. For his part, he's free to jury-rig whatever he pleases, using solder, glue, tape, wires, bolts, nuts, and
screws. Somehow, we manage to coexist, me with my drawers full of
melon ballers and heated eyelash curlers, him with the same bicycle
he's had since college. It works for us—until we hit the road.

I had argued that we couldn't survive Chicago in March without
serious winter clothes and a double stroller. He strongly disagreed.
So we compromised. We headed to a consignment store to find winter coats for the girls—not an easy proposition in March, in the
South. The pickings were woefully slim. Olivia wound up with a
bubblegum-pink puffy jacket that fit her like a candied sausage cas-
ing. Caramia got a bright purple snowsuit that left her virtually immobilized, with only her peeved little face poking out. Still,
uncomfortable as they looked, it was just for a few days. And at nine
bucks total, the price was definitely right. When it came to buying a
double stroller, though, Mark balked.

"We don't need that. Nobody needs that. They didn't even *exist*
until a few years ago, and people survived. Double stroller. It's so
stupid. You're such a sucker, hon." Calling me a sucker is one of
Mark's favorite debate strategies, although given the fact that I happily purchased Topsy Tail off of a TV infomercial, it's not exactly
the most cutting of insults. Like I don't know that I'm a sucker? I was
practically born holding a credit card, a phone, and my breath to
hear the phrase "But wait—there's more!" Being a sucker is a lifestyle
for me.

I tried to be reasonable. "Yes, we do need a double stroller. How
else were you planning to wheel the babies around Chicago? Now
you're just being stubborn." Calling Mark stubborn is one of my fa-

vorite debate strategies, but since he considers his stubbornness a virtue, he takes it as a compliment.

"No, I'm not being stubborn. I'm being smart. Man, the stores just love to see you coming. You'll buy anything they put in front of you. Double stroller. Oh yeah, better get one of those! We'll never make it a block in the stroller we already have! Ha!" He walked out of the room chuckling to himself like Snidely Whiplash.

Cut to Michigan Avenue, 9:55 A.M., temperature: forty-three chilly degrees. Both babies are stuffed into the single-seat stroller. Olivia, the bulbous pink sausage, is wedged into the rear while Caramia, nearly mummified in her purple snowsuit, is propped awkwardly across her sister's lap. Neither child can move anything but her eyes. Both are sobbing, with snotty noses and red, chapped cheeks. Mercifully, Caramia cannot yet speak. But Olivia can—and does. A lot. A sample of her monologue:

"I want to walk, Mommy! Please can I walk? I don't like this coat. Can you unzip it? It's scratching me! I don't like it! Tiny is crushing me. Get off of me, Tiny! Let me out, Daddy! Unzip it! Unzip it! I want to waaaaaallllllkkkk. I am sad! Pleeeeeeease." And so on. All delivered in a great, hiccupping, wailing sort of a moan. Caramia, for her part, simply yelled—except when Olivia attempted to shove her onto the sidewalk, at which point her yells turned into panicky shrieks. Amazingly, no one so much as glanced in our direction. It's one of the things I like about big cities, the way you can trundle along making a ruckus that sounds like something out of *The Exorcist* and no one even questions it.

Out of the corner of my eye, though, I saw it building. I saw the mounting aggravation. And I saw Mark realize his mistake. It was the I-told-you-so moment and I wanted to savor it, like a glass of rare, fine wine. I wanted to hold it up to the light, breathe in deeply its rich aroma, and delay for as long as possible the thrill of tasting its sweetness. Which meant that I had to soldier bravely along for another block or so before very casually saying, "I guess they'll get used to it eventually. At least they're warm, right? All snuggled up together like that?"

That was all it took. He broke. "Okay! Okay! You were right! We should have gotten a double. Are you happy? We'll go buy one right now. One of these stores must sell one. It's Michigan Avenue, for crying out loud!" He was exasperated right to the point of public kookiness.

"Hon, it's not about being right," I replied serenely. (Admittedly, this was a bit of a lie, since *of course* it was about being right. It's a mark of poor sportsmanship to gloat, however, unless it's done with such covert skill that even the defeated himself is unable to figure out whether you've genuinely taken the high road or are just being extra patronizing as a means of rubbing his face in it.) "This is about trying something that might have worked and didn't, that's all." (Told you so! Told you so!) "Now let's just find a double stroller and then take the girls to the Lincoln Park Zoo."

Three hundred dollars and one shiny new double stroller later, we discovered that even on a blustery cold day, the Lincoln Park Zoo is a fabulous—and free—place for a family in search of a perfect moment. The monkey house was riveting, especially for Olivia, who wondered aloud why her daddy didn't have a big, red bottom like the baboon daddies. I struggled to refrain from comment. We then moved on to the seals. We stood, noses pressed to the glass, watching them turn and glide before us like sleek, otherworldly birds. As each seal skimmed past, Caramia would clap her precious baby hands. When those seals would inevitably disappear to the other side of the pool, Caramia would screw up her face into a furious howl. Happy clap. Angry howl. Happy clap. Angry howl. "She reminds me of someone else I know, someone who wants what she wants right this very second or else Everyone Must Pay," my husband observed darkly. He was obviously still smarting over the stroller incident. But all was forgotten the instant we stepped into the giant, see-through Madagascar Hissing Cockroach habitat. Lit by lurid red bulbs and outfitted with microphones, it was a wretched peek straight into hell. The roaches were making a dreadful clicking sort of noise and, yes, hissing, and they were massive in size, obscenely plump, with glossy hard bodies and evil little hairy-looking legs. Olivia started to cry and I would have joined her, if I hadn't been so busy nearly clawing my own skin off. "Oh, calm down!" Mark said cheerfully. "It's not like they're walking around inside your clothes or tangled up in your hair." He chuckled with satisfaction, pleased to be a man untroubled by an overactive imagination or the bloodcurdling fear of a good roach mauling. Sadist.

Equally entertaining were the Hancock Observatory, the Shedd Aquarium, Navy Pier, the Chicago Children's Museum, and the Art Institute of Chicago. The Hancock Observatory provided, in addition to a breathtaking view of Lake Michigan, a delightful opportunity to introduce an old phobia to a new one: Fear of Heights, please meet Fear of Skyscraper Window Suddenly Disintegrating While My Toddler Is Leaning Against It. I think you two will get along famously. At the Shedd Aquarium, we accidentally made Grandpa Dean miss most of the much-heralded Whale Show by spending too much time waving at the diver who was cleaning the walls of the saltwater tank. (This episode is symptomatic of the well-known Empty Box disorder, in which small children are seen to prefer empty boxes and wads of spent Scotch tape to the pricey toys those boxes once contained. Likewise, such children will stare endlessly at a man wearing scuba gear while completely ignoring far more exotic phenomena, for example, a moray eel pretending to be a sock puppet while standing on its head.)

Mark and I saved the Art Institute of Chicago for last, knowing that our success there would depend entirely on the whims of our daughters. Would they gaze in goggle-eyed wonder at *American Gothic*? Might they be influenced in some small but meaningful way by proximity to a real Edward Hopper? Or would they topple and destroy a priceless sculpture, resulting in our arrest, bankruptcy, and a lifetime of being reviled by art lovers everywhere? After much strategizing, we hit on the only plan that made sense: run them completely ragged all day long, deny them naps, and then drag them into the museum two hours before closing. Maybe then, in all of that silence and splendor, they'd pass out cold in their fabulous new double stroller and let us wander the halls in peace.

It didn't exactly work out that way. The girls were comically groggy by the time we rolled them into the Art Institute, but the almost gymnastic effort required to free them from the bondage of their winter coats, coupled with the temptation of all those signs warning "Please Do Not Touch," was enough to completely revive them. In fact, it energized them. Why is it that a bone-tired adult turns into a big, dopey slug while the very same level of fatigue makes a child behave like a coked-up nutcase? When I'm overtired, I snore. When my children are overtired, they take hostages. Think how much more productive we'd be if exhaustion made us hyper instead of, well, exhausted.

Anyway, before Mark and I could look at a single painting, we had to buckle the girls in like miniature test pilots, remove all toys that could potentially be used as projectiles, and bribe them into silence with fistfuls of Pepperidge Farm Goldfish. Then we had to dash from painting to painting, room to room, cramming them full of Goldfish and periodically bending down to whisper-sing "The Itsy-Bitsy Spider." We rounded a corner and came upon what must have been a group of art students and their teacher. They were contemplating some statue or another and sketching furiously away with charcoal on large, white pads. "I want to color, too!" Olivia shouted. "It is coloring time! I want a big crayon for me!" It's worthwhile to note here that this is one of those moments that parents find utterly precocious and adorable but that strangers—for example, students who view themselves as budding Picassos—find disruptive and pretty stupid. Also, as we've now observed firsthand, budding artists

generally do not describe their work as "coloring"; nor are they interested in sharing their "crayons."

Worn out by Olivia's repeated pleas to be allowed to walk "like a
big girl," Mark and I eventually made the critical mistake of parking
in a wide hallway and releasing both girls from their wheeled cage.
The instant their feet hit the ground, they took off in opposite directions. Olivia immediately tripped and sprawled face-first on the
floor, screaming like she'd been shot. Both Mark and I sprang toward
her, never thinking that Caramia would seize that moment of inattention to do anything other than try to bite her own foot. As I frantically pushed Olivia's hair away from her face and looked for
bruising, I heard Mark gasp, "No, Tiny! No!" I wheeled around just
in time to see my youngest standing on her tiptoes and clinging
tightly to a small bronze statue of a naked woman. And what was
she doing to that statue? Was she giving it a big, warm hug? No, she
was trying to nurse. I snatched her away from her new surrogate
mommy ("Only a little colder than the real thing," Mark cracked)
and shoveled her into the stroller next to her blubbering sister.
"Move, now, before Security comes!" I hissed. I never even got the
name of the statue my baby tried to replace me with. *Winged Leche?*

Mark threw the stroller into high gear and we zoomed out of
there. In typical melodramatic fashion, Olivia began to carry on like
a hired mourner at a Mafia funeral. Her heartbroken sobs echoed off
of the stone floors, bounced around the high ceilings, and reverber-
ated throughout the long, wide corridors. Never one to let her sister
suffer alone, Caramia joined right in. Beaten at last, Mark and I slunk
toward the museum exit, pausing only at the gift shop, which had,
naturally, closed just five minutes before we arrived. At the sight of
display cases filled with what were undeniably toys, more deafening
screams and sobs issued from the stroller. Pointing a tiny, accusatory
finger at a bin full of Beanie Babies, Caramia let loose a particularly
raw, anguished bellow, as if to say, "You forced me to look at a bunch
of paint smears on some wall and now you can't even get me a

stuffed penguin for my trouble? What kind of heartless fiends are you?"

If there is a dirty look that the human face is capable of making, we saw it that night. We experienced the full range: scorn, disgust, derision, irritation, rage, impatience, disbelief, horror, contempt, and loathing. Pariahs that we were—*"Can you believe those idiots brought those two crying babies into a museum, for God's sake?"*—we were ridiculously grateful when one woman paused, her face a mixture of sorrow and pity, and murmured, "I remember when mine were that age. It's only a phase, you know. They can't help themselves, poor things." Like neglected dogs slavering over a kind word, Mark and I very nearly knocked that poor woman down and licked her face in joy. Compassion! Decency! And us so undeserving of anything more than a swift, hard kick.

"Screw it," Mark announced. "Let's go get some pizza."

Hours later, Mark and I were abruptly awakened by the sound of crying, Olivia's voice wailing, "Daddy! Daddy! Daddy!" We stumbled out of bed, switching on lights as we went, and were greeted by the sight of our elder daughter crouched on the sofa bed in what looked like a puddle of orange and red paint. Two things to remember: First, never, ever feed a thoroughly exhausted toddler a late dinner of deep-dish pizza and Twizzlers. Ever. Second, deep-dish pizza and Twizzlers look exactly the same coming up as they do going down, so if you do happen to disregard the above warning, brace for the likelihood that you will be unable to eat either item again, separately or together, for the rest of your life.

After a bath that was accompanied by so much screaming and struggling that I frankly expected the police to start banging on our door at any moment, Olivia was finally calmed and coerced into clean pajamas. Having chimed in with a companionable bout of aggrieved weeping herself, Caramia eventually rolled over and went back to sleep. Meanwhile, Mark and I stood at the scene of the crime: the spattered and fouled Embassy Suites sofa bed. Olivia had cleverly managed to throw up in the space between where the pull-out mattress meets the back of the sofa. At first glance, that seemed like an awfully considerate plan. But closer scrutiny revealed that she had gotten vomit into places that only a maintenance worker with a set of screwdrivers and a power washer could reach. It was after two in the morning; even if someone from Housekeeping could come, we guessed that they'd probably bring something noisy, like a carpet shampooer. We were faced with the choice of once again waking the baby, dying from the reeking stench, or cleaning it up as best we could ourselves.

Like a pale, reproachful ghost, Olivia stood by our side sniffling and hiccupping while we held our breath and mopped up the mess. (When I say *we*, I actually mean *he*, since I didn't do any of the cleaning myself. I did hold my breath, though.) Using a Hilton Hotels Do Not Disturb door placard, Mark carefully scraped regurgitated pizza off of the sofa upholstery. My job was to hold the empty wastebasket he was using as a bucket. While he worked, he talked to Olivia in a quiet, soothing tone. "You know, honey, I don't like Paris Hilton, either. I sure don't. But believe me, she's not the one that Hilton was going to send up here to clean our room, okay? You want to punish the Hilton family for inflicting her on the rest of us—I get that. She makes me sick, too. But the next time your tummy feels funny, sweetie, you need to go into the bathroom. Just get right up and head for the bathroom. Okay, honey? Do you think you can do that, hmmm?"

It was kind of a heartwarming moment, I suppose. Perhaps not *exactly* the one I'd envisioned when I first imagined our fun family adventure in Chicago, but it was memorable, and that definitely counted for something. Just because I'd had something a little less chaotic and disgusting in mind didn't mean that I couldn't appreciate the good things we'd experienced on our trip. And there were many. Like seeing the river dyed green in honor of St. Patrick's Day, and the guy disco dancing for cash on Michigan Avenue, and the giant dinosaur skeleton in front of the Field Museum that caused Olivia to squeal, "I *told* you the dinosaurs were real!"

We'd only been in Chicago a few days, but it felt much longer. Maybe there was truth to the theory that having new experiences made time seem as though it were moving more slowly. Probably *very* slowly at the moment for my husband, wearily blotting puke from the carpet. Watching him, I tried to figure out whether or not our trip had been a success.

"Maybe you could give me a hand here, hon?" Mark inquired. "Start cleaning the couch or something?"

"I would, but you know that vomit makes me sick."

"Oh yeah, I forgot about that. I forgot that it makes you sick. 'Cause it makes me happy, right? I love it." Exasperated and muttering to himself, Mark resumed scrubbing.

Returning to my thoughts, I wondered if perhaps there was an actual scientific or mathematical way to measure how successful our adventure had been. It was clear that before I could arrive at a real answer, I'd have to subtract any emotion or drama from the equation. To do that, I'd need numbers. I calculated that from arrival to departure, we'd spent roughly one hundred and fourteen hours in the city of Chicago. Of that, we'd slept about forty hours—a low estimate, but for the sake of argument I was willing to pretend that we'd logged eight hours of shut-eye per night. Eating took up another fourteen hours and fifty minutes—again, a number that was probably on the low side, but better that than a rampant exaggeration, right? We spent at least ten and a half total hours just getting dressed and out of our hotel room. Sightseeing and/or cultural activities consumed another twelve hours. That left thirty-six hours and forty minutes for crying, consoling, arguing, strategizing, and schlepping from place to place. Over a period of six days, that worked out to approximately six hours and six and a half minutes per day of crying, consoling, arguing, strategizing, and schlepping from place to place. Which sounded just about right.

It came down to this: we spent just slightly less than 90 percent of our time in Chicago engaged in activities that could far more easily be done in the comfort of our own home. A pessimist would probably argue that, from this perspective, the trip was a complete disaster. But I'm not a pessimist. You can't sit around waiting for everything in your life to be perfect before you dive in and start living it. Life is messy and inconvenient. It's designed that way. Families are even messier. And what a queasy two-year-old who's eaten way too much deep-dish pizza can do to a sofa is messiest of all. By those standards, a barely more than 10 percent adventure in a big city with two children under the age of four is pretty good. It might even be great. Chicago, Chicago! I love this place!

4

Terrific Today

If you hope to have a reasonably calm, stress-free, easy life, then I do yourself a favor and never greet the day by announcing, "I'm going to be a terrific mom today!" In fact, if you happen to catch yourself even thinking such a thing, immediately grab the nearest pillow and try to smother yourself. It won't be easy, but you'll suffer far less in the long run, I promise. It might not seem possible for a statement so seemingly innocent and positive to wreak major havoc on a woman's life, but it can—and will. Don't believe it? Why don't we pretend we're back in sixth-grade grammar class learning to diagram sentences, and let's take this sentence apart word by word. (But remember, only hopelessly old, decrepit people who grew up in a world without computers or mobile phones call it *grammar;* the new, sexier name is *language arts.* I'm guessing the name change is part of a well-meaning attempt to make all of those tiresome gerunds and dangling participles a little more appealing to kids weaned on electronic screens instead of paper pages. There's just not much call for grammar in an IM: *u r 2 funny lol!*)

I'm

You can't be blamed for interpreting the word *I'm* as a relatively neutral option. After all, unless you're going to start referring to yourself in the third person as though you were the queen, *I'm* is the only real choice for the job. The problem with *I'm* is that it dumps all the responsibility for whatever happens next squarely onto you. Unless you've worked out some sort of polygamous sister-wife arrangement at your house, you'll be stuck dealing with any mess, trouble, or disaster that *I'm* is able to conjure up. And *I'm* is practically a professional troublemaker. You can never, ever trust her: *I'm* will have you finger-painting in the living room or trying to make your own soap out of olive oil and orange peels or hosting a bead-your-own-necklace slumber party for a gang of rowdy ten-year-old girls before you even realize what's happening. When it comes to fabulous ideas, *I'm* is a genius. Just don't forget that *you'll* be the one stuck living with smeary blue handprints on the couch, scrubbing burned soap out of your pots, and waiting for the cat to stop barfing up beads.

Going to Be

This whole phrase strongly suggests that your past record isn't all that stellar. It also doesn't leave much room for error in the way that *hoping to be* or *planning to be* might. *Going to be* is too definite, too authoritative. It represents precisely the sort of rigid, one-dimensional thinking that makes failure so difficult to swallow. Since failure is often more educational than success, why slam the door on the very real possibility of learning something new? *Going to be*, like the words *always* and *never*, has virtually no place in an enlightened relationship—especially the one you're having with yourself. It's a good idea to hedge your bets by sticking to verbs that are just a little more ambivalent and forgiving. Politicians, fearing the commitment demanded by the direct action verb, do it all the time. Why shouldn't you?

Terrific

This word, much overused by advertisers and anyone who interviews celebrities about their latest movie/TV show/hit song/perfume, seems harmless enough. But *terrific* is actually a surprisingly dangerous adjective. *Webster's Third New International Dictionary* (Unabridged) defines it as:

> 1a: exciting fear or awe: TERRIBLE, TERRIFYING
> b: very bad: AWFUL, FRIGHTFUL
> 2a: of an extraordinary nature: ASTOUNDING, TREMENDOUS
> b: exceptionally strong or violent: POWERFUL, SEVERE
> 3: unusually fine or gratifying: exciting admiration or enthusiasm: MAGNIFICENT, MARVELOUS
> synonym see FEARFUL

If Webster has it right, then *terrific* more accurately describes the Four Horsemen of the Apocalypse than the average woman who has somehow become fixated on the notion that constructing a replica of the Eiffel Tower out of dried linguini would be a really cool rainy-day activity. It's fine to have terrific days, if by that you mean terrible, terrifying, awful, frightful, astounding, tremendous, powerful, and severe days. By that definition, many of us have had terrific weeks—months, even. But those are quite possibly what pushed you to the point of lying in bed and vowing to be the very opposite of terrible, awful, frightful, or severe. Choosing the word *terrific* to describe yourself is like trying to lose ten pounds in a week: you might pull it off, but you'll never be able to sustain it. *Terrific* is not only unrealistic; it's bad for your mental health.

Mom

The word *mom* is so potent that it's practically nuclear. What is a mom but the most selfless, loving, devoted, patient, clever, wonderful, amazing, tireless creature alive? And unlike some other very important jobs that may come with more impressive and intimidating titles, for instance, *genetic biodiversity ethics research fellow*, pretty much everyone knows what the heck it is that a mom does all day. And that makes everyone a critic. Announce that you intend to be a terrific baker today and basically, as long as nothing burns and everything winds up frosted according to schedule, you're okay— and even if something does go horribly wrong, it's just dough, and it's unlikely they'll cart you off to jail for it. Plus, since even the surliest croissant can't rat you out for screwing up, you have a fighting chance of at least being able to hide some of your mistakes. But dare to make one wrong move in a Kmart checkout line and you risk revealing to the whole world what an unfit, belligerent, miserable troll hag of a mother you really are. It's brutally unfair, isn't it?

It's not entirely our fault that we've been brainwashed by a lifetime's worth of laundry detergent commercials, TV shows, and hypnotic magazine articles with titles like "Easy Meals in Minutes!" and "Five Minutes to a Fabulous Face!" and "Rainy-Day Fun for Frazzled Tots!" into trying to be robotic superwomen. No one actually succeeds at this loopy task because one, we're human and fallible, and two, even a high-end European appliance can't take the wear and tear the average superwoman gets. The system is diabolically designed to defeat us no matter what we do. You try, you fail, you feel guilty. But if you don't try at all because, honestly, all of that superwoman multitasking looks absolutely exhausting, you feel guilty for being too lazy or selfish to bother. It's a big circle of insanity, and if you let it, it'll take over your reality. Everyone you know will be only too delighted to let you, the madwoman, rush about dealing with all of the remembering, scheduling, plotting, finding, fixing, buying, cleaning, transporting, and outright coping that needs to be done in order for everyone else's life to run smoothly? They figure, well, if she's crazy enough to take it on, let her have it. After all, she's going to be a terrific mom today!

Today

The word *today* is the final warning that you're in real trouble. *Today* implies that yesterday, last week, and perhaps even tomorrow, you were most decidedly not a terrific mom. You yelled, cursed, threw toys, slammed doors, yanked hair, or maybe just feigned a sudden violent stomach virus and barricaded yourself in the bathroom with a bottle of wine and the latest Pottery Barn catalog. *Today* is a word loaded with expectations and—scariest of all—a ticking timer. Locking yourself into an arbitrary time frame like *today* puts unnecessary pressure on your resources, not to mention your sanity. So forget *today*—that's the kind of basic mistake that only a beginner is crazy enough to make.

Recognize *I'm going to be a terrific mom today* for the dangerous propaganda it is. Rather than being undermined and set up for failure, why not begin the day by making the sorts of promises to yourself that you're more likely to actually keep? Start by giving yourself plenty of time in which to accomplish your goal—and be good and vague about it. Avoid absolutes—words like *must, will, always, forever, never*. Emphasize your positives and, finally, celebrate past accomplishments. If that seems impossible, then at least learn from my mistakes—one of us ought to, and since it's obviously not going to be me, it might as well be you.

If you must motivate yourself with a mantra, at least reach for something sensible. Or borrow one of mine. Some samples are listed here, each engineered for maximum ambiguity. You'll note that even the holidays can be approached in this sane, low-stress manner:

At some point, I hope to improve at this parenting thing.

One of these days, we sure could talk about how cool it would be to have a home-cooked meal every night.

You never know when or how this clutter might be dealt with.

No one is bleeding or on fire—an excellent day, so far.

Size 4? Me? Who can say what the future holds?

Perhaps this might be the summer we all go canoeing or camping or something fun like that. Or not. Whatever.

Maybe we'll think about decorating the house for Christmas pretty darn soon.

Making your own wrapping paper sounds like a pretty neat idea for somebody.

You get the idea. Now take a few deep breaths. Ambiguity feels good, doesn't it? It feels like a place where a woman might finally stretch out and hear herself think. It's all part of the simple new three-step philosophy I've developed after years of running in circles like a stressed-out gerbil: Attempt less, fail less, feel better. It's not an argument for slacking off, or becoming defeatist, or giving up on your dreams. It's about setting limits. It's about taking on the things that really matter to you, and *only* the things that really matter. So you never get around to making your own outdoor furniture out of pinecones. So what? Or maybe you'll never grow your own organic herbs—which you'd planned to transform into either a pesto that no one in your family would dream of eating anyway or a potpourri that would probably wind up smelling weirdly like cat urine—but is that really such a tragic loss? As long as everyone that you're responsible for is alive, reasonably well, and not in serious trouble with the law, who really cares about all of that other stuff?

I had plenty of time to mull over my new philosophy on the afternoon of the day that I decided to be a terrific mom. We were a good four months into our new happy-family lifestyle, and I'll admit it: I was feeling cocky. The minor successes were beginning to add up, one cookie-baking or finger-painting session at a time. We'd also had a fairly major success: the trip to Chicago. That had gone off pretty well, minus the wailing, runny noses, fever, food poisoning, and hotel room barf assault, of course. After all, we did make it home with most of our stuff, which firmly counts as a victory. So, with an entire Saturday stretching before me, no big chores, no obligations, I made the fateful announcement. *I'm going to be a terrific mom today.* And then I rolled straight out of bed into hell.

Okay, so *hell* is an overstatement. But not by much. Because if hell isn't crawling with incontinent, yowling dogs, then Satan sure missed a rich opportunity. Champ had wet his bed. Again. After wrestling the urine-soaked cover into the washing machine, I realized that he'd also popped into the kitchen to have a nice, quiet retch onto the rug underneath the table. Heading for the carpet cleaner, I was intercepted by Olivia, with the morning's list of demands.

"Can I watch something now? Please? I want to watch something," she pleaded. The TV wasn't even on, but so great were its hypnotic powers that she was already standing in front of it, wringing her little hands and rocking back and forth on the balls of her feet like a junkie anxious for a fix.

Terrific Challenge Number One

A terrific mom does not allow television but instead encourages her children to explore creative, intellectually stimulating activities, often incorporating flash cards or modeling clay.

"No television, Olivia. How about if you draw some pictures instead?" I responded, in a tone that was both firmly reasonable and firmly encouraging.

"NO! I don't want to draw! Ever! I want *Tiny Planets*! Let me watch it!" (This was accompanied by various *boo-hoos* and *waaagghhs*, gradually building to a piercing crescendo that the neighbors could probably hear. Sooner or later, one of them would feel obliged to call in the law.)

"You are not starting the day with television," I replied, from beneath the table where I was crouched, carefully blotting dog puke. *Tiny Planets* is a computer-animated children's program on cable that stars two space aliens, Bing and Bong. They travel from planet to planet, where they usually come into contact with creatures called Flockers. It's hard to say what's going on with the Flockers, who are alternately clumsy, helpless, and sometimes even vaguely malevolent. Nothing can stop Bing and Bong, though, from climbing onto their special flying couch and zooming off into Flocker-filled space. All of which is surely some giant inside joke, since there's nothing funnier than hearing your three-year-old shout, "Look, Mommy! I want to play with those crazy Flockers like Bong!" The first few times you hear a toddler's mangled pronunciation of the word *flockers* will get your attention, I guarantee it.

"I want Bing and Bong! Bing and Boooonnnnnnnnggggg!" Long, wailing sobs now. And Mommy understands wanting Bong, oh yes, she does. As Mommy hauls a paper towel full of partly digested Eukanuba to the trash can, Mommy is also muttering something to herself that sounds very much like *flocker*. Naturally, this is my husband's cue, dressed in full mountain-biking regalia, to appear on the scene with Caramia. Unfortunately, in a burst of wifely charity, I'd given my blessing for him to disappear for most of the day. Was it too late to change my mind?

"*What* is going on here? Olivia, I'll turn on *Tiny Planets* for you. Did the damn dog have another accident? I'm telling you right now, this is the last pet we're ever going to have. Here, take Caramia. She wants you." Mark surveyed the room and, satisfied that all was in complete disarray, reached for his keys. "Okay then, I guess I'd better get going."

Terrific Challenge Number Two

A terrific mom does not let minor hassles diminish her aura of cheerful competence. If necessary, she fakes an aura of cheerful competence.

"Right! Have a good ride! Oh, no, everything's fine here. Please, like I can't handle it? Go. Now, time for breakfast, girls!"

After the standard breakfast of bananas, Cheerios, scrambled eggs, multiple spills, and wails for them and a protein bar, despair, and enough caffeine to cause the shakes for me, I got everyone dressed for a trip to the playground. Then I got everyone dressed again, because in the time it took me to find Olivia's jacket, Caramia removed her shoes. By the time I got her shoes back on, Olivia had the barrettes out of her hair and in her mouth, trying, I was ready to bet, to remind me that choking hazards lurked everywhere and that I'd damn well better be paying constant attention to her every move. I hustled them toward the door, and then turned back for the diaper bag, which several minutes of wild ransacking revealed had been cleverly stored under a pile of unfolded laundry on the counter. Finally, we made it to the car! Of course, we couldn't actually leave the driveway, since I couldn't find the *Dora the Explorer* CD, and driving even a mile without it was out of the question.

While Olivia rambled on about Dora and Boots, and could I please play the Dora songs now, and why was Dora missing, and did Dora die out like the dinosaurs, and so on, Caramia simply bellowed and pointed at the dashboard as though to summon Dora from the speakers by sheer force of will. Desperate, I called upon Saint Anthony, the patron saint of lost objects, for an assist: Saint Anthony, Saint Anthony, please come around. Dora is lost and cannot be found.

Leaving the girls in the car, I raced back inside and tore through the piles on the kitchen counters. There she was, peeking out from beneath a Lillian Vernon catalog. Dora! Thank you, Saint Anthony! I ran back to the car, shoved in the CD, cranked up the volume, and peeled out of the neighborhood. We were on our way.

The playground is a terrific mom's best secret weapon because (a) it's free and (b) kids will happily tear around like jacked-up lunatics, and may, with any luck, even require a big, long nap afterward. Watching my girls scampering about with the other children, I felt that the morning's insanity was now miles behind us and that we were well on our way to having a truly terrific day. Caramia dug happily in the sandpit as Olivia climbed on the monkey bars with a group of girls. Every now and again, another mother would make an amusing comment and we'd all have a laugh together, just a bunch of mommies whiling away a sunny hour or two at the park. This suburban idyll was abruptly shattered by the sound of Olivia's voice crying out my name. "Mooommmmy! I need you, Mommy!"

Any mother can tell the difference between a cry meant to impart serious melodrama ("Someone took my red bucket!") and a cry meant to signal real emotional or physical pain ("There's a fire ant in my diaper!"). This maternal sensitivity has nothing to do with instinct and everything to do with repeated exposure. Kids cry enough to give anyone with working ears plenty of practice in deciphering their intentions. I'd heard enough of Olivia's fake cries over everything from a lost plastic dinosaur to a single green bean to know that this time, she really had something to cry about. I sprinted across the playground and grabbed her, quickly scanning for anything obviously bleeding, broken, bitten, or impaled. She looked fine, but she was walking strangely. Was it a sprain? A torn ligament? And then the wind shifted, and I knew the terrible truth.

A portable outdoor toilet is a fine convenience, but it's not the ideal place to take a wailing three-year-old and an inquisitive one-year-old. Especially not at the same time. But what choice did I have? I had to clean Olivia up, and I couldn't leave Caramia alone in the sandpit. Sure, there were other mothers there, but they were strangers. What if one of them turned out to be a psychotic kidnapper? How would it sound to the authorities—not to mention my husband—if I just left our baby with some random nut job? Even explosive diarrhea, which Olivia most certainly had, didn't warrant my taking that kind of risk. So the three of us piled into the Porta-John, where I promptly discovered that I'd neglected to put wipes in the diaper bag. Olivia was sobbing while Caramia was busily laying her hands on every filthy surface she could reach. Pinning the baby against the wall with my knee, I frantically swabbed Olivia down with all of the cheap one-ply toilet paper I could grab. To add to the fun, it was the kind that only begrudgingly comes off the roll, one rough and miserly square at a time.

Wadding the soiled clothes into a ball, I hoisted Caramia onto one hip and half-carried, half-dragged Olivia to the car. A fastidious child who'd never had even a minor potty-type accident, she was nearly hysterical by this point. Much as I tried to murmur reassurances, she wasn't having any of it. Caramia took one look at the car, realized that we were leaving the playground, then arched her back and attempted to jackknife out of my arms. Because it was a beautiful day, there were plenty of bystanders to gawk. Their facial expressions varied, in keeping with their own life circumstances. The childless stared in horror, the other parents in pity, mixed with the blessed relief of knowing that this time, at least, it was somebody else's problem. Both girls screamed and flailed as I stuffed them into their car seats. I fired up the engine and nearly jumped out of my skin as "I'm the map I'm the map I'm the map!" blared out of the speakers. Driving the few miles home as fast as I dared, I shouted, "Hang on, Olivia! Just another minute and we'll be there! How's your tummy feeling now, sweetie?" I glanced in the rearview mirror just in time to see her grimace, and yelled, "No! Not in Mommy's car, okay, baby? Please, not in Mommy's car!"

We burst through the door, both girls in tears, Olivia naked from the waist down. My husband, just back from his relaxing day of cycling alone through the majestic and hushed, pine-scented forest, squinted at us in aggrieved disbelief. "What have you done with Olivia's clothes?" he asked. "She's not wearing any pants. What goes on here when I'm not around?"

Terrific Challenge Number Three

The terrific mom expects adversity, actually prepares for it, and handles it with grace, never succumbing to the cheap and easy allure of sarcasm.

Here marks the spot where I lost it. It appeared that I wasn't going to be a terrific mom today, after all. It clearly wasn't meant to be. Instead, I was going to be a mom with a vein throbbing above her left eye, a mom with wildly flared nostrils, a mom with a now-reeking car, and, thanks to my husband's frankly accusatory tone, a mom just itching for a fight. Not good. Not good at all. I took a deep breath, considered my options, and then replied, "Yes, this is exactly what goes on here when you're not around. We all poop ourselves and go out in public without our pants. And then we cry and cry and cry. Yep. That's just what we do. While you're out. Riding. Your. Bike." *Bike* is one of those deliciously hard-edged words that can be just absolutely spat out, in the most wonderfully satisfying way. If you're going to throw down the gauntlet, might as well do it with a flourish, right?

The rest of the day deteriorated from there. Shocking, really, after such a promising beginning. The dog got himself locked in the baby's room during her nap and, despite the fact that he typically sleeps twenty hours per day, chose that precise moment to be wide awake and alert. He stood by her crib and howled mournfully until

Mark and I raced to the door to set him free. Unfortunately, we weren't quick enough. The baby was startled awake by his canine banshee routine, and remained awake—and ferociously pissed off— for the next six hours. Olivia's diarrhea continued unabated. Desperation soon had me groveling in front of the TV, begging for its forgiveness. "Please, TV, keep them occupied for half an hour and I swear I'll never say anything nasty about you again." Dinner was a grim, tasteless affair starring boiled rice and dry toast. Bedtime sounded like a hollering contest. I practically crawled to the bathroom for a dose of Tylenol PM, which I washed down with an extra-large, frosty-cold mug of bitter mommy guilt.

All of my good intentions had added up to nothing. I wasn't a terrific mom today; I was a bitchy lunatic. Disorganized, scattered, easily overwhelmed—a mess. Where was my stamina, my can-do spirit? Where was my composure? And where in the hell was my inner June Cleaver? No wonder our family didn't have the happy sheen of a television family. I couldn't even remember to check the diaper bag for baby wipes, much less successfully drag us all toward a deeper, more fulfilling life of close-knit adventure. There, in our darkened bedroom, I finally gave voice to my deepest secret worry. "Hon? Do you think that maybe I should be on some sort of medication? You know, for, like, high-strung, nervous people?"

There was no answer for a long time, and I guessed that Mark had already fallen asleep. Then, finally, he spoke. "Doesn't that stuff kill your sex drive? It's not like you have all that much to lose anyway, but still. That'd be bad for me."

He might have had more equally thoughtful, compassionate, husbandly things to say, but by then I was mercifully floating away on a magic carpet of Tylenol PM. I'd attempted too much, I'd failed, and now I felt awful. But tomorrow was another day. Tomorrow was another chance to be a terrific mom. Not that I was crazy enough to try it. No, I'd learned my lesson. Instead of obsessing over being terrific, tomorrow we wouldn't even attempt to leave the house. Maybe we wouldn't even bother getting dressed. No cooking, no cleaning, no crafts. Just lots of watching TV in our pajamas. I felt better already.

The Surly Llama

Three things I swore I'd never do:
  1. Become a bridezilla
  2. Rent a llama for a child's birthday party
  3. Time

Jail is the only thing on that list that I've missed—so far, anyway. I morphed into such an abominable bridezilla that, on the eve of our wedding, my groom-to-be nervously asked if I was planning to tear his head off after the ceremony and eat it, like a praying mantis. "Ha-ha-ha," I laughed, before seizing him by the throat and snarling, "Don't even think about ruining My Perfect Day, buddy, or they'll never find your body. Now, run along and get those gifts wrapped for your ushers. Kisses, Boo-Bear! Can't wait to be your wife!"

I'm not able to explain exactly *how* I became possessed by the bridal demons, but once they had me in their clutches, no one was safe. Not even my passel of pint-size bridesmaids, all of them children, most of them under six. At the peak of my madness, I actually issued those helpless innocents a set of written guidelines on every possible nuptial matter, from jewelry to the color of their nail polish (clear or sheer silver, thanks for asking). And here's the psychotic part: *I knew they couldn't read.* Yet I did it anyway. I wish now that someone had taken me aside and Tasered me. Would have saved everyone a whole lot of aggravation.

But, as the saying goes, live and learn. Or, in my case, just live. I can't seem to make time for the learning part. Which is how, one lovely May afternoon, I came to have two goats, a pig, six ducks, a pony, and a llama camped out in my front yard for my daughter Olivia's birthday party. I blame my parents for this. Not because they captured me, held me for days in an underground bunker, and threatened me with torture until I broke down and agreed to book Sue's Mobile Zoo at one hundred dollars per hour. No, I blame them because they showed their usual poor judgment when they stopped fighting long enough one April night to sneak off to the bedroom and conceive me. Make a baby in April, and the odds are, she'll be born in January. The month after Christmas, when everyone is broke and surly and in no mood for a celebration. January 11, in my case. Less than three weeks separated Christmas and my birthday, and long before I figured out just how I'd been brought into this world, I understood all too well how lousy my timing was.

People who are born in the month of December think that they have it rough. But even a combo birthday/Christmas celebration seems like a better deal than what I got for my twelfth birthday. For starters, my parents forgot it altogether. When my older brother reminded them a day later, my mom had the decency to look sheepish. My dad, however, squinted at me in disbelief, then bellowed, "Jesus Christ! You just had Christmas! Whadda you want from me? A parade?"

My sixteenth birthday followed a similar theme—amnesia plus belligerence. In fact, the only thing sweet about my sixteenth was the entire bottle of Boone's Farm Blueberry Hill that I drank that night in my boyfriend's car, and then barfed all over my father as he opened the front door of the house to let my drunken, puking self in.

Birthdays just weren't lucky occasions for me. I soon came to feel guilty for being born so close to Christmas, and didn't want to be a burden on anyone's calendar or Visa card. After a while, I simply stopped paying attention to my birthday and didn't bother mentioning it. It would come and go, and I would mark the occasion by going out to the mall and buying myself a really nice present. I wasn't maudlin or sad about it; I just didn't have any enthusiasm for the anniversary of my birth. What was the big deal?

And then I had kids. Even before my daughters were born, I took great interest in Eric's birthday. Every year, we'd ask him the same question: "What would you like to do for your birthday this year, Eric?" And every year, he'd give us the same answer: a shrug. We'd end up taking him and a few friends bowling, or to play mini-golf, or to one of those seizure-inducing video arcade places where the kids piss away your hard-earned money for a shot at winning paper tickets that can be redeemed for a crappy little pencil eraser or, if you're superlucky, a whoopee cushion. It took us only about six years to realize that what Eric wanted to do for his birthday was something, anything, with his mom. We could have thrown him a live grenade/all-you-can-eat candy fest and it still wouldn't have made him happy.

Once Mark and I finally caught on, we got together with his mom and suggested that the three of us throw him a big party at a place called Frankie's Fun Park. Since all of the guests were Eric's friends from school, their parents were strangers to me. This was Wife Number One's turf, leaving me to play the unpopular role of His New Wife: That Home-Wrecking Tramp. I didn't really *love* being thought of as the Other Woman, but I knew the truth. Mark's ex opted for an alternative lifestyle. At the time, she wasn't out, which probably accounted for the good old-fashioned shunning I'd already endured at various school functions and soccer games. The funny thing is, she and I would make a far more compatible (and cuter) couple than she and Mark had ever been. The two of us had a lot more in common than merely a husband; Mark definitely had a type—and we were it. Still, between flinching from the icy stares of the other parents and the insanely beeping, dinging, whizzing, chirping din of the video games, I was glad when that party was over. Like I said, birthdays just weren't my thing.

So how did I end up violating one of my own personal life vows and leasing a llama? It all began with a bunny rabbit—the gateway drug of the animal kingdom. Olivia was barely eleven months old, just starting to walk. We were at the park, and we spotted a sign. "Free Petting Zoo," it read, and there was an arrow pointing east. We followed the path and soon came to a fenced enclosure. There was a woman there, wearing denim overalls and a big straw hat. "Come on in and bring that little one!" She beamed. She was surrounded by a milling, bleating crowd of baby goats, lambs, chickens, ducks, potbellied pigs, and shaggy Shetland ponies. Cradled in her arms was a giant, fat, fluffy, flop-eared bunny rabbit. Olivia staggered toward it like a drunken Frankenstein, her arms outstretched, plowing past the goats and nearly tripping over one of the pigs. The look on her precious baby face as the woman knelt down and held out that ridiculously adorable rabbit was one of pure rapture. And we have approximately three hundred digital photos taken that day to prove it.

If you're reasonably sane and love your kids, then one day you're bound to experience the curious sensation of having all logic and sense sucked out of your brain by the nearly hypnotic force of their enthusiasm. The instant your baby likes a person, place, or thing, you will like it, too. What's more, you will go to every extreme to deliver this person, place, or thing to your child as frequently as you can, simply for the joy of watching their little face light up with happiness. These discoveries will strike you with the power of a revelation. "Olivia likes *animals!*" I whispered to Mark as we watched our firstborn daughter take a swing at a seriously panicked duckling. Now, if I hadn't been crazy in love with this child and deranged by my own hormones to boot, I might have been able to get a grip and realize that liking animals wasn't particularly amazing. Of course she liked animals—who doesn't? It wasn't as if she'd lit up over something odd or esoteric, like a nuclear submarine. It was a farm animal, for heaven's sake. Roughly 90 percent of all children's literature revolves around the adventures of farm animals. *Pat the Bunny*, anyone? *Make Way for Ducklings*? Bunnies and piglets and sheep were the creatures who populated Olivia's bedtime stories, her toy box, and even her wardrobe. It was only logical that she'd like the real thing, too, right?

Screw logic. If my little girl wanted animals, then animals she would have. Thus began our odyssey of driving into the country in search of cows and horses, of stomping through acres of goose poop at a nearby pond for the momentary thrill of getting close enough to one of those hissing monsters to toss it a cracker. I can't tell you how many miles we traveled in search of animals—but I can tell you that most cows just don't give a damn about making your acquaintance. You can stand at a fence all afternoon yelling, "Hey, cow! C'mere, cow!" and the most you'll get for your trouble is a sideways glance and a disdainful tail swish. More likely, they'll do what cows who spend their days munching grass do, i.e., defecate, which will fascinate your child more than anything else they have ever seen. Have a kid who isn't much of a talker? Let them get a peek at Mrs. Cow making a poo-poo. The kid will talk then. You won't hear about anything else for hours, maybe days. I spent many a nice afternoon hanging over a stranger's fence and discussing manure with Olivia. It's just a good thing that we live in the South, where farmers are friendly and patient and generally forgiving when they catch a high-strung woman with a Philadelphia accent trespassing on their property and hectoring their livestock.

So, since Olivia liked animals, it only made sense to throw her

an animal-themed birthday party. Mark needed his usual bit of persuading. "A petting zoo? In our front yard? I don't want a bunch of
goats eating the bushes or whatever. And crapping everywhere!
Who's cleaning that up? No, wait, let me guess: *I'm* cleaning it up,
right? A petting zoo. You're nuts. No way." He strode off, shaking his
head.

That felt like a *yes* to me, so I immediately gave Sue's Mobile
Zoo a deposit over the phone. "Great news, hon!" I hollered after
him. "Sue says that she'll shovel up any droppings her animals leave
behind! You're off the hook!" With that one-hundred-dollar deposit,
Operation Over-the-Top Animal Birthday began.

The party soon developed its own momentum. First there was
the matter of refreshments. Rather then ordering a single cake in the
shape of a cow—my original idea—I decided to save the work of all
that cutting and serving and just hand out cupcakes instead. Wanting to have plenty of cupcakes for everyone, I ordered five dozen
from a bakery near my office. Apparently I didn't pay close enough
attention when the baker quoted her price. It was not twenty-eight
dollars *total*, as I had thought, but twenty-eight dollars *per dozen*.
And the cupcakes, I realized when I picked them up, weren't the
dainty little treats that I remembered from my childhood. These
were massive, each one easily the size of a Boston terrier's head, and
thickly slathered with bright blue frosting. It took me three trips to
carry all of the boxes out to my car. Total cost: $147. (It's a safe bet
that my first six or seven birthdays *combined* didn't cost my parents a
hundred and forty bucks.)

Then there was the question of seating. Where would all seventeen of those darling youngsters perch when it came time to enjoy
their giant blue sugar bombs? Having gotten just enough of that blue
icing on my hands to know that it was all but indelible, I sure as hell
didn't want a herd of hopped-up preschoolers buzzing around my
living room and wiping their greasy blue hands and faces on the
sage-green drapes. So Mark, who by this point had finally given up

grousing and embraced the whole shebang, called up one of those party stores that rent out gear for weddings and reserved a half-dozen tiny table-and-chair sets. Cost: $235.

You can't really have a party without balloons, can you? Of course not. Balloons *make* a party. The most sensible plan seemed to be the purchase of our own mini helium tank and a bag of one hundred balloons. When it comes to little kids and balloons, everyone knows that you can't have too many. Luckily, Mark found just the thing at BJ's: a balloon party kit that included a disposable helium tank. To be on the safe side, he went ahead and bought two. I congratulated him on his good shopping sense. He replied that he bought the tanks only because he knew perfectly well that if he didn't, I'd nag him until he blew up a hundred balloons by himself. "Well, you wouldn't want your little girl to be disappointed, would you?" I asked. No, he wouldn't. Cost: $30. Each.

Party favors have become a critical component of the modern juvenile birthday party. I've been to parties where the favors bestowed upon departing guests appeared more costly and elaborate than some of the gifts they'd brought. But price alone won't impress; it's all about creativity. Lacking any ability whatsoever in this highly competitive field, I was gobsmacked by some of the party favors my toddler daughter had already toted home from her first few forays into the social swim. There was the charming pink suitcase packed with costume jewelry, candy, and a medieval-style beribboned princess hat. There was the canvas bag loaded with brand-name art supplies and a high-quality T-shirt embroidered with the word *Artist*. She'd come home with stuffed animals, magic wands—even a charm bracelet. This was quality, expensive stuff. Studying her various bags of party loot, I couldn't help but wonder whatever happened to those flimsy noisemakers that unfurled a funnel of paper when you blew into them. Yes, they got soggy from saliva and fell apart pretty quickly, but they were good for a lot of entertainment while they lasted. Not bad for something that cost about a nickel.

Feeling the pressure to keep up with the other (clearly superior) moms, I tried to discuss the matter of favors with my husband. He was dismissive. "*Favors?* I think we're doing them enough of a favor by buying them a pony ride and an overpriced cupcake. Aren't they the ones who're supposed to bring gifts?"

Still, with only five days to go, our lack of a clever party favor gnawed at me. Even knowing that there were far bigger problems in my life and the world to dwell upon, I found myself obsessing over it. It was embarrassing and stupid and yet, once bridezilla became momzilla, no power in the Universe could derail me from my mission of toddler birthday terror. Except maybe Valium. Too bad I didn't have any. There ought to be a squad of suburban sanity keepers who patrol neighborhoods like mine in search of rampaging breeders like me who need to be taken down with a tranquilizer dart for the good of everyone. Fortunately, just when I thought that we'd have nothing to offer our guests but a bag of Gummi Worms, I stumbled across twenty-four toy sheriff's badges on a dusty shelf at Big Lots. "Check this out—you'll issue each child a badge after they take their first pony ride!" I informed my husband. "How perfect is that?" The badges were tin, big and shiny, and three dollars apiece. Cost: $72.

My friend Allison popped by one afternoon a week or so before the party and informed me that her teenage son, Joel, had taken a filmmaking class at school and hoped to make a little cash off of what he'd learned. Was I interested in having him videotape Olivia's birthday, and then edit the footage into a documentary of the event? You bet I was. In just a few short years (seventeen, to be exact), Olivia would be grown and gone and all I'd have left would be my increasingly fading memories and the hope of an occasional collect call from her college dorm room. A documentary of her animal birthday party might well become my most treasured possession, and the comfort of my old age. I pictured myself all shriveled and forgotten but still able to relive the enchanted days of my elder daughter's babyhood. The very idea of it made me feel better about the future. Having been taught by MasterCard that there are some things in life that you just can't put a price on, I didn't have a clue what amount we should offer to pay for a custom birthday documentary. Joel didn't have that problem. His price: $100.

With animals, treats, balloons, tables, and a filmmaker all onboard, the only thing left for me to control was the weather. The day of the party dawned cloudy and hot. I unhappily abandoned my dreams of blue sky and sunshine, but at least the little ones wouldn't be fried to a crisp as they meandered through the petting zoo. Which arrived right on schedule, to the disbelief of our neighbors. A hastily assembled chicken wire enclosure on our front lawn held ducks, chickens, rabbits, and a baby pig. The goats, llama, and pony were tethered to a tree by the curb. Sue and her helper spread some straw in the street and then proceeded to saddle up the pony. The animals, sensing that showtime was near, were warming up with grunts, bleats, squawks, and whinnies. The guy next door stood in his driveway, staring and shaking his head.

When was the last time you truly examined a goat's face? They have narrow, yellowish eyes and a small mouth with thin, smirking lips. It might be those vacant yellow eyes, but goats look pretty much the way you'd expect Satan to look: evil and inhuman and slightly mocking. Satan probably wouldn't gobble up your shrubs and trees, though, something these goats wasted no time doing. I knew that Mark would have a fit when he saw them, but for the moment he was preoccupied with the baby pig. It was black and silky and plump as could be—an absolutely darling creature. It was also using its snout to vigorously root up our lawn. "Aarrrgh! Make it stop! I just put that sod down!" Mark yelled, waving his arms and charging toward the piglet. Meanwhile, behind his back, one of the devil goats calmly stripped another branch off of the freshly planted dwarf maple and swallowed it whole.

Olivia, the eminence for whom this entire barnyard spectacle had been staged, was thoroughly delighted. When she grew weary of menacing the ducks, she roughed up the rabbit and then stomped around the pen in pursuit of the alarmed baby pig. She was afraid of the llama, which suited the llama just fine. In fact, that llama was the first animal I'd ever encountered capable of rolling its eyes and sneering. It stood there, bored and impatient, occasionally pawing at the asphalt and snorting at the kids when they came too close. Not realizing the severity of its birthday party burnout, I hoisted the baby up in the air for a closer peek and cooed, "Look at the pretty llama, punkin! Look at its beautiful eyelashes!" The llama responded with a look of pure disgust: *Yeah, whatever. Man, this place is a dump.*

The reaction of the other sixteen guests spanned the full range from terror, to indifference, to malice. Any time you get a group of kids together with a group of animals, there will always be one child bent on capturing and strangling, one child who bursts into anguished tears and refuses all comfort, and one who puts a pellet of rabbit dung into their mouth. That same group of kids will be accompanied by their parents, one of whom will sue you for everything you've got if their child is pecked or bitten, one who wrings their hands and worries aloud about salmonella, and one who looks the other way while their kid tries to capture and strangle a chicken. This is why serving beer and margaritas at your child's birthday party is an excellent idea, but, unfortunately, one that hadn't occurred to me. Parents who are enjoying a pleasant buzz tend to pay far less attention to trivial details, like liability or rabies.

After pony rides, an event so fraught with screams and tears that you'd have thought we were sending those kids over the Donner Pass in a blizzard instead of just leading them in a leisurely clip-clop around the cul-de-sac, it was time to sing "Happy Birthday" and have cupcakes.

Predictably, the frosting was the only part of the cupcake that most of the kids ate. They dropped the decapitated remains wherever they were standing, and needless to say, the charming balloon-festooned napkins we'd provided were left untouched. In no time at all, our young guests looked like a miniature Blue Man Group after a bender. By now, everyone was totally keyed up. Kids were caroming off of each other like electrons, snatching at cups and balloons and packages in a sugar-induced frenzy. I caught the eye of another mother, a woman so driven by obsessive worry that she made me look positively tranquil. *Overstimulated*, she mouthed, in the understatement of the day. *Someone's going to get hurt.* As I yanked her son's thumb out of his neighbor's cupcake and used my hip to block yet another kid from swiping my sunglasses off of the table, I could suddenly hear my father's voice in my head: *Jesus Christ! You kids are worse than animals!* Trying to wipe a smear of blue frosting off of my T-shirt—which only made the stain bigger and bluer—I considered the possibility that the old man might have had a point for once.

As Mark corralled the kids into a circle to open presents, my best friend, Marsha, jogged up and panted, "That boy who went after the chicken? The future felon? He's poking the rabbit with a stick now. Where the *hell* is that kid's mother when this shit is going on? And what's-her-name with the petting zoo? She says that time's up and that she needs to get a check." I privately wondered—and not for the first time—what would our family do without Marsha. How would we survive? If polygamy meant having a clever, fun, supportive ally hanging around the house 24/7 to help get it all done, then show me where to sign up for a sister wife. I was more than willing to share at this point.

"Thanks," I answered. "Please don't ever leave me. Listen, while I'm getting my checkbook, can you keep an eye on Crew Cut over there? He's trying to pop the balloons."

As soon as Sue opened the doors of the Mobile Zoo, her animals barreled for the safety of their trailer like rock stars leaving the stage after a gig. The assistant swept the remaining straw and manure into a neat pile, shoveled it into a trash bag, and before the ink on my $125 check had a chance to dry, Sue's Mobile Zoo chugged out of the neighborhood and was gone. The only thing they left behind was a patch of pig-rooted soil and a few goat-gnawed trees. Oh, and some feathers. Apparently that poor chicken had given the future felon quite a fight.

Olivia's guests were soon grabbed by their parents and dragged, filthy and blue and most of them sobbing, into their respective car seats. One by one, the vans and SUVs pulled away, eventually leaving us alone in our driveway, surrounded by piles of wrapping paper, half-eaten cupcakes, and frosting-smeared tables. As Olivia moved from one toy to the next, Mark and I cleaned up the mess. And I finally faced something that I had spent weeks avoiding, something that up till now I dared not admit, even to myself: the total cost of this shindig.

Eight hundred and thirty-two dollars. Throw in another $25 to cover plates, napkins, and juice boxes, and that brought the total to $857. I felt sick. I felt like someone who went to Las Vegas with $20 worth of quarters for the slot machines and wound up having to pawn her wedding ring in the middle of the night. I had completely lost my mind. How could I, a coupon-clipping, bargain-hunting former welfare recipient, have become such a ridiculous spendthrift? I knew better. I was ashamed to have spent that kind of money on a birthday party. It was borderline obscene. There was no way to justify it, not even to myself. And then there was my husband. Oh my God—what kind of huffy lecture would I have to suffer at his hands? How many times would he get to say "I told you so" and "Everything has to be perfect with you"? Eight hundred and fifty-seven dollars! It was a mortgage payment, a couple of car payments, a week's salary at my old TV job. I wanted to throw up—and the four bites of that nasty blue cupcake I'd eaten didn't help.

"Hon," I croaked. "I have to tell you what today cost. Get ready. Please don't yell."

He didn't even look up from his sweeping. "I know what it cost."

"No, you don't. I didn't even add it up until just now. It's horrifying. You're going to freak out."

He put down the broom and sighed. "About eight hundred bucks, right?"

I was amazed. "How did you guess that?"

"Come on—look who you're talking to. I kept track of it as you went." He heaved a trash bag full of wrapping paper into the garbage can. "It's okay. You got it out of your system. You finally got to have the ultimate birthday. Are you happy now?"

Marriage is a strange thing. One day you fight like mortal enemies over something stupid, like a cheeseburger; the next, you barely blink when your spouse basically hands almost a thousand dollars to a goat. Relieved to have dodged the sermon, if still nauseous about the spending, I collapsed into one of the miniature rented chairs. Olivia climbed into my lap, sugar-smeared and glassy-eyed.

"If you knew it was that much, then why didn't you stop me?" I moaned.

"You never got to have this kind of stuff. I know that."

That was certainly true. Even my most recent birthday, just a few months earlier, had been blown off. Mark had gotten himself a ticket for some sort of indoor motocross event. (After I pointed out that he'd chosen to watch grown men jump their dirt bikes over hay bales on the anniversary of my birth instead of spending the evening with me, he insisted, "I didn't even *think* about it being your birthday when I bought that ticket!" Not surprisingly, this failed to comfort me.) In an effort to make it up, he took us all out for brunch the next day, a brunch that began with Caramia screaming inconsolably for half an hour and ended with Olivia dumping a full glass of ice water into my lap mere seconds after my omelet arrived at the table. Not a happy time for anyone, I'm afraid. But pretty typical for my birthday.

Olivia burrowed into my chest. I kissed the top of her head and squeezed her tight. She was sweaty and limp, and apparently too exhausted to even talk—a rare event for such a rampant little chatterbox.

"Yeah, it's out of my system now. And it was really wonderful. But I can't believe I went so crazy. *Eight hundred and fifty-seven dollars.* We can never tell anyone about this, okay?"

Mark sat down in his own tiny white plastic chair. "They can figure it out for themselves, believe me. You brought in a petting zoo, hon. *A zoo.*" He shook his head. "Olivia, did you have a fun animal party?"

Olivia roused herself to beam. "This was my best birthday ever." She sat up and clapped her hands together. "Wasn't it, Mommy? Wasn't it my best birthday *ever*?"

It sure was.

6

Relentless

June. Dinnertime. Rather than eat a single green bean, Olivia is facedown on the table sobbing, her hair trailing in her plate. Eric is performing microsurgery on a grilled pork chop, carefully cutting away every last trace of browned or blackened meat. At this rate, it'll be morning before he actually finishes eating what little meat he hasn't succeeded in scraping off. The baby has firmly rejected everything on her plate, then howled like she was being tortured until we let her out of her seat. Not surprisingly, we've had no uplifting family conversation, no good-natured bantering, not even an earnest "What was your favorite thing today, kids?" We have opted instead to practice the following imperfect family mealtime strategies:

Yelling
"Back in your chair this instant, Olivia!" I said. "Sit down! Finger out of your nose! Now!"

Lecturing

"What are you doing to that meat, Eric? 'Black stuff'? It's grilled, for
heaven's sake. You can't cut off every single grill mark! Just eat it. And
be happy. You should have been around for *my* mom's pork chops.
You couldn't even chew them, they were so tough. At least you can
chew these. You don't know how lucky you are, mister. You could be
starving to death, like plenty of kids in this world are, and then you'd
beg for a blackened pork chop. Ask your dad. He'll tell you."

Pleading

"Just taste it. How do you know you don't like it? Hmmm? Just pop it
right into your mouth and chew it up! I bet Elmo likes green beans.
Doesn't he? Doesn't Elmo love green beans? That's right, he sure
does. Just ask Daddy. He'll tell you all about it."

Bribery

"Special dessert for everyone who eats their dinner! No, I can't tell
you what. It's a surprise. But it's only for people who eat their dinner.
Yummy surprise! Ask Daddy. He knows all about surprises."

And Finally, Outright Threatening

"Don't you dare throw that bean or you'll go straight to your bed
right this very minute. With no stories! Do you hear me? I said, *no
stories*! Don't you dare ask Daddy! I told you no stories!"

And so on. How could we possibly have fun family quizzes about
things like the state capitals or new vocabulary words under battle-
field conditions like these? Then there was the unbearable stress of
watching children who'd gladly eat raw sewage—as long as it came
packaged with fries, a drink, and a plastic toy—painstakingly dissect
a meal prepared from scratch as though they feared we might deliberately attempt to poison them. Taking a deep breath, I tried to get us

back onto the happy family track. "Mealtimes are special times," I began.

I never got to finish that thought, because my husband interrupted me mid-soliloquy. "Where are the hidden cameras? Where are they? I know you've got them in here somewhere." He pointed toward the sink and, shaking his head, stared at me reproachfully.

I turned and saw something that might have made me nauseous once upon a time but that now barely registered as out of the ordinary. It was our baby, squatting on the floor at the dog's bowl. Her cheeks bulged, and she drooled a bit as she happily chewed, swallowed, and reached for another fistful of Purina.

Paranoia is one of the unexpected side effects of obsessively dwelling upon the dynamics, behavior, and attitude of your own family. It didn't take long for Mark and me to begin to suspect that perhaps there was a secret world running parallel to our own, a conspiracy of small children bent on global domination by any means possible. Worried of appearing insane, we didn't dare voice this suspicion. But we began paying more attention, began noticing how seemingly random events, for example, my toddler flushing my mobile phone down the toilet on the very day that I was expecting a call confirming an out-of-town business trip—a departure the baby simply would not permit—weren't quite so random after all. Call it conspiratorial dementia, but there's no way that Olivia poking herself right in the eye with a wire clothes hanger on the same night that I had to work very late and her father was half-dead from an intestinal virus was a mere coincidence. Not to mention the wire hanger. Where'd *that* come from? It takes someone with a particularly cunning mind to borrow a prop from *Mommie Dearest* to terrorize her own parents. Was it all part of a sinister plot to destroy our minds? It had to be. And once we started looking, we could see evidence of it everywhere: formerly functioning adults rendered stupid, desperate, and helpless by their own offspring. Now it was happening to us, too.

Mercenaries have *Soldier of Fortune*; fishermen have *Field &*

Stream; people with no sense of irony have *Real Simple.* What if kids had their own superspecialized publication? Think about it: a magazine that cut through all of the usual cutesy childhood homilies and offered its readers the kind of gritty, practical information they really wanted and needed. There'd be lots of do-it-yourself articles on everything from effectively clogging a drain to painting a car using Mommy's nail polish. There'd be an advice feature, "Dear Brianna" ("Dear Brianna, I'm only six, but my mom and dad are already pressuring me to get a soccer scholarship for college. I'd rather just hang out on the bench with my friends and make daisy chains or something. Should I bite the goalie on the face to get kicked off the team, or just keep puking in the car on the way to the field?"); beauty tips ("Cool Haircuts with Cuticle Scissors!"), and even recipes ("Hershey's Syrup Shooters"). The big feature every month would be an interview, in which a gifted juvenile hell-raiser would discuss methods, philosophies, and approach to the work—very much in the style of the fawning analyses of celebrities that currently choke the newsstands every month.

And then one afternoon, I found it. I was on my knees, as usual, pawing through the mess of books, stuffed animals, hair barrettes, miniature teacups, and half-naked baby dolls that spilled out from beneath Olivia's bed. It was tucked half inside a larger book, and it was a bit battered, the front cover torn and doodled on in green crayon. But there was no disguising those two grinning faces. I was holding in my hands something no parent was ever meant to see. It was *Relentless: The Magazine for Kids Committed to Chaos*—and my daughters were on the cover. Trembling, I crawled into the closet, pulled the door closed, and started to read . . .

> "I'm not eating carrots *ever,*" Olivia declares, pushing the offending vegetable to the side of her plate. In person, she's smaller than expected: barely three feet tall, with small, plumpish hands, feet, and knees. The famously deep dimples in her

cheeks are there, though, and she flashes these at the waiter, who is clearly starstruck and flustered. "I want more chocolate milk! Get it for me now!"

As he stammers and hurries off, Caramia rolls her eyes. "You forgot to say *please*, Olivia." Caramia leans close and confides, "She's always doing that. You should see her at the playground. Mine, mine, mine. Unbelievable."

Shaking her head, Caramia grabs for the last chicken nugget on her sister's plate. The two tussle good-naturedly, shrieking and yanking at each other's hair. It's typical enough behavior between sisters. But these sisters are real pros, veterans of enormous mayhem, not to mention seasoned punishment negotiators. Don't let their tender ages fool you: beneath those *Dora the Explorer* T-shirts beat the hearts of a couple of real killers.

Discovered in a bit part in the low-budget thriller *Night of a Thousand Screaming Babies*, Olivia quickly nabbed a starring role in the harrowing *Tyranny of Toddlers*. Her acclaim made it almost inevitable that her younger sister, Caramia, would crawl in her footsteps. The two hit box office gold together with this year's runaway comedy smash, *Time Out!* The girls seem unaffected by their success and disinterested in fame. "It's all about the work for me," said Olivia. "It's easy to get hung up on the toys. But we've got enough LEGOs, you know?"

Caramia nods in agreement. "She's right. We're more focused on our craft. Everything else is just a distraction."

The girls sprawl on the floor to talk, taking only the occasional break to nibble a Fruit Roll-Up or visit the potty. Their parents are nowhere to be seen. "Oh, them," sneers Caramia. "Listen, any time another adult comes within ten feet of this place, those two take off like they're on fire. It's, like, so pathetically obvious how desperate they are for a break." Olivia snickers.

The two exchange a look, then burst into maniacal laughter. "Good luck, Mom and Dad!" they hoot. "It's a long way till college!"

Relentless: Olivia, talk about *Night of a Thousand Screaming Babies.*

Olivia: I just loved the script, you know? The story itself is
really claustrophobic—these two completely exhausted
parents, trapped in a small house with an insomniac infant.
It was foreboding and desperate, but darkly comic at the
same time. The script originally called for my character to
be dealing with reflux, which I thought was just a fantastic
touch. At the last minute, though, we decided to have me
get my head stuck in the crib rails instead.

R: That's right; it was one of those old-fashioned cribs—

O: Exactly! It was supposed to be a family heirloom or whatever, and once they got my head unstuck, Daddy took it
outside and smashed it to bits with a crowbar! Very funny
stuff! I was a little apprehensive about the amount of stunt
work involved, but it proved to be a wonderful challenge.

R: How did you prepare for the role?

O: Since there was a tremendous amount of screaming in the
script, I had to get serious and do major vocal training. We
basically alternated a high-pitched whining moan with a
deeper, more guttural bellow. I probably screamed for, like,
five hours a day prior to shooting. It got intense around
here, which actually helped me get into that frantic, do-
anything-to-make-it-stop mind-set.

R: You're in practically every scene of *Toddler Tyranny.* That
must have been difficult.

O: Not really. I was two at the time, just loaded with energy—
double that if you sneaked me a little sugar! (laughs)
No, seriously, it felt more like play than work. The trick
lies in keeping it all believable. For example, I couldn't
ransack the refrigerator because most kids my age can't
exactly get those doors open without help. So I would tear
the pantry apart instead, or dump Mommy's purse into
the trash.

R: Caramia, you made your debut in *Toddler Tyranny.* Do you
remember much of that?

Caramia: They were looking for a newborn, and there I was. Lucky timing. My first scene with Olivia was pretty quick—we meet in the hospital, just kind of look each other over. But the moment that made me think, Yeah, this is what I want to do, is the one a few weeks later when Olivia tried to smother me with the yellow blanket. The emotions were so powerful, but cathartic, too. And I loved the attention I got, there's no question about it.

R: And you must also be enjoying the power that you now wield?

C: It's not really about that. I mean, we pretty much totally control our parents' lives, right? All we have to do is cry or barf and they're stopped right in their tracks. (shrugs) A lot of people were afraid of us anyway just because we might poop on them or give them a cold or something. You know how it is—babies really gross some people out.

O: When I'm in the middle of a scene, crying until I make myself physically sick or cramming a whole cheeseburger into my mouth at once or whatever, I'm not thinking of anything beyond making my parents suffer as much as I can at that moment. That's always the ultimate goal, no matter what.

C: She's right. I feel the same way. In *Time Out!* the script called for Olivia to slam my finger in the door, then keep trying to pull it closed while I'm slowly building from a silent scream into a full-on howl. I told her, "Look, just go for it. Don't worry about me. Slam and pull. Hard as you can." I wanted that scene to be as real as possible. I think you can always spot a [stunt] double, or a faked move that's choreographed to look real.

O: So we went for it. Took six takes—her finger was flattened!

C: (holding up her slightly misshapen left pinkie) It's my little souvenir from that day. I was more freaked out by my parents' reaction than I was by the pain. You'd have thought I'd been shot, the way they carried on. I'm not saying they were unprofessional or anything like that; it was just . . . I don't know. Over the top. I'm glad they were totally panicked and all, but come on! Especially Mommy! Her face went dead white! We thought she was gonna keel over!

(The two girls leap to their feet and dance about in a manic pantomime of parental concern. Giggling and shrieking, they scream, "Oh no! Get an ice pack!" and "Oh my God, do you think it's broken?" It's at least ten minutes before they collapse, breathless, back onto the floor.)

R: Speaking of *Time Out!*, what was it like to work together as equals?

O: Caramia has really taught me about teamwork. I'd gotten a little cocky—like, I can make any trouble you need all by myself. I resisted the partnership at first. I just couldn't see the benefits of sharing the stage, if you will. But together, wow. We're able to do some pretty spectacular damage. And from an emotional standpoint, there are so many opportunities for parental manipulation. You know—*you love her more!* That kind of thing. It's very rich material.

C: Olivia has the size advantage, which was hard for me to deal with in the beginning. It forced me to approach the role differently. Which was ultimately for the best. I can pull off the unexpected. Everyone's like, "Oh, look at the cute little baby," and quick as a wink, I've got a steak knife off the table and I'm stabbing it into the DVD player, or pouring my milk into the heat register on the floor. Also, I can pull the *hell* out of Olivia's hair and not get into trouble, because, hey—I'm a baby! I don't know any better, right?

R: That reminds me of the scene with the screwdriver—

C: The Phillips head! When I spun around and shoved it up Olivia's nose! And *she's* the one who got yelled at! That was all improvised, believe it or not.

O: (shaking her head and laughing) The things we do for our art, right?

R: Describe a typical day.

C: We're morning people. Me, I like to lie in my crib and cut loose with a good earsplitting, piercing scream. It really clears my head and wakes me up. Olivia's all about the stealth factor.

R: Which means . . .

O: Slip out of bed, tiptoe through the house, sneak into my parents' bedroom, and *wham!* Smack the mattress like a marine drill sergeant! (cracking up) You should see them jump! Another good one is to get right up into one of their faces, then announce, "It is time to be awake." The trick to that one is keeping your voice monotone and your expression blank—very *Children of the Damned.* Totally freaks them out every time.

C: Then there's breakfast—

O: Or, as we call it, the dawn disaster—

C: And trust me: it is. I'm more of a physical performer, so I really go for it. I feel like any kid can just sit and scream, right? But swipe a handful of soggy Cheerios and chuck it at the window and *woo!* Big reaction! So I watch Olivia, and wait for her to burst into tears over something like what color vitamin she's been given, for example. When that happens, all I have to do is ride her wave of energy. We're very improvisational, I think.

O: Her brilliance knocks me out, too. Truly.

C: You're embarrassing me!

O: No, really. Shoving a soggy shredded wheat square into the dog's ear? Pouring orange juice into your own shoes? Come on! I *love* that stuff! And that time you yanked my place mat—

C: —and sent pancakes, maple syrup, and orange juice all over the room! (giggling) It was so *Three Stooges!* It's an old shtick, but man, it still really, really works.

O: Bottom line: the only thing stickier on earth than maple syrup or orange juice is the oozing muck they make when combined. It had to take at least an hour to clean that up, don't you think, Caramia?

C: It took Daddy all day to recover.

O: It was genius, pure genius.

C: Aw, thank you.

R: And after breakfast?

O: The rest of our day is pretty much devoted to training. We train using a method of play called "Dismantle." It's controversial, but we've found it extraordinarily effective. (thumps her sister in the side of the head) How would you describe it?

C: Ouch! (kicks Olivia in the leg) Um, well, you basically just tear apart everything you can reach. You aim to empty cabinets, shelves, tabletops, and what have you, and scatter their contents. It's aerobic, and very good for hand-eye coordination. The goal is to increase your total speed of destruction. It takes a good bit of practice, more than you'd think. Right now we can all but obliterate a bathroom in less than three minutes. We're kind of proud of that, actually.

R: What makes it so controversial?

C: Because the focus is on found objects in the environment, not on traditional toys. Dismantlers ignore dolls and blocks, for example, choosing instead to play with ballpoint pens, car keys, and bottles of Windex. It not only encourages creativity, we think, but it also drives your parents right out of their minds. And that's always good.

O: It builds your memory skills, too. Because you need to know at all times where the lotions are, the baby oil, the Magic Markers, the lipstick. Then, when the opportunity strikes—and it will, because no parent can watch you 24/7—you're prepared. It's about being able to destroy without thinking. You know, get into the zone.

C: Meals are a great time to practice dismantling. Because sooner or later, they [parents] get lazy and accidentally leave their wineglass or a saltshaker within reach and then *bam!* Disaster! We also get into a lot of heavy emotion at mealtimes. Olivia always says, "A dinner without tears is something Mommy and Daddy won't be having tonight." She means it, too. I once watched her go from laughter to sobbing in a split second, all because the dog scarfed up a piece of meat she'd dropped. She was inconsolable! It was riveting. You can learn a lot just by watching the choices she makes.

R: What about bedtime?

O: What about it? Ha! I don't go to sleep; I pass out. And I try to take as many people down with me as I can. I force my parents to read certain books aloud over and over and over again, knowing they'll be absolutely flattened by the repetition. They can't get through it! There's nothing sweeter than to watch one of them fall asleep with a book on their head, snoring. That's a good night for me, a very good night.

C: Bedtime has been a real challenge for me. I'm pretty tired at the end of the day. All this growing is really wiping me out. So I've been fairly reasonable about going to sleep. I'm hoping that will change, though. As soon as they move me out of my crib to a big-girl bed, I'm planning to wander this house like Hamlet's ghost. And the first place I'm headed is the kitchen. Olivia showed me where they keep the knives. (beams happily at her sister) And I've always wanted to try my hand at wood carving.

In a cold sweat, I slid *Relentless* back into its hiding place beneath Olivia's bed. My head was spinning. They were out to get us. Who would ever believe me? Downstairs there was a sudden crash, followed by whispering and giggles. And then the voice floated up the stairs.

"Mommy! You have to wipe me!" Trembling, I rose to do her bidding. Who's paranoid now?

7

Children of the Corn Maze

On the way home from work one muggy August afternoon, I impulsively stopped at a coffee shop for a chai tea (low-carb, soy—somewhere along the way I mysteriously turned into one of *those people*) and found myself standing on line behind an elderly couple struggling to make sense of the faux-European java offerings. He was glaring at the menu board and muttering. She was questioning the clerk and then loudly repeating every word back for her husband's benefit. Since he either wouldn't or couldn't speak for himself, she ordered for both of them, declaring, "I'll have the real coffee and he'll have the decaf. And some soup. What's that?" She bent her head toward him as he—and there's no other way of putting it—snarled at her. She turned to the clerk. "Make that soup hot, please. Very hot. And some crackers, too. Now, be sure that you give him decaf. Are you sure that's decaf?" The clerk and I exchanged a glance.

"Tell her sugar!" the old man hissed.

"He takes sugar," she said.

"It's right over there." The clerk pointed. "You have to put that in yourself."

Cursing under his breath, the old man shuffled toward the condiment station. His wife leaned over the counter and whispered, "He's just awful, isn't he?" Then, taking her change, she made her slow way to the table where he was already waiting, a look of sour fury on his face.

"That'll be us one of these days," I said to the clerk. "Old and crabby and pissed off at the world. Or *his* wife. You've got to wonder why anyone gets married, don't you?"

"Tell me about it. And then has kids on top of it," she replied.

"If my husband ever treats me like that, I'll smother him with a pillow. Put the old bastard out of his misery."

The two of us started laughing. Nothing like a little pitch-black marital humor to bond complete strangers.

"Listen." She giggled. "I already did. I didn't kill him, though, just divorced him. But don't even get me started. It's a lot harder being a single mom, believe me. *And* he's still alive, which means I still have to deal with him all the damn time. I don't know what I was thinking. But those two." She nodded in the direction of the table where the old couple were seated. "They come in here a lot. And he's always like that—just mean. He's mean to her, too. It's like she doesn't even notice it, though, or she just ignores it. She's probably used to it by now, though I don't know how anybody ever gets used to that. There—one low-carb soy chai. Anything else?"

Walking back out to my car, I was in a reflective mood. Maybe it was the tea. Or maybe it was the image of the elderly couple, twinned in mutual dependency, so used to being a pair that even their simplest interactions were like a well-practiced duet. He growled; she translated. He demanded; she provided. I wondered if things had always been this way between them, or if something had happened to make him so bitter, her such a doormat. Was it illness? Infirmity? Did he rage at retirement, or at the loss of his former physical strength and power? He was gruff and unpleasant—nasty, even—and yet I'd watched him as she turned from the counter and walked toward him. He never took his eyes off of her. As she sat down, he reached across the table and very tenderly squeezed her hand. They remained that way for a long moment, and then, without a word, began eating their soup.

Marriage is either the noblest romantic experiment in the history of civilization or the craziest idea anyone's ever had. Take two individuals, throw them together in a confined space, limit the available resources of food, money, and sleep, then add in a child or two or four, and watch what happens. Things can get pretty brutal in there—not to mention loud and messy. It's pretty amazing that people do it, especially knowing that about half of all marriages will end up in divorce. Since a thorough shark mauling will leave you with fewer scars than the average divorce will, a wedding might well be the most breathtaking leap of faith any sane person ever takes.

My older brother married a woman with two young children. They then promptly had three more of their own, creating a household of seven, the three youngest all in diapers, all at the same time. My sister-in-law—let's call her *Nancy*, which happens to be her real name, but, since most of the people she deals with just scream, "MOM!" right in her face before demanding money or a ride, she'll never guess that we're talking about her—would slump, dazed, on the living room floor amid towering piles of laundry, those three babies crawling all over her, gnawing and drooling on everything they could cram into their toothless little mouths. With the heat cranked to hellish, near-suffocating levels to help keep the babies toasty, that poor soul would then struggle to find mates for dozens and dozens of white socks, all different, all fiercely resistant to the very idea of meeting their match. It was a chore so daunting, so horrible, so hopelessly repetitive, that it bordered on the surreal. It was practically Kafkaesque—except that even Kafka would have flinched at subjecting a character to such a bleak and futile task.

When Nancy wasn't folding socks, she was mopping up an endless river of spilled apple juice, or coaxing a peanut butter sandwich out of the VCR, or searching for the perennially missing other shoe. Every now and again, to break up the monotony, one of the kids would decide that it was time for a rollicking trip to the local emergency room for an X ray or stitches. So they'd get together and negotiate whose turn it was to climb up onto a high perch, like the roof, and jump. Equally good was a deep laceration with something sharp, filthy, and covered in rust. And there was, for those rare occasions when their imaginations failed them, the always-reliable fastball to the head. These kids were like the postal service: neither rain, nor snow, et cetera, et cetera, could keep them from their sworn duty to wreak havoc against their own parents. What would have been long, boring months of dreary winter for other people instead proved to be an excellent opportunity for this family to contract any virulent stomach flu that happened by, and, when the kids were babies, every available ear infection. For years and years, no matter what the season, someone was always sick with something nasty and, preferably, contagious. Even the pets got in on the action. The sheepdog had ear infections of his own; the cat had irritable bowels. The bird seemed healthy enough, but when you're talking about some tiny, generic bird bought cheap at, say, Kmart, and then parked in a cage dangling two and half feet from a blaring television set, who really knows? If nothing else, the unfortunate creature had very likely gone stark raving mad from living in a state of such unnatural, unbirdlike bedlam. At the minimum, it surely suffered from debilitating paranoia, the result of the countless hours it spent being stalked and harassed by one very frustrated and dyspeptic cat.

And yet, in between hauling buckets of barf to the bathroom and trips to the pharmacy for antibiotic refills, my brother and his wife pawed each other like a couple of horny teenagers. How? Why? Amazingly enough, neither seemed to blame the other a bit for the expensive, noisy, unpredictable mayhem in which they routinely operated. In fact, they laughed at it. Laughed! As though everyone lived in a whirling vortex of screaming, spilling, clattering, crying, bashing, breaking, and barking, and and their little corner of paradise was no louder or crazier than anyone else's. To tell the truth, they seemed downright relaxed in the midst of it all. Even more perplexing, they'd steal any opportunity they could to sneak off somewhere and make out. It was like they hadn't yet figured out that too much heavy breathing is exactly what brought about all this racket and pandemonium in the first place. What on earth were they thinking? Even Pavlov's dog was a faster learner, and the only thing *he* was forced to listen to was one measly bell.

It was a real mystery, their happiness. I couldn't fathom it. How could anyone stare down that much dirty laundry, pour that many bowls of cereal, chase that many wailing kids through three floors of a very old house that, though charming, had neither a dishwasher nor an air conditioner, and still have even one ounce of enthusiasm left over at the end of the day for a good, raunchy spousal grope? I tried to picture myself in Nancy's shoes, riding herd on that wild brood, waiting all day for the moment when my husband would walk into the house. Would I greet him with a big happy smile and a lusty kiss as she did? Or would I hide behind the holly bush at the front door and, as he put his key in the lock, leap out and club him with a baseball bat while screaming, "You! You did this to me!" Oh sure, in between visits to their house, I was able to delude myself about what a great wife I'd make. But once I'd actually gotten there and stayed a few days, even I couldn't hide from the truth: I was a bat-wielding psycho just waiting to happen. Which explains why, after leaving their house, I'd rush home, swallow a fistful of Ortho-Novum, and then curl up in the fetal position on my bed mumbling, "Never, ever, ever, *ever*. Never."

So what was it about marriage and children and a life of backyard barbeques in the 'burbs that had such a hold on me? I certainly wasn't trying to recapture the sun-drenched bliss of my early life—

my parents were no role models for the joys of the nuclear family. Their entire marriage could essentially be held up as an object lesson in what *not* to do, summarized in three easy-to-follow rules.

Rule Number One
Do not marry a sociopath.

Rule Number Two
If you disregard Rule Number One, do not, under any circumstances, breed.

Rule Number Three
In the event that you stubbornly violate Rules Number One and Two, you'd better pray that none of your kids grow up to be talk radio hosts, because that kid will one day enthusiastically tell the world every single vile or deranged thing you ever did or said, and believe me, there's no shortage of material to work with.

An editor of a fashion magazine in Paris. A geologist in the Peruvian high country. A member of Doctors Without Borders. A Las Vegas showgirl. A wine pourer in Sonoma County. There were so many other dreams to be had, more dreams and ambitions than could ever be cataloged or even described by one person. Poet. Inventor. Astronaut. Think of it: strapped to a rocket, launched into orbit, floating for months aboard the International Space Station, brushing one's teeth in zero g each night, gazing through portholes at clusters of alien and unknowable stars. And here I was, loading up on Froot by the Foot and hauling a carload of yelping kids to the zoo for an hour and a half so that they could witness howler monkeys doing the kinds of sinful things to each other that their father and I no longer enjoyed the privacy or energy to do for ourselves.

When you got right down to it, being a wife and mother was exhausting. Here I was, eight months into my happy little experiment, and I was fried. I wanted to sneak off to someplace tropical, collapse into a hammock, order a margarita, and bury myself in a book. I didn't want to talk, I didn't want to think, and I didn't want to have to blow anyone's nose for at least a week—maybe longer. It had nothing to do with love; I loved my children more every day. I adored my husband. It was just that being so damnably perky and chipper and together was *work*. Hard work. Thirsty work. It was driving me to drink. And that probably wasn't good. After all, when you find yourself agreeing to dinner at Chuck E. Cheese on the grounds that, loud and awful as it generally is, at least you can get a beer there, well, it might be time to reevaluate your choices.

With much less than my usual gusto, I paged through the weekend entertainment section of the newspaper. Fireworks at the lake. Hmmm. We could bring a picnic. But then there'd be the mosquitoes, and the girls wouldn't want to stay on our blanket, which meant they'd be tearing around in the dark with a bunch of strangers, me in hot pursuit, probably stepping on people's hands and kicking over their wine bottles. . . . No. It was tiring just thinking about it. There was a crafts festival about thirty miles south of us. That sounded reasonably okay. A charming small town, some interesting pottery, the girls having little fairies or butterflies painted onto their flushed and happy cheeks, begging us to be allowed a second and third spin on the merry-go-round—and then puking corn dogs and funnel cakes all over the backseat of the car on the ride home. Pass. Just as I was beginning to think that America's most adventurous madcap family might be spending a quiet weekend in our very own backyard while Mommy logged some hard-core napping, I saw it. It was an ad for the A-Maize-ing Maze: a giant maze etched into a living cornfield and, according to the newspaper, an ideal outing for all ages.

Intriguing, I thought, scanning the fine print for details. I imagined a delightful stroll along winding, shaded paths, a soft breeze whispering through the silken-tasseled stalks of corn, the sounds of nearby highways muted by dense, fragrant greenery. Nice. On top of that bucolic Zen splendor, the ad also promised a veritable journey of self-discovery. It said that people revealed their truest selves in the maze, that relationships could be either strengthened or destroyed after just a few simple hours spent navigating the corn. Was this not exactly what I was looking for? An experience that might elevate our family to a higher plane? It would be a test of our family dynamics. We'd find out what we were made of. We'd see just what kind of marriage we had. And we'd be the kind of people who spent their weekends tramping around in wholesome, sunny cornfields instead of holing up in dark, overly air-conditioned rooms, freebasing cocaine and watching pay-per-view porn. In short, the exact opposite of my childhood—always the strongest selling point for any activity.

Here are some things I didn't stop to consider before loading up the family and heading for the maze:

Mid-August in North Carolina means blistering heat. Heat so intense, relentless, and muggy that even Satan pisses and moans about it—and then stays inside watching DVDs.

There are many synonyms for the word *maze: labyrinth, confusion, muddle,* and *intricacy,* to name just a few. None of these words are particularly cheerful words, and two or three sweaty hours of torment in a corn cauldron won't change that.

Never, and I do mean *never,* take a logical, rational, trained engineer into a corn maze and think that you'll be able to ask for help or cheat in any way to get the hell out of there. That would be quitting, and quitting is for other people, people who are not nearly as clever as the above logical, rational, trained engineer.

We arrived at the maze after much driving and at least seven wrong turns. Not an auspicious beginning. Undaunted by our failure to follow the relatively simple directions printed in the newspaper, we finally rolled into a parking space near a stack of hay bales, square in the middle of nowhere. Mark and I unloaded the girls and their stroller, and trudged toward what looked like a ticket kiosk. We were issued an orange flag on a long pole and a sheet of paper with a grid printed on one side and a series of what looked like riddles on the other. After being pointed toward a dispenser of sunscreen, we were told to gather in ten minutes for orientation. While we waited, we were invited to explore a "practice" maze, a roughly ten-by-ten area marked off by more hay bales and tape. In a worrisome portent of things to come, I couldn't make heads or tails of it and, as soon as the maze coordinator wasn't looking, ducked under the tape and went in search of some shade.

The rules of the corn maze were simple: Keep your flag aloft at all times so that the maze master, seated in a high tower overlooking the field, can keep track of everyone. Stay on the paths, and don't trample or damage the corn. And, we were warned, if we did go into the corn, we'd be really sorry, since the leaves were blade-sharp and covered in something that was guaranteed to make you itchy and miserable for hours and hours. Once we were inside, our job was to decipher the clues on the sheet of paper we'd been given, which would then lead us to a series of postboxes, each containing another tiny square of paper. Pasted together properly in the grid, these tiny squares would form a map, which, if correctly interpreted, would then lead us out of the maze. Oh, and the riddles? They were a collection of weirdly cryptic hints and queries pertaining to specific and apparently famous battles of the Revolutionary War. Do you have any idea what could possibly be meant by the phrase *General Nelson, after a rainy hour in a chicken coop*? Neither do I. I stared at the maze coordinator in disbelief. Suddenly my fantasy of a lovely stroll in the country had turned into something that more closely resembled the hunt for Osama bin Laden. I risked a glance at my husband, expecting—and this time, actually *deserving*—a look of pure, exasperated scorn. To my shock, he was glowing. A puzzle! A baffling, obnoxiously hard, insanely complicated puzzle. It was right up his alley. It was obvious that he couldn't wait to get started. I knew then that we were in trouble.

We set off. It was all very pleasant at first. The corn was well over six feet tall in places, and so thickly planted that it practically formed a solid wall of gently undulating green. The dirt paths were smooth and wide enough to accommodate a stroller. We trundled along for a bit, following the path that twisted and turned through the stalks. Chattering with excitement, Olivia led the way, as I pushed Caramia, ensconced in her stroller like a tiny, sweaty queen. Mark studied the map, frequently pausing to ask me if I'd figured out any of the clues yet. "Working on it!" I'd cheerfully respond. That, of course, was a great big lie. I'm not a puzzle person. Some see the Rubik's Cube, for instance, and wonder, How? I see the Rubik's Cube and wonder, Why? As a kid, my husband could happily spend a two-hour car trip amusing himself with one of those cheap plastic maze toys, the kind with the itsy-bitsy silver balls, each destined for an equally itsy-bitsy indentation, the whole thing sealed in a clear plastic box, and guaranteed to frustrate the living hell out of anyone lacking the patience or the attention span of a Nobel Laureate. Give me that same maze toy and I'd sneak the window down a crack, poke the toy through the opening, and let it fall to the road below just for the pleasure of hearing it crunch beneath the tires.

Besides, I figured that these riddles were just busywork. The whole idea of needing a map to find our way out of a cornfield seemed ridiculous. For starters, it wasn't very big. How lost could we get? I figured that we'd be able to just sort of feel our way through the corn, intuiting which paths to take, which to avoid, and so find our way to Victory Bridge by sheer gut instinct alone. This method, or Jersey Girl Mall Navigation System (JGMNS), is much like the better-known Global Positioning System, or GPS. However, where GPS is pitifully dependent for its data on a network of satellites in geosynchronous orbit, JGMNS requires no technology to operate and demands only that the user be a regular and attentive shopper. JGMNS is calibrated by extensive, repeated exposure to retail landmarks like Ann Taylor, Nordstrom, the Limited, Abercrombie &

Fitch, Cinnabon, and The Body Shop. As an example, my own JGMNS is so acutely tuned that you could blindfold me, stuff me into the back of a truck, drive aimlessly for days, shove me out in the parking lot of any mall anywhere in the United States, and, if there's a Banana Republic within three hundred yards, I'll find it for you in about two minutes flat. While at first glance this may seem to be a highly limited and therefore not terribly useful skill, you never really know when you might be marooned in a strange city, in desperate need of a dusky pewter silk tank top *right this minute*. For that kind of navigational emergency, I'm your girl. For everything else, you'd be better off choosing your route by flipping a coin than by handing me a map.

Unbelievably, we'd now been roaming in circles for three quarters of an hour. Muttering under his breath, Mark suddenly wheeled around and sprinted back down the row we'd just traveled. "Got it!" he hollered, reappearing seconds later, waving a little square of paper. "The first clue! We're on the right track. Who's the man? Who found the clue? All right! Now come on, hon; I need you working on that riddle!" I carefully pasted the square onto the grid and noticed with a sinking heart that we needed about fifteen more little squares in order to solve the maze and escape to someplace cool with a liquor license. Based on our current rate of progress, that would take roughly more than eleven hours, which should get us out of the corn at about 3:00 A.M. or so.

I started thinking about cornfields and what I knew about them, and sad to say, it wasn't much. I'd never actually been in one before. My entire experience of corn came from either Del Monte or Holly-wood. Since corn was the one vegetable my father would eat, we had it for dinner every night for the first twelve years of my life. Back then, the only tool I'd ever needed to find my way through the corn was a can opener and a fork. As for cornfields, I gathered from the movies I'd seen that they made excellent hiding places. Especially for the ghosts of famous baseball players in Iowa, or creepy little pale-faced parent-murdering demon kids in Nebraska, or even aliens. Corn, it turned out, was spooky stuff. Inside the maze, it even made strange whispering sounds, and I couldn't shake the feeling that I was being watched. Of course, I *was* being watched—by Caramia. She stared at me from the comfort of her stroller with weary contempt, as if to say, "Heatstroke coming. Hello? I'm *one*. What were you thinking, Mommy? How's this gonna sound to the folks at the emergency room? Who takes a *baby* into a freaking cornfield in August? Hmm? Got an answer for that? You're gonna be needing one. A good one, too."

Here was our first Lesson of the Maze: My husband was a rational, analytical being who thrived on a challenge and used all of his wits to survive. I, on the other hand, suffered from a deranged and overactive imagination coupled with a complete inability to follow directions. Also, I knew nothing about the Revolutionary War beyond George Washington crossing the Delaware River—and truth be told, my knowledge of that one event was pretty sketchy. What to do? Cravenly use the well-being of the children as an excuse to wave the orange flag and call for rescue by the maze master? Admit that this was a wretched idea and beg for release? Before I had a chance to properly weigh my options, Mark triumphantly spun the stroller around a curve and announced, "The second clue! Stick with Daddy, girls! We're going to solve this maze!"

Hour number two. There is a reason that farmers wear boots rather than cute, strappy Italian leather sandals. It's also rare to see much harvesting or threshing or whatever it's called being done in capri pants and skimpy tank tops. Farmers know better. Hoping for a little sympathy, I mentioned that I might be getting a blister or two and wondered aloud whether or not we might be close to the finish line. "That's what you get for wearing stupid clothes like that. You knew we were going to a cornfield. Why on earth didn't you wear sneakers?"

Offended, I replied, "You saw what I was wearing when we left the house. Why didn't you tell me to change?"

"Oh, right. Then I get accused of trying to control you and boss you around."

"Which is not a problem for you any other time. How come today is the day you pick to suddenly stop being so damn bossy?"

"Don't try to make what you're wearing my fault. Besides, if you'd pay attention and help out with these clues, we could get out of here."

"If you'd let us ask the maze master for help, we'd already be out of here," I snarled.

"What's the point of even coming here if you're going to cheat?" he shot back.

"What's the point of suffering for no good reason other than your stupid genius pride?"

"Oh, my stupid genius pride! Let's don't forget that this was all your idea in the first place. Now, wait a minute—haven't we been down this row twice before?"

How would I know? All the corn looks the same. Which brings us the Second Lesson of the Maze: No matter how light you think you're traveling, when you enter the corn, your baggage comes with you. Here Mark and I were lost in the middle of a sweltering field, and instead of putting our heads together and coming up with an answer for the bewildering query about John Patrick Henry that stood between us and blissful freedom, we were quarreling over the central dispute in our marriage: control. How stupid was that? Bickering was the last thing I wanted to do. Bickering would lead us into a far more treacherous maze than any farmer ever carved out of his corn. Bickering just wasn't the happy-family thing to do. I stared at the girls, both napping now in their stroller, and took a deep breath. "Okay. Let me see that riddle again."

By this point we were over three hours into our little agrarian adventure, and just six clues shy of solving the puzzle. Admittedly, I hadn't done much of the navigating, and my intuitive sense of the corn had turned out to be just about worthless. And when it came to solving riddles, it appeared that desperation, thirst, and even ruined shoes weren't enough to inspire one of those eureka moments. "Maybe we could just get a hint?" I ventured. "Not the actual answer, but just a little hint."

Mark sighed. He kicked at the dirt with his shoe and thought about it. Much as I wanted to beg, I said nothing. Mark had to think it was *his* idea, or I knew we'd be trapped in the stalks till the harvest. Finally, he looked up. "All right. You raise the flag, and I'll get a hint. Listen to what they say, okay? Don't be off daydreaming or whatever. I need your help with this."

Giddy with relief, I held our flag aloft and swished it back and forth. From her lofty perch high above the field, the maze master spotted us and called, "Need some help? You've sure been in there awhile!"

"Just a hint," Mark called.

The maze master laughed. "Okay, just a hint. You just came down the row you needed, one back. There's a turn there, one that you don't want to take, and a turn that you do. The one you want comes later. That's your hint! Good luck! You're almost there!"

Mark stared at me. "Did you get that?" Uh, no, not really. It's not like it made a tremendous amount of sense, did it? As hints went, I thought it was definitely on the fuzzy side. Also, I suffer from a brain disorder yet to be recognized by the medical establishment, which causes me to completely tune out any communication involving directions, numbers, percentages, or beginning with the phrase *I had the weirdest dream last night.* . . . But, since I'd committed to being a team player, I knew it was time to play along.

"Yep. Got it! We start by going one row back, and don't take the first turn," I declared enthusiastically. "Come on! I'll push the stroller for a while."

Note: one reason that you've probably never witnessed anyone pushing a baby stroller through a cornfield is that it's a lamebrained idea. The same stroller wheels that virtually glide along cement or asphalt instead dig into plowed earth and grip it for dear life. This gives whatever hapless baby is stuck inside one heck of a bumpy and unpleasant ride. More important, it's exhausting for you, the pusher. The only consolation comes from knowing that you're getting an excellent upper-body workout. But really, isn't that what gyms are for?

Sweating, grimacing, limping a little, we trundled back down the row we'd just covered. There was the first turn, and I saw now that it looped around in a big circle—a circle we'd covered at least twice, maybe three times. Then we came to the next turn, the right one, and there was the trail we needed. Although I knew it had been there all along, it seemed to have materialized out of thin air. Spooky.

"I don't remember seeing this spot before," Mark said excitedly. "This must be the way!"

Down another dusty row we trundled, and then another, and by now, the sun was so low in the sky that the shadows cast by the stalks stretched long and deep across the path. My blisters had blisters, and we were out of water. "Now this way!" Mark said, as I jerked the stroller into another sharp turn. Suddenly, there it was, looming in front of us: Victory Bridge. Olivia woke up and rubbed at her eyes with filthy, gritty hands. Lifting her from the stroller, Mark and I slowly climbed the steps to the top. From there we could survey the entire cornfield. Mark immediately grasped the entire pattern of the maze. "Look." He pointed. "It's a cannon. See? There's the barrel, and that little place over there is the fuse. That place where we were so stuck makes the wheel. Do you see it?"

Let me be completely honest: I didn't see it. All I saw was a blazing sunset over a big field full of corn that had a straggling handful of lunatics stomping around in it and waving flags. I wanted to see the cannon shape; I tried to see it. But in the end, no matter how I squinted my eyes or cocked my head, the only thing I could see was corn, corn, corn, and more corn. And I knew that it was hopeless.

Remember those Magic Eye posters that were all the rage about ten years ago? At first glance, they seemed to be nothing more than abstract washes of color and patterns. Then, if you focused your eyes in just the right way, suddenly an image would emerge, like a dolphin or a teapot. I'd stare at those things till my eyes crossed and my head hurt, and I never once saw anything other than a blurry blob of color. Never. I got so tired of people saying, "Do you see it? Do you? Huh? Do you see it? What do you mean, you can't see it? It's right there? It's so obvious! Do you see it now?" that I started faking it. I faked Magic Eye like some women fake orgasms. It was the easiest way I could think of to survive that fad without being hounded to marvel at images that I just couldn't see. My brain must not be properly wired for pattern recognition or tacky art recognition or whatever skill it is that's required to spot a cannon cut into a cornfield or a porpoise hiding in a poster. Standing there on Victory Bridge, I flashed back to one particularly grueling episode in a Deck The Walls store at the mall when Mark absolutely could not accept my inability to see the Magic Eye image in front of me:

Him: Just stare at it, then relax your focus, and *bam!* You'll see it.

Me: Nope, nothing happening.

Him: Try again. Make your eyes go soft.

Me: I don't even know what that means. You mean squint?

Him: No! Just try harder. Monkeys can probably do this. Just focus and relax and stop thinking about shoes or whatever it is that you're thinking about right now that's keeping you from concentrating on this.

Me: I don't see anything. What is it?

Him: I'm not telling you.

Me: Fine. Who cares? It's probably something stupid, anyway.

Him: Your bad attitude is probably why you can't see it. Ever think about that?

If I told my husband that I couldn't see the cannon, I'd be stuck on that bridge for at least another ten minutes. But if I lied and said that I *could* see it, then I'd cheat us out of our key Lesson of the

Maze. That is, we each brought our unique and separate strengths into the corn. Without me, Mark never would have driven forty miles into the country and spent an afternoon prowling around an acre or two of vegetables for no good reason. And without him, I'd have given up hours ago without really even trying. I brought adventure and novelty into his world, and he brought logic and reason into mine. I got us into trouble, and he got us out. Sometimes we worked well together, and sometimes not. But so far, we'd always managed to find our way out, even if it took all day.

"I can't see anything but corn and you know it. We could stand here for an hour and I still wouldn't see a cannon. Let's go get some dinner before we get arrested for child abuse. Look at these poor tired, hungry, grubby little babies!"

"Who's the man, though? Who's the maze-solving man? No help from the three of you. I could have done this a lot faster if I didn't have to push a stroller. When we come back next year . . ."

He kept talking, analyzing moves, gesturing at the now-tattered map in his hand. I set my brain on spousal autopilot, making a noise of agreement or surprise every so often, just enough to maintain the illusion of attention, and in this way, we slowly stumbled back to our car. "Girls," I said, as Mark and I buckled the babies into their seats, "I know that you're really young right now, but we want you to try very hard to always remember this day. Mommy's parents would never have spent an afternoon wandering around a cornfield with my brothers and me unless maybe they were hoping coyotes would eat us. This has been a very special family adventure, hasn't it? Hasn't this been fun? Daddy was a very good navigator, wasn't he?"

"Ock!" said Caramia.

"I want pizza!" said Olivia.

"I need a beer," said Mark. "What's around here, other than cows? Oh, wait. Let me guess: you've got an idea, right?"

8

Just Do It

With a sigh, she dropped the last of the dirty silverware into the basket and bumped the dishwasher door closed with her knee. Standing there at the sink, she scooped her hair into a careless ponytail, savoring a brief moment alone in the now-deserted kitchen. Lost in her thoughts, she didn't hear him enter, didn't see him move purposefully toward her in the gathering darkness. Then suddenly, his lips grazed the back of her neck, his arms encircled her waist, and she was enfolded in the rough, male hardness of his embrace. "Dinner was fantastic," he whispered, his mouth brushing the tender hollow beneath her earlobe. "Can't wait for dessert. What do you say we meet for that a little bit later, hmm?" Watching him saunter away, she felt the familiar weakening in her legs, and a sensation of heat, as though her body concealed a flicker of desire that needed only his touch to be ignited.

In a moment she would follow him upstairs and stand at the doorway of the children's room, watching as he tossed the kids in the air or crawled around on the floor pretending to be a monster. It was her favorite part of the day, seeing the man she loved playing and laughing with their children. Sometimes, just the sight of his strong, bronzed hands tousling their hair or smoothing their blankets was enough to melt her. And tonight, as she leaned against the baby's dresser and listened to his deep, almost musical voice chanting the familiar singsong words of Dr. Seuss, she felt like the luckiest woman alive. He was hers.

Soon they would walk downstairs together, turning off lights, locking doors, performing all of the comforting end-of-day routines that reassured her of their family's safety. Tonight, those rituals would take on a delicious, teasing edge, as each step pulled them closer to the moment when all cares and stresses would fall away in a tangle of limbs and hands, mouths and breath, in a shared ecstasy that had somehow deepened and grown more intense with each passing year. "My God, you're beautiful," he growled, pulling her close. She felt herself dissolving in his arms, her hunger matching his own, their bliss a storm that drowned out all thought, leaving them both spent, drowsy, content. As she drifted into slumber, a smile playing at the corners of her mouth, she whispered a silent prayer of thanks for her marriage, and for the glories of his touch.

Of course, as any sane married-with-kids person knows, the preceding 416 words are pure fiction. Work a couple of jobs, juggle housework, yard work, pets, relatives, bills, kids, and the myriad school and sports commitments created by those kids, and you'll very quickly watch the romance in your life evaporate into the ether of fantasy. The reasons for this are both really simple and terribly complicated. First, kids wear you completely out. You must understand exactly how they operate. Think of comic book villains, like the evil genius who invents some sort of brilliantly insane contraption to suck dry every power and energy resource around the globe, leaving the world chaotic, confused, and ripe for eventual takeover. Simply put, your children are both evil geniuses *and* insane contraptions. And, like most evil geniuses, they are not just single-minded but also unreasonable and generally reluctant to negotiate. They *will* have what they need or desire or they *will* scream. And when they are screaming, it's no use lighting candles and cranking the volume on the Barry White CD. Because they will keep screaming until you attend to them, and even then there are no guarantees that they will be appeased. Older children, their screaming days behind them, will instead insist on remaining awake right up to the moment that you yourself are virtually incoherent with fatigue, thus ensuring that you will be too tired for anything more gymnastic than brushing your teeth and collapsing into your bed.

From the age of twelve on, children develop even craftier methods. For example, requiring emergency late-night assistance with homework in subjects that hadn't even been invented when you were in the ninth grade. This last serves the dual purpose of keeping you from having a minute alone with your partner and generating proof that you are, as your teen probably suspects, hopelessly stupid.

So, despite my best efforts to keep those bedroom fires blazing, I quickly discovered that the first obstacle to hot marital monkey love is the crushing tyranny of one's own children. Incidentally, this same tyranny is one of the world's best-kept secrets. We all assume that the people we see in public being bossed around by snotty-nosed belligerent little beasts are merely too dumb and disorganized to get their houses in order. We think that it will be different for us, because we are calm, clever, and have our act together. FYI: we are wrong, wrong, and wrong some more. The only people who never have an awful, out-of-control day with their kids are either big phony liars or so wealthy that they can afford to hire nannies to have awful, out-of-control days with their kids for them. People like this are so unbelievably irritating and smug that it's best to just avoid them altogether. Let them hang out with each other, congratulating themselves on their clean houses and packed social calendars and multiple orgasms. They only act happy in order to spite the rest of us—deep down, they're miserable, stuck-up, and ashamed of their own shallowness. At least that's what I tell myself. Anyway, the important thing to remember is that sex very often leads to kids, and kids very often lead to involuntary celibacy. This is the fundamental truth buried in that vast body of knowledge known collectively as the facts of life.

The second, more complex barrier to getting your married groove on springs from one of the most basic yet profound differences between the genders. In some cruel practical joke of the Universe, men need sexual contact in order to feel loved, while women need to feel loved in order to desire sexual contact. Whose brilliant idea was this? It's a system all but designed to cause misery and misunderstanding. Sure, there are always those exceptions that one hears tell of at parties—the husband who feels cheap and used if his wife demands a quickie, the raging nymphomaniac wife who needs sex twice per day in order to keep from pouncing on the FedEx man. These tales are a lot like urban legends. The foreplay-crazed husband is always some former neighbor's brother-in-law; the nympho once worked at a cousin's office. They're just like Bigfoot—we've all heard the stories, but not one of us has ever actually witnessed these amazing phenomena with our own two eyes.

Considering the entire industry of women's magazines trumpeting the need for more foreplay, it shouldn't come as news that women want it. But it might come as news to some that foreplay isn't necessarily just a hurried two tweaks, a grab, a swipe, and a squeeze. After a long day of working, driving, chasing, washing, scraping, folding, sorting, adding, subtracting, cajoling, coaxing, threatening, pleading, and hollering, the average woman requires something a little more enticing than a blurted "Are we gonna do it tonight or what?" to get herself into the mood for love. Chances are, if you're a man who likes to stomp his feet and holler about being horny, you're going to stay that way for another long, lonely night, maybe three. It's a terrifying thought for men: foreplay for the typical woman actually includes everything that he does, all day long—including what he says and how he chooses to say it. Anger and spite are huge turnoffs. What woman genuinely adores being bullied—especially when it comes to sex? The first rule of thumb when it comes to luring a tired wife into the love lair is: Stop yelling at her.

In a perfect world, the act of bending over to unload a dishwasher would be as much of a turn-on for women as it apparently is for men. Then we could all rut like happy baboons and still have plenty of time left over to watch the game. Too bad it doesn't work that way. Men are more easily aroused by visual stimuli than women are, which explains their ready enthusiasm for action at the mere sight of a bit of cleavage. Men are really, really lucky to be wired this way, make no mistake about it. After a long day at work and a busy night with the family, trust me: it'd be much more fun for everyone if women could somehow get all hot and bothered by the sight of an unzipped fly. This whole visual dynamic is a big part of the reason why retailers like Victoria's Secret are so hugely successful. Women like to buy and wear sexy underwear; men like to look at it, buy it, and then look at us wearing it. As an added bonus, the Victoria's Secret catalog is better than a dirty magazine, because it comes with the ultimate free pass—it's not porn; it's shopping. "No, honey, I wasn't drooling over Tyra Banks. All these models are way too skinny. I was just imagining how much sexier you'd look than her if you were wearing those great big angel wings and a spangled thong."

If men are aroused with their eyes, what's the equivalent for women? Every sex expert has the same answer: their minds. Sex for women begins in the brain. This is why the sight of a man lounging spread-eagle on the bed in a pair of tighty whities isn't typically quite enough to drive a woman wild with desire. Throwing in the phrase "I'm ready!" doesn't much help. The reason that you'll find flowers, candles, soft music, and long, slow, deep kisses that build to raw animal passion in most romance novels and Hollywood love stories is because—brace yourself—women really like flowers, candles, soft music, and long, slow, deep kisses that build to raw animal passion.

Maybe no one can have all of that every single day, but surely there's a happy medium between a rose-petal-strewn bed and a fast grope in the shower.

For all of the talk about what a bewildering enigma the average female is when it comes to sex, we're actually pretty easy. Show us love, respect, and consideration and you'll be amazed at how receptive and eager we are for sex. Treat us with contempt or derision, act like a bully or a selfish bastard, and eventually, resentment settles in. Resentment, the marital equivalent of an ice age, is the ultimate bad news in the bedroom. If you need sled dogs and a parka just to climb into bed at night, the odds of your experiencing much sexual intimacy are fairly bleak. Which means that the second rule of thumb when it comes to luring a tired wife into the love lair is: Act loving.

So what on earth do women want? No one dares speak for weird mutations in the species like supermodels or psychopaths, but most wives and mothers are pretty much looking for two things: be nice, and do your fair share. And get the idea out of your head that everyone else is having more and better sex than you are. They're totally not. As part of the overall reengineering of my marriage and family to better conform to the coveted TV ideal, I did a little informal research on the sexual frequency rates of my married friends, neighbors, and coworkers. This was in no way scientific. However, that didn't prevent me from treating the information I obtained as being at least as reliable as my daily newspaper horoscope. Shockingly enough, nobody was having much sex.

"Let me think about it for a minute," said one thirty-two-year-old married father of four. "Once a week, if we're lucky—maybe. It's kind of been a while. I remember liking it, back when we used to do it, though."

"Don't tell anybody, but hardly ever. Which is weird, because we're pretty young. We're just too tired most of the time. How pathetic is that?" This, surprisingly, came from a woman in her late twenties, who was beautiful, with an equally beautiful spouse. Okay, so she and her husband both worked full-time *and* he took classes at night *and* they had a toddler, but still. It was hard to believe that two people who looked like that weren't having the kind of sex widely presumed to be the birthright of two people who looked like that. No matter who I asked, the answers sounded the same. Not much. Once in a while. Every other week or so. The randiest couple I consulted could only manage twice per week. What a revelation! I raced home to share the data with my husband. He greeted the news that he was not the most sexually deprived man in the southeastern United States and was, in fact, routinely getting more than any other guy I could find by remarking, "Wow. That's not saying much for any of us."

The pornification of America has gradually led us to believe that everyone is having threesomes, installing sex swings, making their own hard-core home movies, and creating their own adult Web sites—or would be, if they were open-minded enough. Not true. There are millions of us out here too damn busy and overworked to make time for French kissing, much less a neighborhood orgy. Even if we could work up an interest in something kinkier than *Cinemax After Dark*, sex, like flossing or filling out a tax return, is an act best enjoyed in private.

The problem is, children abhor privacy the way nature abhors a vacuum. Close a door, and a child will bang on it until it's opened. Tell them that Mommy and Daddy are going off to take a nap, and one of them will promptly fall down the stairs and require stitches. Sneak off while they're watching a cartoon, and you can all but bank on their sudden need for juice, Band-Aids, or help with the potty. Perhaps because they are innately selfish, their instincts warn them that, when parents are left alone for too long, the odds of their being saddled with additional attention-hogging siblings skyrocket. I once witnessed my toddler daughters huddling up for a Friday-night strategy session: "Listen, if for any reason I fall asleep tonight, you scream, okay? Loud, you know, that high-pitched siren thing you do. Just keep them separated and we'll be fine. Here, have a Fruit Roll-Up—one of these will keep you jacked for hours. Now quick—act like you're watching *Dora*. I think Mommy's getting suspicious."

Even after launching a training program for my husband in the dual arts of not yelling and making more of an effort to act in a loving manner, we still couldn't seem to find any time alone when one of us (usually me) wasn't dead asleep. Which meant that he constantly walked around wearing his sad, horny face. You know the one—every guy has it. I began to worry that Mark's face would freeze in that expression and the whole world would know what a sad, horny mess he'd gotten himself into. What to do? Mornings were out. I had to get up at 4:00 A.M. for work; the idea of setting the alarm clock for 3:30 to make time for chitchat and romance was too crazy to even contemplate. At that hour, which sane people rightly consider the middle of the night, a sweaty roll with George Clooney himself isn't worth waking up one minute earlier for, believe me. Nights were also out. At the crispy end of a seventeen- or eighteen-hour day, I couldn't have kept my eyes open if my husband slipped into an eye patch and a mink jockstrap and lit his own buttocks on fire with a blowtorch. And he's a cute guy—especially when he's wearing a fur jockstrap. Afternoons were okay, provided that both girls took a nap at the same time, which was about as likely as an alien invasion. Still, Mark and I gave it a shot, hunching over the crackling baby monitor like a pair of field generals eavesdropping on the encroaching enemy. "I haven't heard anything in five minutes— what do you think?"

"That's a go!" I'd whisper. "Lock the door!"

Within ten minutes we'd hear the telltale thump of two little feet hitting the floor overhead and racing toward us. "Incoming!" my husband would yell as we scrambled for cover.

Date night, that mythical honey-soaked interlude so beloved by women's magazines, became the newest priority item on my perfect-wife to-do list. "We need to schedule date nights," I announced to my husband.

"Date nights? Can't we just go out like normal people?" he whined, looking at me suspiciously.

" 'Date night' *does* mean going out like normal people, except that we plan things to do that are more romantic than just sitting in some movie theater," I explained. "It's like a real date. You do the whole seducer thing, you know, like you did before we had kids."

He looked doubtful. "It sounds like work to me. Do we at least get to have sex?"

"If you do it right. The point here isn't just to have sex, because we can do that anytime, but to have romantic couple time. Time to really just focus on each other for a change."

He rolled his eyes. "If we can do it anytime, then how come we don't?"

The following Friday afternoon, we threw our toothbrushes into a bag, packed the girls off to my friend Marsha's house for a sleepover, and checked in to a downtown hotel. The next twenty hours were all ours, and Room 312 was our playground. Mark opened a bottle of wine and we stretched out on the bed, which was actually made, already a wildly exotic departure from our usual routine. With the late-afternoon sunlight streaming through the windows, and that weirdly antiseptic chill in the air common to hotel rooms everywhere, the whole scene felt illicit in a naughty, dirty-movie sort of way.

"This is what it must be like to have an affair," I said.

"Too tired to move?" Mark asked.

"No. I mean being in a hotel room in the daytime, while other people are at work. With your real life somewhere else, and everything around you so impersonal and anonymous. I bet that makes it easier to be wild and not feel guilty, don't you think?"

In response, he set his wineglass down on the bedside table, rolled over, and, stroking my face with one hand, stared at me intently. It was a moment ripe with possibility and erotic potential. Finally he spoke. "You're getting those crazy Gabor sister eyebrows again. Stop plucking them so much. Let them grow for a change."

So much for erotic potential. "That's a very romantic observation on your part," I replied. "I do *not* have Gabor eyebrows."

"Hey, do you want me to be one of those guys that doesn't pay attention to you?"

"By 'pay attention' I don't mean to notice minute grooming details or flaws. 'Pay attention' means to smother with compliments and notice only the really good things."

He laughed. "Is that what it means? Are you sure that it doesn't mean to point out Gaborian eyebrows?"

"No. You're not even supposed to care what my eyebrows are doing, because (a) you're a straight man and (b) I look damn good for having had two of your babies and busting my ass every day at four A.M. You're supposed to be barely able to restrain yourself from jumping on me at every opportunity. Which is what you should be doing right now instead of analyzing the density of my eyebrow hair, Mr. Queer Eye."

"I just don't understand why you won't let yourself be natural."

I realize that I should be delighted to be with a man who thinks that I'm perfectly gorgeous just as God made me. But I happen to be a firm believer in the saying "God helps those who help themselves." The Lord has seen fit to shower upon the earth an abundance of defrizzing hair serums, lash-enhancing mascaras, self-tanners, and Lycra—are we not therefore morally obliged to help ourselves to this beauty bounty? The whole "be natural" campaign was merely another one of my husband's clever little traps. He only wanted me to sprout caterpillar eyebrows, wear sensible shoes, and be a lumpy, au naturel she-beast so that he could immediately embark on an affair with a perfectly coiffed, lipstick-and-high-heels-wearing exotic dancer. Then, as he and the stripper, probably named Brandi

("That's *Brandi* with an *i*," she'd chirp in her fake sugary voice), rode off in his two-seater midlife-crisis mobile, he'd shake his head and tell me that I'd really let myself go. *Natural.* Oh yeah. Sure.

"The 'natural' you want me to be actually takes a lot of work to pull off," I patiently explained. "I *like* being a girl. I *like* girly stuff. For a guy whose first wife turned out to be a lesbian, you're not nearly grateful enough for how girly I am. Now, quit talking and show me why it is that I agreed to come to a sleazy hotel with you in the middle of the day."

(According to the date night guidelines mandated by women's magazines, Mark and I were right on track for a lovely evening. Splitting hairs over eyebrow hairs didn't exactly qualify as sexy pillow talk, but at least we weren't talking about the kids, the bills, or our jobs—all forbidden topics on date night. Which is a staggering challenge for most couples, since kids, bills, and jobs eat up every waking hour, leaving precious little time to bone up on whatever it was that made us such fascinating people back in the day before kids, bills, and jobs entered the picture.)

After somehow overcoming the libido-killing power of my Gaborian eyebrows, Mark and I strolled out of our hotel an hour and a half later feeling extremely pleased with ourselves. With eighteen hours of childless freedom still before us, the biggest challenge we faced was finding the last restaurant in the city that any parent in their right mind would drag a kid to. Not because we didn't want to be around other people's children, but because we were so sick of pizza, pasta, rice, and string cheese that we were willing to eat a curried goat's nostril on a bed of fresh lawn clippings as long as it didn't taste anything like a chicken finger. We found the perfect place, a charming bistro enthusiastically caught up in the small plate/big price trend. For my midwestern husband, a man who prefers to be served a steak big enough to wrap around his own head, a single shrimp puff in a sea of quince foam for the price of half the ocean was cause to drink himself silly. Two hours and two bottles of wine later, we staggered back to our hotel and both passed out cold until morning. End of Date Night Number One.

Date Night Number Two looked promising. We'd been invited to a huge party at the home of Mark's flamboyantly gay hairstylist. Having been to one of these parties before, we knew we were in for a fabulous time. Great food, great music, great company, great drag queens. We'd looked forward to it for weeks. We planned to go out to dinner first, enjoy a little conversation about something other than kids/bills/jobs, then head to the party. As we were getting dressed and ready, Eric shuffled into our bedroom and slumped on the bed. He sighed.

"What's up, honey?" I asked, hoping that the answer was nothing more than five bucks and a ride to a friend's house.

Eric didn't answer for a few minutes. Not a good sign.

"There's no one to play with. Everyone's gone. I'm *bored*." He blinked rapidly, as though blinking back tears. "I haven't had anyone to play with *all weekend*." He sniffed and hunched over even further, the very picture of misery.

All weekend? It was only Saturday. Knowing how useless that kind of logic is to a kid, I bit my tongue. Sitting down next to Eric, I gave his shoulder a little squeeze and asked, "Honey? What's *really* the matter?"

Another long pause. This was definitely bad. I could feel the fabulous party, the *mojitos*, and the bizarre French disco music slipping away like the fragment of a beautiful, impossible dream.

"I wish we could go to the movies and stuff like we used to before," he blurted. *Before* obviously meant "before the babies came along." Before the babies, Mark and I took Eric everywhere, even on a special honeymoon just for the three of us. Now we were all living under the equivalent of house arrest, and it felt like no one went anywhere anymore. Poor Eric. Everything in his world changed overnight when his sisters were born, and unlike us, he wasn't caught up in the minute-by-minute drama of parenting. He was stuck in the backseat between two squalling tormentors, forced to listen to their maddening baby music, and unable to properly defend himself when one of them walloped him in the head with a toy. Mark and I exchanged a glance, and it was clear that there was only one right thing to do.

Which is how we wound up eating at Subway that night and taking Eric to see *Sky Captain and the World of Tomorrow*. Not exactly a proper date night, although two hours of watching Jude Law dash about in a leather bomber jacket was definitely time well spent. Mark and I *did* consider hitting the party later, after the movie, but our teenage babysitter had other ideas and her own party plans. So we paid her (the going rate is now about what you'd expect your local endocrinologist to pull in) and called it a night. End of Date Night Number Two.

Date Night Number Three. The babysitter was late. The kids were determined to keep Mark and me apart. We were tired, worn down, ready to give up. We didn't have the energy for anything other than a movie, and movies were against the rules. Here's how bad it got: in an effort to be more of a spontaneous temptress, I forced my husband to drive to a secluded spot in a brand-new neighborhood that was still under construction. He parked on a dead-end street and killed the engine. "But we have a perfectly good bed at home," he whined. "Let's just go home. This is crazy."

"No, it isn't. It's hot. Look, we finally got a babysitter, but she's going to leave the minute we show up, then the babies will start crying, and that's it for the rest of the night," I replied, doing my best to sound reasonably alluring. "Besides, isn't this kind of fun, doing it in the car? Risking getting caught, hmmm?"

Fun is a multipurpose word. It can mean all sorts of things. I suppose it can even encompass the contortions of two fully grown adults in a Toyota Camry striving mightily to experience ecstasy while simultaneously keeping an eye out for cops.

"Ow, that's my bad knee."

"Sorry. Ouch, there's a bolt or something right under my back."

"Scoot this way. No, no, the other way. Maybe if you move your leg a little . . ."

It might not have been comfortable, but it really *was* extra steamy, parking and fooling around in front of some stock market McMillionaire's mammoth future dream home. Poetic, even, since you know that someone had probably already gotten screwed in that deal. Alas, on this night, it wasn't going to be us. Neighborhoods like that don't wait for the residents to move in before hiring security to keep riffraff like us out. In a hasty scramble for zippers, buttons, and shoes, we did as the guard suggested and moved along. The last thing I heard was a transmission from his walkie-talkie. Shockingly, it was our three-year-old daughter's voice, unmistakable, even through the static: "Confirm coitus interruptus. Over."

"Roger that," the guard drawled. "It's all over but the cryin'. Heh-heh-heh."

Beaten, chastened, and stripped of hope, Mark and I slunk home. Someday, I thought, the kids will be grown and gone and we'll have plenty of time for date nights. Unless they refused to ever leave home and just mooched off of us until they were in their thirties and we were completely destitute. That could happen. After all, anything was possible. Except for an hour alone. That was the one thing we couldn't have.

9

Betty Briefcase

Nothing screws up the flow of a good heated marital argument like spotty cell phone service. Like many people, my husband and I were successfully brainwashed into believing that we absolutely needed to communicate with each other via mobile phone countless times throughout the course of a day. Patton managed to win a war without talking to his field commanders half as often as Mark and I talk to each other in a single week. Having foolishly signed a multiyear service agreement with the world's most rinky-dink cellular provider, we didn't *talk* so much as spend a great deal of time shouting "What?" and "Are you still there?" into our phones. This kind of confusion occasionally led to misunderstandings but was generally nothing more than a minor annoyance. Unless we happened to be using our mobiles to have a great, big, giant fight—then it provoked us both to the point of yelling, swearing, and launching our nukes.

The best arguments are often over something really stupid and trivial. This was no exception: which one of us should take Olivia to her very first dental checkup. What began as a simple conversation about logistics quickly turned into a brawl. The trouble started when Mark informed me that my presence at the dentist's wasn't necessary.

"Olivia doesn't need you there," he said. "That's all in your head, not hers. She'll be fine." The line crackled and popped. His voice sounded metallic, as though Mark were insulting me from inside an enormous tin can.

"What? I'm her *mother*. You better believe she needs me there. I'll take Olivia, and you can stay home with the baby while she naps."

Through more hissing static I faintly heard: ". . . ridiculous . . . ," *hiss, pop,* ". . . just . . . work . . . dentist appointment!" Then the line went dead. Cursing, I punched the redial button. Six rings, followed by a recording: *"This is Mark; I can't get your call right now,"* which was promptly drowned out by the insistent beeping of an incoming call on my line.

I hit "answer" and barked, "Why didn't you pick up just now? That's me trying to call you!"

"It never rang. Calm down. Okay, so I'll take her. I just need directions—"

"You're taking her?" I interrupted. "No, no, *I'm* taking her. I *want* to take her. Okay? Don't worry about it."

"No, you're *not* taking her. You're not leaving work for a stupid dentist appointment." The line crackled and sputtered; his voice dropped out completely for a couple of seconds and then boomed into my ear, "SUCH A MARTYR! It's one stupid appointment! *I'll* do it!" The line went dead again.

Furious, I screamed at the phone and stabbed at the redial key. This time Mark answered on the first ring.

"Martyr!" I roared. "Don't you dare call me a martyr! That is my *child* you're talking about! I am her *mother*! How *dare* you tell me I can't go to the dentist with my baby!"

"Oh, you're nuts, do you know that?" he yelled back. "It's a checkup. A. Check. Up. It's not some precious moment for the damn baby book! Why do you have to make such a gigantic production out of everyth—" The line went dead again.

I threw my phone across the office. It bounced on the carpet and almost instantly started ringing. I dove for it. "What?" I hollered.

He was indignant. "Did you just hang up on me?"

"No, I didn't. But I would have if the @*$%# phone hadn't gone dead! I can't believe you call me a martyr for just wanting to do what any mother would do. You know what? You just want to exclude me from everything! It's so obvious!" I was apoplectic by this point. Did he really expect me to hang out at the radio station while my little girl braved the dentist for the very first time? Plus, it counted as a rite of passage. There was no way I was going to miss it.

"Aaaarrggghh! This is crazy! Why can't you just stay there and do your job, and let me do mine? It's *my* job to take her to the dentist! Mine! You're so controlling!" He was practically foaming at the mouth. "*I* stay home. *You* go to work. You can't have it both ways!"

I was near tears. "Both ways? What's that supposed to mean? A good mother takes her children to the doctor!"

"A good mother doesn't have a breakdown over a dentist appointment!" he spat.

"A breakdown? Are you accusing me of having a breakdown? That's it! I'm hanging up on you!"

"Fine!" he yelled.

"Fine!" I yelled back, smashing the phone down onto my desk. I was still fuming a good fifteen minutes later when it rang again.

"Hello?" I snarled.

"It's me." He gave a nervous chuckle. "Um, I still need those directions . . ."

Listen, no one has to tell me that I'm a head case; I know that. I'm anxious, tormented by unrealistic expectations, and consumed by guilt every waking minute. I admit it! *ARE YOU HAPPY NOW?*

But this is what happens to some of us when we have children and then leave them in the care of another while we go out to work. Even if the person caring for them is their own father. I had very specific ideas about how I wanted to raise my kids, very specific ideas about what kind of parent I wanted to be. I'd already ceded control of the household to my stay-at-home husband—now I had to relinquish my standards in this area, too? I'd vowed to be the mom who showed up for every doctor's appointment, every parent/teacher meeting, and every game, recital, or school play they threw at me, as long I had the strength to crawl out the front door. Yes, my husband was phenomenally committed to fatherhood, a fact that overjoyed me. I was blessed to have a good career, with an income that made it possible for him to stay home with our babies. But none of that could magically erase or alter my deeply held maternal goals and desires. I'd need a lobotomy for that. And if Mark meant to give me one, he'd have to catch me first.

I discovered just how deep some of my mommy ambitions went when Olivia began preschool. Mark and I hadn't planned to enroll her in school until she was kindergarten age, but she was so clearly ready for *something* by age two and a half that we began seriously investigating our options. Since she already knew her colors, her alphabet, how to count to twenty, and the names and diets of about two dozen dinosaurs, we figured that she'd be reasonably qualified for a good program. I used to crack up at the horror stories other parents told about the competition to get into preschool. The interviews! The waiting lists! But I stopped laughing after running across about the hundredth parent dead set on scaring Mark and me into thinking that our child's entire future depended on precisely where it was that she went to learn *not* to eat Play-Doh or put plastic beads up her nose. And suddenly it didn't matter that shoving beads up her nose actually seemed a whole lot less silly than our competing for admission to the "right" preschool. This was our baby we were talking about. Not only did we love her beyond reason, but let's face it: she was also our little genetic emissary to the future. She carried our genes forward to the next generation, and while mine were a motley bunch of disreputable hoodlums that the species could easily do without, her father's came with a genius-level IQ and a nose that any plastic surgeon would die for. We began to reconsider our position on the importance of preschool. What if those other parents, with their doomsday scenarios of tragically unfulfilled juvenile potential, weren't just a bunch of worked-up ninnies living vicariously through their kids? What if they were, horror of horrors, *right?*

In the late 1980s, the president of the company I work for was faced with the prospect of hurling her son, then three, into the intensely competitive world of Manhattan education. Sitting down for an interview with the director of one highly regarded preschool, she was asked, "What exactly are your son's special skills?" Special skills? He was three, for God's sake. A special skill at age three is not peeing in your pants when you're too busy playing to remember to visit the potty. Expecting a toddler to show up for story time with a dazzling résumé is asking way too much of a person who's only recently begun operating a spoon and fork. Not to mention the pressure that places on parents. Like we don't have our hands full just teaching these kids to walk and talk—now we're expected to tutor them in Chinese and classical piano, too? Mark and I thought we were the bomb every time our daughter remembered to say "please" or "thank you." Now we realized that we had been kidding ourselves. Obviously, it wasn't enough to merely purchase the Baby Einstein flash cards; we should have gone ahead and drilled her with them. Our only hope at this point was that Olivia had absorbed a little knowledge while gumming them into a mangled pulp.

Despite our incompetence and woeful lack of focus, Olivia got into preschool. Amazed by all of the possibilities available, Mark and I decided to enroll her in a British school: British curriculum, British faculty, British sensibility, and even Harry Potter–esque British uniforms. My older brother, the history buff, was baffled. "We won that war—you're *paying* those people to educate my godchild?" I assured him that the British were our allies now and, moreover, that Olivia would be learning French. Wasn't that cool? He snorted. "She's three, Sher. *Three.* How about if you give her a chance to learn to speak English first? You're such a yuppie." It was my turn for mockery—a *yuppie.* Please. How Reagan-era could you get?

"There's no such thing anymore as yuppies," I retorted.

He laughed. "Want to bet?"

For her part, Olivia was thrilled at the prospect of going to school just like her big brother. She'd finally have playmates her own age, and a backpack to carry, and, according to her, "very important homework, Mommy." I was thrilled that she was thrilled, but as the first day of school drew closer, I began to feel sicker and sicker. No matter what anyone said about how exciting or wonderful this was going to be, I knew the truth. When my daughter walked through the doors of that classroom, she would be taking her first small steps toward independence. She would be joining a world that I could visit but never truly belong to. All it took was a glass or two of red wine and I'd begin stewing in melancholy over how quickly she was growing up. School! How could we already be talking about school? Suddenly, her infancy seemed very far away, and I bitterly regretted having squandered it by leaving the house to earn a living when I should have spent every possible moment holding and staring at her. After tucking her into bed one night, I confided to Mark, "I wish I had a pouch, like a kangaroo. Then I could keep the girls in there and tote them around everywhere I went. That would be so awesome, don't you think?"

He shook his head and sighed. "Please get help. Can you do that? For me?"

As the first day of school loomed, I tried to embrace it the way I imagined the perfect mother might. I insisted on hemming all of Olivia's uniforms myself, by hand, even though my sewing skills rank somewhere between Dr. Frankenstein's and the village idiot's. I took her shopping for school shoes and interrogated the poor sales-woman like a detainee at Gitmo. "Are you *sure* these have enough support?" I demanded, as Olivia twirled around the store in a pair of blue leather Mary Janes. "These are *school* shoes, not just play shoes." The clerk was patient; she'd dealt with the likes of me before. She understood, even if I didn't, that preschool wasn't a coal mine, and that most any shoe would be up to the task of getting my child safely through the hokey-pokey.

We'd been informed that Olivia would need to bring a snack each day from home. What rapture for me! I immediately drove to BJ's and spent a blissful hour debating the nutritional merits of Teddy Grahams versus Fig Newtons, and Juicy Juice boxes versus Minute Maid. When I spotted the case of single-serving cartons of chocolate-flavored soy milk, I was in heaven. I called Mark from the car. "Fantastic news, hon! We don't have to give Olivia juice boxes with all of that nasty sugar. I found chocolate soy milk! Can you believe they even *make* that? Isn't that the *best* news! Hello? Hello? Are you still there?"

Since I had to be at work before 6:00 A.M., I wouldn't be around in the morning to cook nutritious breakfasts or brush Olivia's hair or perform any of the other myriad little tasks that a child needs her mother for. This worried me. "Promise me that you'll never take Olivia to school with ratty bedhead, okay?" I begged my husband. "And make sure she eats something with protein. Don't just give her sugary cereal. And don't forget to put a water bottle in her backpack. And put sunscreen on her, if it's sunny. You have to promise me that you're going to do this. Stop making that face."

Mark's eyes were rolled back, his mouth hung open, and he was drooling. "Ugh. I am soooo stupid. I could never figure any of that out without you. Brush hair. Feed. Sunscreen."

I was on the verge of hyperventilating. "I'm going to have to quit my job! I can't be gone for all of this important stuff."

He laughed. "Oh, calm down! Like I'm not going to brush her

hair in the morning? Stop worrying about every last thing. No wonder your skin's breaking out. It's stress."

"It is *not* stress!" I argued. "It's my new alpha hydroxy scrub.
My skin just has to get used to it. I am perfectly relaxed."

"Oh, yeah, obviously. I can see that," he answered with a smirk.

The following week, I took the day off from work and the whole
family accompanied Olivia to her first day of school. She looked so
beautiful in her uniform, a pale blue pinafore that made her resem-
ble nothing so much as a nurse in a Victorian mental hospital, and
insisted on wearing her backpack in the car, even though it was awk-
ward and uncomfortable. The headmaster and teachers were waiting at the door to greet each family. Olivia took one look at them,
then dropped our hands and sprinted for the door. "School time!"
she shouted. "I am going to school!" She didn't bother with a back-
ward glance our way, never mind a tearful good-bye. The only time
she troubled herself to cry was about ten minutes later when we
stuck our heads into her classroom to sneak a peek. Spotting us, she
thought we'd come to take her home. "No!" she sobbed. "I don't
want to leave!" We swiftly backed away—like campers from a startled grizzly bear—scooped up Caramia, and trudged out to our car.
We sat there for a few moments in silence. Even the baby seemed
deep in thought.

Mark started the car. "You okay?"

I was. Which surprised me. I'd expected to fall apart. But Olivia
was so clearly happy about being at school that I couldn't help but be
happy, too. Sort of. Driving away that morning with a lump in my
throat, I never could have guessed that in a few short weeks Mark
and I would come to view preschool as the greatest idea anyone had
ever had. A mere half day with the Brits left Olivia so wiped out that
she'd collapse into bed and be snoring by 7:30 P.M. We rediscovered
quality adult time and HBO. God save the Queen.

Our days quickly fell into a new routine. I'd lay out a clean uniform for Olivia and pack her a snack before leaving for work in the

morning, and Mark would get the girls up, fed, and out the door to school. Since Olivia's day ended at noon, Mark would pick her up and then all four of us would meet at home to have lunch together. I wanted to pick Olivia up myself, but I could rarely leave work in time to drive all the way across town and fetch her by noon. Weeks and weeks would pass between my school visits. On the days I could slither out of work early enough to get her, I'd invariably be greeted by one of the other parents with a hearty "Oh! We sure don't see much of you!" Naturally, I interpreted this innocent statement to mean *"We don't see much of you because you are a bad, selfish mother who cares more about her career than about her own child."*

I'd respond with a weak "Well, I have to work, so it's hard for me to get here by noon most days."

This would be met by something along the lines of "Oh, that's right. You're on the radio, aren't you?" Mark swore I was imagining it, but the word *radio* seemed to be uttered with the kind of distaste you'd reserve for a particularly repulsive insect.

"Yes, I am," I'd apologize, before grabbing Olivia's hand and diving for the car.

Equally uncomfortable were the occasions on which I bumped into the dashing school headmaster, a man with an uncanny knack for catching my show only on the days when we were discussing the most incredibly tasteless or bizarre subjects imaginable. Like the morning we took calls from people who'd accidentally shot themselves with their own guns.

"Hello there!" he'd beam, in his rich, plummy, BBC accent. "You Americans and your guns—that was quite an interesting topic this morning. Yes. Interesting. Armed to the teeth, some of your callers are. It does make one wonder, doesn't it?"

It *did* make one wonder. It made one wonder if one's daughter would see her future prospects suffer as a result of having been born to the broadcasting industry's equivalent of a carnie.

Meanwhile, Olivia, totally smitten with her teacher, and learning all sorts of new British slang and phrasings along with phonics and French, alternated between calling me "Miss Ross" and "Mum." I'm sure that I called my own mother by a teacher's name once or twice—and I bet she was glad I did. It gave her a legitimate excuse to avoid putting down her book and fetching me another cup of grape juice. In the beginning, I struggled with Olivia's new idiom, especially in the first few months of school when I wasn't expecting my three-year-old to follow in Madonna's footsteps by adopting a new, vaguely British accent and identity. I was standing in the kitchen one afternoon, trying to come up with a dazzling new approach to frozen green beans, when she burst through the door. "Mum!" she cried. "I need a plaster for my knee, Mum!" When I successfully translated that into "get me a Band-Aid" and did, she rewarded me with a weepy smile and sniffed, "Thanks, Mum! Right, then. I'll sort myself out." Which apparently meant: "I'll be fine now, without any further interference from you."

Between Olivia's gradual transformation into a member of the British royal family and Mark's hogging all the fun of taking her to and from school every day, I began to feel sorry for myself. Not to mention extra guilty. I wasn't the parent attending the morning meetings and teas. Yes, teas. I didn't even know most of the other parents, much less the other children my daughter spent her days with. This wasn't at all how I pictured my life as a mother. Mark didn't understand my sorrow. He also didn't understand my sudden obsession with stain removal. I might not be able to drop my child off in the morning to go finger-paint, but I could damn sure be available to scrub that paint out of her clothes at the end of the day. Before long, I was going through a bottle of OxiClean a week.

"I don't get it," Mark declared. "You go hang out with your friends every morning and laugh your ass off. I *hear* you. But you think you're missing something at home with Thing One and Thing Two? It's chaos every morning. It's awful, just trying to get them fed and into the car so Olivia isn't late. You're on vacation compared to what I'm doing."

He wasn't exaggerating about the morning chaos. Caramia either refused all food or insisted on having one bite of everything she could point to. If Eric was there, he took thirty-minute-long showers and then stared at his breakfast in puzzled despair as though he hoped it might somehow eat itself. Olivia wanted whatever *wasn't* on that day's menu. She'd argue for pancakes if Mark made waffles, scrambled eggs if he served Cheerios, milk if he poured orange juice—i.e., whatever option proved most inconvenient at the moment. Then there was the matter of choosing a toy to accompany her to school. Again, opting for the greatest possible inconvenience, she always strived to select the one toy that could not be found anywhere in the house. Then she'd turn on her ever-ready fountain of tears and wail, "But I *need* Thoughtful the lizard!" Or Uncle Tyranno Duck. Or Baby Meat Eater. Or any of a dozen other elusive and weirdly named creatures. Trust me: you haven't even flirted with losing your mind until you've torn apart six rooms and a garage in a fruitless search for an Uncle Tyranno Duck who was *never* going to be located anywhere on the premises, because he'd been mistakenly left at school the day before.

"Excuse me, *vacation?*" I huffed. "My idea of a vacation doesn't include waking up in the middle of the night and then being under the gun for ratings and revenue every single day. It might sound like a party to you, but what I'm doing is *work.*"

"Work? It's just talking! What *I* do is work!"

I was indignant. "Just talking? How about all of the research that goes into it? Hours and hours of research—and you know it!"

He raised a condescending eyebrow. "Oh. I didn't realize that looking at 'Stars Without Makeup' in some tabloid qualified as research. Forgive me."

Then there was the morning when Olivia, extremely proud to

have made Number Two in the potty, insisted that her daddy and baby sister come behold her handiwork. As the three of them bent over to admire this natural wonder, Olivia accidentally dropped the hair barrette she was holding into the toilet.

"My hair clip! Daddy, you have to get it!" she screamed.

Mark reached for the handle to flush it away. "No, honey. It's ruined now. We'll just get another one."

She flung herself at his legs. "No! No! That is my favorite hair clip *ever!*" (It was a plain brown barrette from the drugstore, six to a pack. There were five more just like it waiting in a nearby drawer.) "You have to save it! Please save it for me! You have to use a, a, a . . . spoon!"

"Spoon! Spoon!" shouted Caramia. "Want spoon, too!"

"Girls!" Mark yelled. "Out of the bathroom now! Olivia, stop crying. It's just a barrette!"

Olivia dropped to her knees. "Please, Daddy!" she implored. "Please save my hair clip with a spoon! Pleeease! You have to!" Out of either desperation or madness, Mark relented. Demonstrating some of the famed midwestern common sense that I married him for, he at least used a plastic spoon to do the job. How do I know? Because he called my mobile phone immediately after finishing the grim task. I listened sympathetically but failed to mention that while he'd been fishing around in a mucky toilet for a cheap hair accessory, I'd been kicked back in a comfy leather chair in our air studio, feet up, chatting on the phone with one of the stars of the hit ABC television show *Lost*—and nibbling on a tiny filet mignon sandwich that Morton's restaurant had thoughtfully dropped off for breakfast. Given the choice between Matthew Fox and toilet diving with a plastic spoon, even I couldn't pretend that I wasn't absolutely relieved to be at work.

Still, there were times when our arrangement seemed like a bit of a raw deal. If my husband were the only one working, then by golly, no one would dare imply that his job involved nothing more than "sitting around and talking." He'd not only be admired for his diligence; he'd be practically dragged out of the house on weekends for a little much-needed golf or fishing or some other butch activity far away from screaming kids and ticked-off wives. And if *I* were the one staying home, complete strangers wouldn't stroll up to him and coo: "I think it's just so neat how your wife takes care of the kids. And she's adorable, too. Aren't you lucky?" And you can forget weekends filled with personal leisure time for the stay-at-home mom. A guy who works all week and plays golf or whatever on the weekend deserves a break; a woman who does exactly the same thing is a selfish monster who should never have had kids, and frankly doesn't deserve them.

I tried to explain all of this to my mother in a crazed phone call one afternoon, but she only chuckled. "Honey, this is what we burned our bras for all those years ago." I'm sorry—did she intend that to be comforting? Or had the low oxygen levels at her high-altitude mountain home finally begun to erode her mind?

"It's the old double standard, sweetie," she continued. "Welcome to equality. Be careful of what you wish for and all that. Maybe it's time to burn those bras again. Heh-heh-heh."

When had my bright, incredibly well-read mother turned into a talking fortune cookie? I knew all about double standards and the price of equality, but burning my bras was out of the question. After nursing two babies for over two years, I needed the damn things too much to set them ablaze. Besides, I didn't want to protest anything. I wasn't angry. I was amazed. Amazed to find myself living in an unexpected minefield of emotions and role-reversals. Worse, I couldn't tell how much of what I was feeling was real, and how much was swirling around in my own head. For example, if I didn't allow Mark to run our household in whatever manner worked best for him, then I risked being a controlling nag. Because he was right: being at home, with all that entailed, *was* his job. I had to trust him to do it properly. As we wrestled and negotiated over our shared domestic territory, I began to understand that what I feared wasn't losing authority over what my children ate for breakfast or how we folded the towels; it was the idea of being our family's sole provider that scared me to death. Not the financial responsibility—I could handle that. What I worried about was the potential impact it might have on our marriage. I remembered my grandmother's dire warnings when I was in college. She'd shake her head, exhale a puff of cigarette smoke, wag her finger at me, and mournfully declare, "You and your career-girl ways—keep it up and you'll never get a husband! Men have a very fragile ego, Miss Library Lips! They don't want a girl smarter than they are, mark my words."

The fragile male ego! I tried to tell myself that my grandmother was of another era, that her reality wasn't mine, that things had changed between the sexes, that we'd come a long way, baby. Besides, didn't women have fragile egos, too? All it took for me to develop a lifelong complex about the size of my head was hearing one nasty remark at age nine from a stunted punk named Joey Brett who told me that I had a blowfish face. As tears filled my (admittedly) huge eyes and trickled down my (undeniably) puffy chipmunk cheeks, the rotten little twerp laughed and threw a rock, hitting me square on the top of my (inarguably) jumbo-sized head. So I had the facial proportions you'd expect to see in a Japanese cartoon—I eventually grew into them. I think. But *blowfish* was a low blow indeed. We all have fragile egos. In fact, we're all pretty much just a bunch of fragile egos walking around in bags of skin that we're convinced are so much more hideous than they really are. If you want to know what a fragile ego looks like, try being a woman in a culture that spits on you if you're not a size 4 with smooth, bouncy hair and zero wrinkles. Go ahead and talk about your penis anxieties— they've invented pills to take care of most of those. But we're still waiting for a pill that'll keep us twenty-five years old and perfect forever. The fragile male ego! The more I thought about it, the madder I got at the unfairness of it all.

As Mark sent me out the door each morning with a kiss, I was uneasy. Did staying at home while I went out to slay the mighty paycheck beast leave him feeling emasculated? Did he secretly hate me, even as he smiled and waved from the front door and called, "Have a good show!" Exactly how much trouble was his so-called fragile male ego stirring up behind my back? Clearly, we had to talk. I hunted Mark down in the garage, where he was tinkering with one of the cars.

"Hon," I demanded. "Tell me something, please. Where's *my* three-martini lunch? *My* Saturday tee time?"

He stared at me in bewilderment from beneath the hood of the Camry. "Your tee time? What are you talking about? I thought you had to work on Saturday."

Exasperating! Why did he never listen?

"You know what I'm talking about!"

He shook his head. "You don't even play golf."

"That's not the point!" I cried. "The point is, I couldn't even if I wanted to."

"You want to play golf now? Is that what you're telling me? Where're you going to find time for that?"

Like many of my previous attempts at explaining my deepest inner thoughts and feelings, this one came off like the disjointed ramblings of a crazy woman. I took a deep breath and then tried again.

"I work and then come home and I feel like a bad mother *because* I work, and then I feel like a bad wife because I'm always tired. I never finish anything anymore, and no matter where I am, half of my mind is somewhere else, and I feel guilty all the time. And it seems like no matter what *you* do, you get to be Mr. Amazing and Wonderful and Selfless."

"Mr. Amazing? Says who?"

"Says the world. And you have your fragile male ego, so I'm not supposed to be negative or critical or you'll take it personally or whatever." What was my point again? When you start confusing yourself in a debate, it's never a good sign. I could feel my chances of victory rapidly slipping away.

He set down his tools. "Tell me again what we're talking about?"

We were at the point in the discussion where I deeply regretted saying anything and wished I'd sneaked upstairs to take a nap with the baby instead of choosing to "work" on my marriage.

"Here's the deal: you go to school every day and chat with Olivia's teacher and her little friends and then it's off to the park and I'm not a part of all of that. Yes, I'm here in the afternoon, but I still miss so many things. And then you treat me like Betty Briefcase when I want to take my daughter to a stupid dentist appointment. You have the job that I always assumed would be *mine*. I'm having a harder time getting used to that than I thought I would."

Shaking his head, Mark answered, "But everything's going great."

"Then why do I feel like such a failure?"

"Because you're insane," he replied, gingerly patting my back, the way you might pat a dog with a reputation for biting. "You're a great mother. And you're a pretty good wife, most of the time. When you can stay awake long enough. Nobody thinks you're a failure but you. Just stop doing that to yourself."

That's my husband's idea of therapeutic advice: Just stop it. Whatever your problem might be—fatigue, illness, anxiety, fear, self-loathing—if you can give it a name, he'll urge you to just knock it off. Just quit it and move right on. Next! He's like a cyborg Dr. Phil.

"All right, I'll work on that. I just want to make sure you don't feel emasculated by this arrangement. You don't, do you?"

Mark laughed. "Oh yeah, it's *killing* me. I'd feel much more manly working seventy hours a week and never seeing the girls. I wish I could have stayed home with Eric. But we needed my income too much then. I really regret that. I know that some people think a guy who stays home with his kids is just a lazy bastard. Or that he couldn't cut it in the 'real world.' I just don't let people like that bother me."

"What about your fragile male ego?"

"It's hanging in there; don't worry about it. Stop looking for problems. It's all good. Maybe you need to stop trying to do everything, because you can't. *Relax.*"

Relaxing was definitely on my to-do list. Along with everything else I was supposed to stop doing. But if I didn't do everything, who would? And what should I cut? My job? Nope—without it, we'd starve. Fretting over nutrition? Dicey—left to his own devices, Mark would bomb most vegetables out of existence and happily live on jelly beans and Diet Coke. Trying to be a sex kitten? Even though it was an unrealistic goal, I still felt obliged to pursue it. Stain removal? Here was one I could probably surrender. So my children would walk around looking like the "Before" part of a Tide commercial—I could try to live with that.

No sooner had I committed to kicking the OxiClean habit than the voice inside my head—it had to be either Satan or Procter & Gamble—whispered, *Dirty children are the sign of an uncaring mother.* For once, I ignored it. I *could* relax. I *could* calm down. I could even take an infinite number of schoolyard greetings that sounded like "Oh, we haven't seen much of you!" because, effective immediately, I was a sane, mellow, go-with-the-flow working mom. A celebration of my newfound serenity was definitely in order. That's when I heard the glorious news about the State Fair. All of the fun was set to begin in just four days. How lucky was that?

10

State Fair

Only after you've gotten—at the minimum—a cornfield maze, a picnic, a petting zoo, a bout of heat rash, a public vomiting, a visit to a giant flea market, and maybe even a war reenactment or a medieval festival under your belt should you dare take on the awesome challenge of a visit to one of the ultimate old-fashioned family fun destinations: the State Fair. Be warned: this is expert-level stuff, and if you hope to make it through without publicly shrieking at your spouse or smacking your kids, you're going to have to get serious and train. The State Fair is almost like a final exam, combining everything you've learned so far about high costs, higher expectations, nasty food, squabbling children, a pissed-off husband, and just exactly how hideous you can look after a long day of schlepping around in the sun. We were a good ten months into my happy-family experiment before I felt confident enough to load up the brood and tackle the Fair.

Who doesn't love the idea of a Fair? Prizewinning farm animals and handmade quilts achieve their moment of glory side by side

with blue-ribbon pies and fresh-faced 4-H kids basking in the spot-
light of momentary fame and acclaim. The Tilt-A-Whirl beckons;
music blares from the Himalaya. The midway is crowded with food
trucks offering everything from candied apples, to the ubiquitous
"bloomin' " onion, to deep-fried Twinkies. There's a smell in the air
of grease and sugar and diesel fuel, and it's a smell you've known
your whole life: the smell of raw, uncomplicated happiness. Barkers
holler from every stall, promising easy wins on games of chance,
their booths hung with massive stuffed toys—gigantic clown fish
and pug dogs dressed up as pimps. Immersed in color, noise, action,
excitement, and the knowledge that the Fair comes but once a year,
you find yourself pulling cash out of your pockets and flinging it into
the air like so much fluffy green confetti. Darts? Sure! Ringtoss? You
bet! Who wants some frozen lemonade? How about a funnel cake?
Or some elephant ears? With hot fudge sauce? Why not have both!
Calories don't count at the Fair and there's no such thing as a rip-off
when it's all in the name of fun. Yes, everyone loves the idea of the
Fair, and no one more than me. The memories we'd make! I could
hardly wait to arrive.

The Fair was about a hundred miles away, which meant we'd
have to make it an overnight trip. Indulge me in a moment's nostal-
gia here, as I reminisce about the road trips of *my* childhood. My
parents would load my two brothers and me, along with the dog,
into the back of our old Chevy Malibu. No seat belts were ever in
use, of course, which allowed us to fight for the opportunity to lie
across the back dash. My younger brother was generally made to sit
on the floor with the dog, so that my older brother could enjoy the
full length of the rear seat. We were not allowed to speak, because
the sound of our voices and the nonsense we spewed irritated the
living hell out of our father. With the windows tightly closed, my
parents would proceed to chain-smoke their Pall Malls, crank up
Johnny Cash on the eight-track, and drive—with barely a stop—
from New Jersey to Wyoming. This is a distance of roughly two

thousand miles, which, as you might imagine, is a very long time for three children to remain still, silent, and reasonably well behaved.

At feeding time, my parents would buy a bucket of KFC and chuck it into the backseat, where we'd fall on it like jackals. Or they'd pull over at a truck stop and leave us sleeping in the car while they enjoyed a leisurely breakfast and another good smoke. We'd get their leftover toast—minus the jelly, which would have been far too sticky for the likes of us to be trusted with. Beverages were strictly rationed, as bathroom stops would only slow us down and prevent us from making good time. Taking in minimal food and water not only meant producing minimal waste; it left us with very little energy for squirming or bickering. We could barely muster the enthusiasm to cough from all the cigarette smoke. This was a good thing, because when we did cough or wheeze, our dad was sure to shake his head and say something folksy, like "I don't know what's wrong with these goddamn kids, but they're always frigging sick."

Not that it was all misery. The dog was spectacularly flatulent, which broke up the monotony, and my older brother would sometimes amuse us by putting my younger brother in a choke hold and inflicting what he called Chinese water torture on him. It's a revolting game, and not at all politically correct, but there's no denying that a thread of saliva will dangle almost indefinitely when you've got a long, flat expanse of Nebraska highway unwinding beneath your wheels. Our mother liked to stop at roadside markers and learn a little something about the landscape we were passing through, so every now and again our father would sigh heavily, then pull over and let us out of the car. To our disappointment, we never seemed to hit a marker commemorating the Donner party, or the great buffalo migration, or Lewis and Clark. But we did acquire a bit of knowledge about the Eisenhower Interstate System and various local irrigation projects, and my brothers got to sneak off into the bushes to pee. Then it was back into the polluted Malibu for another six or seven hours of non-stop driving.

If I did any of this to my children today, the authorities would immediately remove them from my home. My case would make the CNN crawl: *Psychotic Mother Subjects Children to Starvation and Smoke-Related Abuse. Children Being Treated at Local Hospital. Charges Pending Against Parents.* Instead, my children travel in comfy safety seats featuring three-point harnesses that would pass muster on any thrill ride in America. Mark and I invested in a tiny portable DVD player so that they could be entertained on long journeys by such edifying fare as Baby Einstein, The Wiggles, and Thomas the Tank Engine. The CD changer is stocked with kiddy faves like the sound track to *Dora the Explorer*, and the Raffi classic *Bananaphone*. They are served cool drinks in colorful watertight containers and are offered an array of tasty tidbits to munch on should they feel even a twinge of appetite. When a DVD fails to amuse, we swiftly provide them with LeapPad educational toys, or books, or crayons and drawing paper. We are constantly swiveling our heads around to check on them, to make sure that they are comfortable, happy, and, above all, satisfied with the onboard amenities. In short, they travel in exactly the manner that I, as a child, assumed the Queen of England might deem appropriate.

Although snoozing in a moving car with a gassy Lhasa apso on my head was plenty good enough for me, my kids are as delicately calibrated as sports cars. Sleep for them is a sheer impossibility unless they are tucked into a proper bed, accompanied by their special blankies and other assorted fetish objects. The room must be darkened, and the baby must be alone, since even the sound of another human being's breathing would disturb her fragile slumber. Having finally learned this lesson the hard way (Chicago, Orlando, Charleston, Saint George, et cetera), Mark and I reserved two rooms at the Comfort Inn. The baby and her monitor would share one; we would share the other with Eric and Olivia. Try as we might to reserve adjoining rooms, we never succeeded. In fact, the only time I could ever get a hotel room with a connecting door was when I traveled alone on business. Invariably, I would bump into the guest in the adjacent room in the hallway, where I couldn't help but observe how eerily he resembled a portly Charles Manson. Every. Single. Time. No matter what city I was in. Go figure. You can't get a room next to your own kids, but a creepy-looking loner with squirrelly eyes? Not a problem.

Does anything promise romance in a marriage like an exotic night away from home in a plush Comfort Inn with your eleven- and three-year-old youngsters bouncing on the bed eight inches from your head? Even if you wanted to fool around—which seems unlikely, given how aggravated you'll be after a long, loud car ride to the hotel, followed by a chaotic swim in the hotel pool, followed by a dinner of chicken fingers and fries, followed by an epic struggle to get everyone into pajamas and bed—you won't be able to. It took nearly a year's worth of ghastly nights at various hotels for Mark to finally accept this truth and wipe the look of horny expectation off of his face. By now he had learned to hope for nothing more than a swim in a halfway decent pool and a restaurant with a liquor license.

Hotels with indoor pools are paradise for small kids. They don't care how cold the water is—they want in. And because they cannot swim, you'll be going in with them. And that water is cold, very cold. For some reason, the pool heater will always malfunction at whatever hotel you show up at, on whatever day you check in. It's one of the enduring mysteries of the Universe, and no one at the front desk can explain it. You, the hardworking, taxpaying, perpetually sleep-deprived adult, are not being unreasonable to desire an indoor pool to feel like a bathtub. Your kids, on the other hand, would wade buck-naked into a frozen stream if you let them. That's how much they like water, any water. Stepping in, I reminded myself that (1) I didn't want to be one of those prissy, horrid women who won't swim for fear of mussing her hair, and (2) splashing around in something that felt like a penguin habitat was probably very good preparation for our pending assault on the State Fair. No point in being relaxed or comfortable with Operation Midway just seventeen hours away. Spying my hesitation, my husband boomed out another of his jolly and blatantly untrue yet sincerely wholesome encouragements: "Jump in and get your head wet! You'll warm right up!" Lies.

Bedtime. Eric couldn't find his toothbrush. Olivia had stuffed her already-lumpy sofa bed full of plastic dinosaurs. The baby had wriggled behind the television and disconnected the cable. I belatedly realized that Mark and I had forgotten to get good and drunk at dinner. We unearthed the baby monitor from the suitcase and set it up. Changed a diaper. Found the Maisy books for Olivia. Sent Eric to the front desk for a toothbrush. Read stories, kisses, more stories, turned off the lights. The baby monitor fell silent; in a miraculous turn of events, Caramia fell asleep next door. In the adjacent bed, Eric began snoring lightly. Not Olivia. She kicked repeatedly at her mattress, whining and mumbling until 4:30 A.M. At 7:00 A.M., a loud, insistent buzzing filled the room. Was it the alarm clock? Not exactly. It was the sound of the alarm clock going off in the baby's room, as heard through the baby monitor. With the baby screaming like an angry piglet, I staggered across the room and fumbled through a stack of room keys for the one that would unlock her door. The baby was rescued, but she was angry and now would not be appeased. Which was perfect, because it was time to go to the State Fair. My husband cheerfully hollered from the bathroom, "Everyone will calm right down after a little breakfast!" More lies.

We arrived at the South Carolina State Fair just before it opened. Dew sparkled on the grass growing in patches in the parking lot. From behind the closed gates we saw not one but three Ferris wheels, and a roller coaster, and a big sign advertising pork chops on a stick. Suddenly, the wearying drive, the chilly pool, even the bad, sleepless night were forgotten as we gazed upon the splendors of the Fair. Mark and I paid our entrance fee, pushed our double stroller through the turnstile, and pointed ourselves in the direction of the animals. First stop: the draft horses.

After five minutes of watching an elderly cowboy scrutinize the withers of a young Percheron, we realized that when it comes to animals, the Fair isn't anything like the circus. What Mark and I thought would be a horse show, involving some bravura riding and a few dazzling tricks, was actually just some horses being walked around a ring once or twice. Not too exciting for the kids—especially Eric. "This is totally boring," he remarked. "Here's a horse. Here's a different horse. Like, who cares?"

Olivia probably would have agreed had she not been too busy licking the metal bleacher we were seated on. "Olivia! Get your mouth off of that!" Mark shouted. Muttering darkly about trench mouth and other communicable diseases, he scrubbed at her tongue with a baby wipe. The announcer called for the next group of horses. Two handlers carrying shovels trotted into the ring. Eric yawned. "Look, they got stuck cleaning up horse crap. That's a crappy job."

Pause. "Hey, do you get it? A crappy job? Because they clean up crap. So it's like a crappy job for real. That's funny. Heh-heh-heh." Clearly, it was time to move on to the next bit of entertainment.

We opted for the petting zoo. The usual suspects milled around in their picket fence enclosures: goats, sheep, a handful of lambs, a donkey. There were also a few star attractions: a zebra ("You can't pet them because their jaws lock down when they bite and they could, like, tear off your whole hand or something," Eric informed us; a camel ("Cool. I hope it spits on somebody while we're here"), and even a deer. The deer had all of the petting zoo angles figured out and, immediately upon spotting us, sidled over to the twenty-five-cent chow dispenser and began coyly batting her big, chocolaty-brown eyes at the kids. Minutes later, Caramia had her arm halfway down the deer's throat, while Olivia carefully inserted one nugget of food at a time into the saliva-foamed maw of a baby goat. Eric was busy staring the camel down, while Mark skulked around with his camera, aiming to capture that one perfect shot worthy of gracing the annual Christmas card. Animals were clambering onto the fence rails, twisting their heads through the bars, and licking the baby's face, head, and hands. Pulling her out of the way, I stood up in time to catch a wet, drooling swipe across my cheek from the deer's surprisingly large, black tongue. I didn't mind all that much—I figured it was the most action I'd see all weekend.

After a tour through the Small Livestock Barn, we learned that roosters cock-a-doodle-do pretty much constantly and not just at dawn. Those birds were squawking, yelling, and jerking their bodies like a preschool class after too much birthday cake and punch. Like true city folk, we couldn't help but gawk at the larger rabbit breeds, some of which were just fantastically huge, like bunnies bred downstream from a nuclear power facility. We also discovered that the words *meat* and *rabbit*, when affixed to the wire cage of something that looks suspiciously like the Easter Bunny, combine to form a profoundly unappetizing phrase. Since the Cattle Barn beckoned from just across the way, we took a quick spin through aisles crowded with Angus and Charolais bulls, some lying down, others stamping their hooves and swinging their massive heads from side to side. We watched as one farmer carefully vacuumed his bull, suctioning up bits of straw and dust from the animal's glossy coat. Olivia was full of questions. "What is that man doing, Mommy?" And "Why does this cow have that ring in his nose, Mommy?" And "What's that black cow's name, Mommy?" And "What is that big, pink thing sticking out from that cow's tummy, Mommy?" (I should note here that official prizewinning stud bulls *really* live up to their billing.) Overhearing this last inquiry, the farmer looked up from his vacuuming and snickered at us. I smiled right back, as if to say that explaining massive bovine genitalia to a three-year-old was something I dealt with each and every day, and firmly answered, "That, my precious, is Mr. Cow's pee-pee. Now, who wants to go for a ride on the Ferris wheel?"

Either I've forgotten a time when I actually enjoyed being spun around and dangled upside down on amusement park rides or I've always been a morbid, death-obsessed freak unable to simply relax and put my fate in the hands of a squinty-eyed, tobacco-chewing carnie, but I found the Ferris wheel to be a fairly stressful experience. For starters, the much-heralded view—in this case, the miles of blighted-looking industrial outskirts of Columbia, South Carolina— wasn't quite magnificent enough to distract me from the very real possibility of my toddler leaping out of the car to her certain death fifty feet below. Also, the little swinging door to that car didn't latch or lock closed, and we weren't restrained in our seats by anything stronger than common sense.

While Eric scanned the midway below for games to piss our money away playing and Mark studied the motor and hydraulics of the Ferris wheel for interesting engineering components, I clutched the baby in my arms, squeezing her till she grunted, and took deep, cleansing breaths. While it may be possible for the extremely neu- rotic to have a good time, I'm here to tell you that the amount of ef- fort required to get to that point is exhausting. Oblivious to my rising panic, the carnie did the unthinkable: he doubled the length of our ride. "You're my first riders today!" he called merrily. "Enjoy one on me!" Excuse me, but who ever heard of a carnie giving something away for free? Leave it to me to find the one ride operator on the State Fair circuit burdened by a heart of gold.

Midway through that second go-round, as we hovered at the very top, our car swaying in the chill morning breeze, the baby lung- ing crazily in every direction, I realized that parenthood had forever changed me. My old irrational fear of a horrible death had been pushed aside by my new irrational fear of a horrible death for my children. In effect, the intensity of my morbid psychosis was now at least triple what it had been pre-*Kinder*. At this rate, I'd soon be com- pletely unable to function, much less protect myself against a lunchtime onslaught of foot-long corn dogs. The Fair was proving to be a bigger challenge than I'd thought.

After dropping twenty bucks or so on various games involving softballs, darts, rings, and a slew of prizes that no gullible mortal had any shot at actually winning, we bellied up to the food wagons for a little snack. The low-carb options ranged from giant turkey drumsticks, to various meats skewered on sticks, to cheeseburgers minus the bun. International fare included spaghetti, gyros, and yakitori. On the side were giant bags of cotton candy, along with kettle corn, caramel apples, fudge, ice cream, cookies, and whatever could possibly be crammed into a deep fryer, from Oreos and Twinkies to onions and candy bars. It was an orgasmic sea of fat and sugar, a parade of the saltiest, chewiest, gooiest, creamiest, crunchiest, crispiest, most awful for you, and yet irresistibly delicious food that mankind knew how to make. Fairgoers were double-fisting caramel corn, inhaling bucket-sized servings of soda, wolfing down bulging kielbasa and slabs of fried dough. The grim news of the coming American obesity epidemic hadn't yet hit the midway, or if it had, no one gave a damn. Inspired, Mark and I did our part, ordering up sausage pizza, Cokes, cotton candy, a caramel apple rolled in chocolate chunks and glazed pecans, and, to crown it all, a deep-fried Milky Way candy bar. Nothing tasted as good as it looked, of course, especially the deep-fried candy bar, which bore too close a resemblance to what we'd seen being shoveled out of the horse ring earlier that morning—and tasted suspiciously of the bloomin' onion that preceded it out of the fryer. Delicious or not, it was authentic Fair food, and the kids were overjoyed to see it.

They were overjoyed, period. They loved everything about the Fair. Eric couldn't wait to win a basketball; Olivia nattered on about the bumblebee ride and the carousel. No one cried or sulked. No one was angry or disappointed. We still had the roller coaster to look forward to, and the Cuckoo House, and the live shark tank. There was the gigantic sand sculpture waiting to be admired, and the Junior 4-H Cattle Competition to attend. Mark and I bobbed in a sea of happy, expectant faces, with money in our pockets and high hopes for the afternoon. Mark leaned over between bites of pizza and whispered, "I don't care if we've got to drop forty bucks to do it, but let's make sure that Eric wins one of these stupid prizes, okay?"

I agreed. It was the right happy-family sort of thing to do. Never mind the caramel smeared in the baby's eyebrow, or the cotton candy stuck to the side of Olivia's face. All of my plans for our family were finally coming together. Surrendering to the magic of the midway, I said, "Let's just spend all the cash we brought! We won't leave till it's gone. Let's do everything that everyone wants to do. Yes, yes, honey, we'll ride on the bumblebee ride. What? And the strawberry ride, too. Yes, and the merry-go-round. Yes, honey, I promise. It's family fun time! How does that sound, Eric? You having a good time?"

Eric munched down a mouthful of candy, shrugged, then nodded. His eyes were glued to a nearby ride, something that looked like a whirling giant octopus in the throes of an electrocution. Its victims—I mean *riders*—were swooped up, then dipped down, then flipped upside down, then swung from side to side in a big, nauseating arc that made me weak in the knees just watching it. Since Mark, some years ago, had slyly developed his acute-dizziness alibi, I was stuck being the designated rider on anything that spun or twirled. And that meant if Eric wanted to ride the wild octopus, I'd have to ride it, too. I didn't want to be an evil stepmother, much less a wimpy one. Worse, I didn't want to be a buzzkill. So I tried hard to swallow my terror. "Um, sweetie? Did you want to go on that one?" I asked, trying to play it cool.

"Nah," he replied. "But you know what, Sheri? Your hair looks like you already rode it. It's like—*wooooo!* Crazy! You should see it." With that, he returned to his cotton candy and his thoughts.

Crazy hair or not (and don't even bother explaining to a preteen kid that you look like a wreck because you spend all of your time, attention, and energy on their needs instead of your own, because, truly, they did *not* ask to be born and do *not* want to hear it), we had as close to perfect a family day as anyone could have. The proof? We ultimately walked out of the Fair with five prizes, one sleeping baby, two happy kids, two grinning adults, and exactly two cents in Mark's pocket. Two cents—down from the $120 we'd started with. The Fair had taken our money, to be sure, but it didn't get our spirit. The Fair had shown us a good time—and what we were made of. Nothing could rile us: not rickety rides, or too much fat and sugar, or rip-off games of chance, or even staggeringly well-endowed livestock. Our clan was *solid*. Eric had been generous and patient with his sisters. Mark and I had been patient with the kids—not to mention with each other. We'd all bonded over lots of wholesome spectacles, including sheep shearing and cattle grooming. We'd done it all, tried it all, seen it all, and spent it all. After hours and hours in the suffocating South Carolina humidity, pressed on all sides by equally sweaty fellow fairgoers, bloated from junk food, and reeking ever so faintly of the many varieties of manure that clung stubbornly to our shoes, we actually strolled out of there laughing. Just like a family on TV. So we were broke and sticky? It was worth it.

11

The Smug Race

Marriage, a union of two souls committed to sharing a lifetime together, might just be the noblest experiment a human being can embark upon. What an act of faith such a partnership is for creatures so selfish, locked as we are inside the prison of our own consciousness, trapped by the crude boundaries of our skin and our limited senses. We hurtle through the universe in desperate solitude, yearning to connect, to be reassured that we are special and unique, that our existence matters. Marriage offers the promise of that connection, the hope of peace and security. And that commitment, deepening over time, grants us the freedom to grow and mature, to soar to greater heights than we could ever dare aspire to on our own. Marriage is an expression of our finest selves and a sanctuary in this unpredictable and lonely world. What a blissful and glorious thing is marriage!

What a crock.

Marriage is rarely the trip to the moon on gossamer wings one hears about in so many love songs. Marriage is more like an overbooked plane ride to an uncertain destination in which most of the flight is spent bumping and swaying in search of smoother air. And you don't always get to be the pilot, either. Sometimes you don't even get a seat. Marriage is tricky, tricky stuff. Inviting two human beings to swap their innate, factory-installed selfishness for a lifetime of negotiated compromise is a tall order. Which explains the 50 percent divorce rate in the United States. In fact, the only thing harder than marriage *is* divorce—and divorce has the advantage of being a mostly temporary condition. But I believe in marriage. I also believe in extraterrestrials, psychics, and skin-rejuvenating moisturizers, though, so maybe I'm not the most credible spokesperson for the institution.

You can call marriage a poem; you can call marriage an adventure; but what marriage most resembles is the fragile détente between superpowers locked in the dance of mutually assured destruction. Don't go looking for this information in any bridal magazine. You won't find it buried between articles on making honeymoon sex hot or choosing the wedding day updo that's right for you. This info is locked up tight in the top-secret, eyes-only folder. By the time you figure it out, you'll be very, very married and long dug into your bunker. Instead of weapons, you'll be stockpiling incidents. Who did or said what, and when. Who won the fight or had their way, and when. Whose turn it is, and for what. Who screwed up, and how bad was the mistake.

They say that you shouldn't keep score in a marriage. They say that you should never go to bed angry. They also say that you should defrost your freezer twice a year, wash your makeup brushes with gentle, cleansing shampoo once a month, exercise for five hours a week, and eat four to six cups of vegetables every single day. They say a lot of crazy things, which is why no one ever listens to them. I don't care if you're from Mars, Venus, or Uranus: if you're married, you're going to argue, you're going to nag, and in one way or another, you're going to keep score. We're all products of our highly competitive culture, a culture that worships the individual above all else. We take protection of individual freedoms so seriously that we went ahead and put it down in writing when our country was founded. The Bill of Rights is a uniquely American document. And while you can interpret the phrase *pursuit of happiness* a million different ways, however you interpret it, you're bound to feel absolutely entitled to your share of it. It's an American birthright. That can-do individual mentality doesn't just magically evaporate the instant you slip on a wedding ring.

I once had a boyfriend who used to pout that my problem was I wanted to be an *I* instead of a *we*. Without we-ness, he explained, there could be no us-ness, and the two of us would never achieve a Vulcan mind-meld together. That sounded like a bunch of crap-ness to me. How and, even more important, why would I surrender my I-ness to be in a state of we-ness with a guy who actually borrowed his relationship metaphors from Mr. Spock on *Star Trek*—and wasn't joking about it? First of all, what woman really wants to know what you think her problem is? We don't, you know. We might ask to be told, we might even *beg* to be told, but deep down inside, we don't want to hear it. And second, good luck finding *any* female interested in picking up tips on emotional intimacy from an actor wearing pointy latex ears. Aren't relationships difficult enough to pull off all by themselves without also attempting to merge brains like a couple of TV space aliens? Isn't achieving simultaneous orgasm a sufficiently daunting challenge for most of us? How much more can one simple Earth woman be asked to do? I beamed myself straight out of there.

Back to marriage, that state of legally binding we-ness. You can love your spouse beyond reason. You can be prepared to sacrifice anything for their happiness, suffer any discomfort for the pleasure of their company, maybe even take a bullet, if doing so might spare their life. Friend, lover, companion—you can be all of those things. But you'll also be tormentor, jailer, and goad. Not intentionally, at least not most of the time. It's just that when you agree to share your life with another, you can't possibly realize what exactly that entails. Picking out cute stuff for the house and taking long romantic walks is only a teeny-tiny part of marriage. The rest of it is one long, delicate, carefully nuanced treaty negotiation, broken up by alliances, border skirmishes, outright hostilities, trade agreements and violations, aid missions, embargoes, natural disasters, political campaigns, scandals, labor strikes, all punctuated by periodic photo ops. And that's if you're lucky, able to communicate, and can manage to create something resembling a democracy. Some couples wind up living in a hellish dictatorship or a frostily civilized but desperately unhappy Cold War. Better a little conflict brokered with diplomacy than the icy silent treatment or a lifetime spent pretending to the neighbors that everything is wonderful and couldn't be better.

Around our place, I try very hard to be the perfect wife/mother/sex kitten who doesn't nag/carp/complain. Naturally, I fail miserably, but how about some points for the effort? Besides, my husband does exactly the same thing, in his own way. He's extremely interested in being seen as the perfect husband/father/stud puppet. As a result, we live in a state of feverish, near-Olympian competition, each of us jostling over who deserves the daily gold medal for doing a better job of managing the house and kids. As in any good arms race, there's lots of vigilance, surveillance, and covert operations, not to mention plenty of plausible deniability and loads of good cover stories. Mark and I plot, scheme, and scramble, all while vying for a taste of one of the most exquisite pleasures left to the married-with-children: the right to be smug, smugger, and smuggest. The Smug Race is one of the dirty secrets of marriage. It's included in the long list of things they say you're not supposed to do once you're married. You know the drill: Don't go to bed angry. (That again. How about seething? Can we agree to go to bed seething?) Don't make major financial decisions without consulting each other. Don't get all worked up and accidentally call your husband "Johnny Depp" in a moment of passion. It's a nice ideal, but these things do happen in marriage, and not only because we're all imperfect and human, but also because Johnny Depp is spectacularly hot.

Cunning and strategy are critical to coming out on top in the Smug Race, but don't make the mistake of thinking that's all it takes. And don't fall into the trap of expecting much cooperation from your kids. They're usually unreliable little traitors who'll enthusiastically sell you out for a doughnut—or less. You're in this battle alone. And to win it, you'll need the scarcest, most unpredictable commodity of all: luck.

Opportunities to don the crown of smugness take many forms.

February 4, 11:10 A.M. My office. The phone rings. It's my husband. "Um, listen, when you come home, you need to brace yourself for Olivia's face, okay?"

In a microsecond, the scenarios—more vivid and horrifying than any Hollywood screenwriter could manufacture—run through my mind. The neighbor's child-hating terrier snapped its leash, bolted into our yard, jumped onto my baby girl, and viciously chewed off half of her face. Or maybe she grabbed the handle of a pot of boiling water—admittedly a stretch, since Mark doesn't cook, but what if he were boiling a spark plug or a carburetor or something equally bizarre that he'd read about in one of his car magazines, which is exactly the kind of freak accident that you read about but think could never happen to you—and she burned her whole face? Or scissors! She somehow got a pair of scissors and sliced her cheeks open. Or she fell face-first onto a fork! Or she put her head through a window! Anything awful is possible. With my heart in my throat, I barely manage to croak, "What happened? What happened?"

Heavy sigh on the other end of the line. "We were running down the driveway, and she tripped and fell down. She scraped her face up pretty good. It looks kind of rough. It's going to be scabby."

Brain now frantically searching hypochondriac database for relevant links. "Does she have a concussion? Are her pupils dilating? Don't let her fall asleep! Stitches! Do you think she needs stitches?" As I interrogate him, I grab my keys, handbag, and coat.

"Calm down. She's fine. I'm only telling you about this now so that you don't freak out when you see her." Much as he means this to reassure me, it has the opposite effect. *Brace yourself? Freak out?* These aren't phrases one chooses in conversation about one's off-spring unless things are very bad indeed.

I practically fly home, leap out of the car, race into the house, and dive at my daughter. Her nose and chin are livid and oozing. It really is just an abrasion, albeit a bad one. After sneaking a peek at her pupils just to be sure, I dab Neosporin onto her face while she whimpers and squirms. As I casually wonder aloud why it is that *he* never comes home to a weeping, disfigured daughter, Mark squirms, too. Verdict? Mark is a bad, careless, crazy daddy who chases his toddler down a steep, cement driveway. Smug Point: mine.

April 16, 5:00 P.M. Kitchen. Here's the thing about having a husband who chooses to stay home and take care of the kids: He will *not* be the wife you've always dreamed of. More to the point, he will not be *any* sort of a wife. The stark reality is, he may neither share nor even fully comprehend *your* domestic priorities. He may not cook or clean the way you would. He may not schedule his days in a way that makes any sense to you. He may not fluff the throw pillows properly—or at all, for that matter. He may even go so far as to de-scribe your charming decorative knickknacks as "a bunch of junk that just gets dusty and clutters up the place." And unless you want to be the shrewish gorgon from hell, you'll need to make peace with it, whatever *it* turns out to be, as quickly as possible. Because the minute he takes over the full-time management of the home, you have to stifle almost every control-freak impulse you have and let him do it his way. Anything else would be unfair. This is much harder to accomplish than you'd think.

Grocery shopping was our earliest battleground. It's a simple chore, right? Figure out what you need, go buy it, bring it home, and put it away. Little did I know that the supermarket was actually a working laboratory for the study of gender-based sociobiological differences in human beings. Wired by nature to be a hunter, my husband would peer in the refrigerator, see that we were out of milk, then head for the nearest dairy case, where he would stalk and capture a gallon of 2 percent, and bring it home to our cave. While he was hunting milk, all other products were invisible and irrelevant. Milk is what he went for; milk is what he got. The one significant difference between him and Neanderthal man was that Mark didn't get to bag his prey with a spear.

Wired by nature to be a gatherer, I would peer in the same refrigerator, see that we were out of milk, and also observe a shortage of eggs, apples, cheese, and yogurt. I would then draw up a list and head for the nearest market to snatch up that all-important gallon of 2 percent, along with the fifty-seven other items we required in order to keep our family fed and going. When I gently suggested to the Great Dairy Hunter that he might consider improving his efficiency by purchasing more than one item at a time, he shot me a look that said, *Woman, don't be such a ball breaker. I do things my way around here.*

I bit my tongue as I repeatedly watched him ferry a single loaf of bread and three bananas from the grocery store to our kitchen, and that wasn't easy for me. But it was nothing compared to the kitchen sink. I didn't know how enraged a sink filled with dirty dishes could make me until I started coming home to one on a daily basis. Bloated clumps of half-eaten breakfast cereal shared the sink with soggy sandwich crusts and wadded-up paper napkins. There were gobs of peanut butter slowly hardening into cement on the knives, and egg yolk glued to the plates. The inner 1950s white-glove-wearing hausfrau that I didn't even know I possessed rose up inside me and howled like Joan Crawford after a weekend's worth of freebasing coke and chugging Starbucks: *"Clean! Up! THIS MESS!"* Toys, puzzles, books, newspapers, shoes, and jackets were strewn across every surface. The place looked like the FBI had tossed it looking for evidence. It was bad.

Staring at the chaos one spring afternoon, veins throbbing in my head like a madwoman, I announced, "Girls, while Daddy is off picking up your brother from school, we're going to clean this place up and prove that it can be done. Mommy knows how to clean a house, oh yes, she does."

I had about an hour. Tearing through that place like Martha Stewart on a weekend furlough, I shoved toys into boxes, books onto shelves, and dishes into the dishwasher. With minutes to spare, I wiped off the countertops, stuffed a pile of unopened mail into my bag, and for good measure lit a scented candle. Perfect. I heard Mark's car pull into the garage. I was mere seconds away from triumph! Both girls were playing together at the kitchen table; the house was tidy and quiet—a gorgeous tableau right out of a commercial for Mop & Glo. Deciding that it was far more thrilling to cruise into Victory Lane in a blaze of glory than just be standing there waiting for my trophy, I quickly darted out of sight. I heard his hand on the knob, his footsteps in the hall, then his cry, "What the hell is going on here? Caramia, get out of there!" I came around the corner to the sight of the baby on all fours, her head practically submerged in the dog's water bowl. Olivia was still at the table, though she'd used my fifteen-second absence to find and line her lips with a green Magic Marker. Caramia came up for air, laughing and clapping, and then bent down for another long slurp from Champ's dish. "Is this what happens when I'm not here?" Mark inquired. "I guess the baby is thirsty? Why didn't you give her a drink? And why'd you let Olivia color on her face?" Staring down at Caramia, who by now was completely soaked and sitting in a puddle of water, he sighed and shook his head. "Look at this mess. Were you off daydreaming or something? It's just a good thing that the *right* parent stays home with these two, don't you think?"

My look-how-easy-it-is sparkling house/well-behaved children plan backfired miserably. Verdict? I am controlling, haughty, and totally busted by my own double-crossing offspring. Smug Point: Mark.

August 18, 7:43 P.M. Kitchen. "Olivia, come over here and let Daddy take a look at the boo-boo on your foot, sweetie." Olivia dances over, twirls in a circle, thumps her sister on the head, swipes a magnet from the refrigerator door, and puts it into her mouth. "Olivia," I repeat, much more firmly. "Come. Here. Now. Sit down and let Daddy take at look at that foot." She finally complies, collapsing onto the floor in a giggling heap.

Mark lifts her foot and, as I step forward to take a closer look, peels off the now-ragged Scooby-Doo Band-Aid. Olivia begins screaming. "Oh, for heaven's sake, honey!" I say in my most exasperated-mommy voice. "He hasn't even touched it yet! He just took the Band-Aid off. So much drama! Honestly, I don't know where you get it; I really don't."

As Olivia continues to wail, Mark looks at her, then at me, and calmly remarks, "Hon, you're standing on her fingers."

Ah. So *that's* the problem. I immediately lift my (remarkably well cushioned) Nike off of her hand, and presto! No more screaming.

"Nice going. Just stomp on her hand, why don't you? That's one way to distract her while I change the Band-Aid. Very good." He shakes his head, and as I apologize and attempt to kiss her fingers better, Olivia gives me a look that Pol Pot would have recoiled from. Verdict? I am a bad, clueless, clumsy mommy who cannot even tell when she is standing on her own child's appendages. Smug Point: Mark.

October 27, 9:20 P.M. My car. Had to work late and am finally headed home. After a seventeen-hour day, and a package of vending-machine crackers for dinner, I am ragged with fatigue and wallowing in remorse and self-pity for having missed dinner with my family. Suddenly, my mobile rings. It's Mark. "Where are you?" he blurts.

"On my way home," I answer. "About ten, maybe fifteen minutes away. Is something wrong?"

In the background, I hear screams and sobs—in other words,

nothing unusual. "Just get here fast!" he shouts. "Olivia got a wire coat hanger stuck in her eye!"

The human mind is a magnificent thing. There will never be a computer able to rival it for speed or complexity. Hearing the words *Olivia got a wire coat hanger stuck in her eye* instantly triggers a cascade of images and calculations, all processed at lightning speed. There are the obvious questions, starting with: Why is Olivia not in bed? What was her face doing anywhere near a wire coat hanger? Where was Mark while she was impaling her eyeball on said wire hanger? And where, in a houseful of plastic hangers from Target, did she manage to find a wire hanger in the first place?

Then there are the fears, starting with, Oh my God, she's going to lose her eye! She's going to lose her sight in that eye! That wire hanger is probably rusty and dirty and now she's going to get gangrene or tetanus or whatever and not only lose her eye but possibly her life!

Already well into the opening stages of a full-on panic meltdown, I scream, "Take her to the emergency room! Right now! I'll meet you there!"

From the other end of the phone I hear more shrieking and thumping, then Mark's voice bellowing, "Just get home! The baby's asleep and I don't want to wake her up. If Olivia would just let me take a look at it—Olivia, let me see that eye!" Through the pinhole-sized speaker of my Nokia phone, I hear my firstborn hollering like a terrified bear cub caught in a trap. By now, my stomach is an icy knot, and I'm doing 60 in a 45 mph zone.

I yell, "Take her to the hospital!"

He yells, "I just want to look at it!"

Olivia yells, "Mama! Mama! Mommy! I want my mommy!"

The phone goes dead. Cursing, I punch the speed dial number for home—voice mail. Totally freaking out now. I catch the next four traffic lights red and am ready to abandon the car and run home. Finally—our street! I peel into our driveway, nearly taking out two shrubs and the mailbox. I bolt into the house. Silence. No sign of life. I sprint to our bedroom—nothing. "Mark! Olivia!" I scream.

My husband barrels down the stairs waving his arms and hissing, "Ssshh! They're both asleep. Don't make so much noise."

Asleep? Am I tripping? Did I not, less than twelve minutes ago, get a frantic phone call about my daughter having a wire coat hanger stuck in her eye? Taking a deep breath, I croak, "Asleep? How can she be asleep? She has a wire coat hanger in her eye—remember? You just called me and I nearly had a heart attack and I drove sixty miles an hour the whole way home so that she wouldn't lose her eye and now she's asleep?"

Him: What do you want me to say? She cried herself to sleep.

Me: And we're just going to let her lie there with a gouged eyeball? She could go blind in that eye!

Him: You need to calm down and stop overreacting. I looked at her eye. She's fine.

Me: She wasn't fine just ten minutes ago!

Him: Hon. Seriously. Get a grip.

Me: I can't get a grip. There was a hanger? In her eyeball? Remember when that happened? Like, *just freaking now*?

Him: Man, it's no mystery where Olivia gets the drama from. It's pretty late for you—don't you have to get to bed?

A long time ago, before I was married, I was home from work with the flu, scanning the TV channels in hopes of finding either a good brawl on *Maury* or a juicy *E! True Hollywood Story* when I came across a black-and-white movie on Turner that starred Ingrid Bergman as a woman whose conniving, sinister, manipulative husband played all sorts of devious tricks on her in order to make her believe that she was losing her mind. It was called *Gaslight*. Little did I know that one day I'd find myself in a similar situation, on the receiving end of desperate phone calls about wire hangers and eyeballs only to come home to a quiet house, children nestled safely in their beds, and a puzzled look on the face of my forever-blameless spouse. But I was on to him, oh yes, I was. I wouldn't be carted off to the asylum without a fight. I fix him with my best piercing stare.

Me: I'm on to you.
Him: *On* to me? You're *on* to me? Hon, you're crazy.

And chuckling to himself, Mark strolls calmly, exasperatingly, out of the room.

Hmmm. Nice try. The old brazen-your-way-out-of-trouble scheme. But even the best postgame strategy couldn't save this one for him. After all, our daughter stuck a wire hanger into her eye on *his* watch, not mine. Possession may be nine tenths of the law, but in marriage, you don't even get the benefit of the doubt on that last tenth. In marriage, possession is *everything.* It's like a crazy game of hot potato, in which whoever is caught holding the crying or filthy or injured or crime-committing child is Suspect Number One in the ensuing investigation. In this case, all of my prior convictions paled in the face of a hanger in the eye. Verdict? Mark is a bad, reckless daddy who allows his child to play with dangerous household objects while his back is turned. Smug Point: mine, mine, mine!

Marriage. It's a beautiful thing. A great institution. One thing nobody tells you, though, when you promise to hang tough for better or for worse, is just how much of the "worse" you'll end up cheerfully inflicting on each other. For the rest of your lives. Incidentally, that's how long the Smug Race takes, too. And just when you finally pull ahead by doing something truly amazing and spectacular, like successfully performing CPR on your kid's beloved pet iguana, that's when you're sure to run the baby's foot over with a wheelbarrow, sending yourself straight back to last place. There's no way to win, and no chance of a break. The best you can aim for is to just stay even. Romantic, isn't it?

12

Shiny and Fragile

W hen the Pilgrims gathered to celebrate that first Thanksgiving, they were grateful for so many things. There was the bountiful harvest they'd coaxed from the fertile soil of their new land, the forests thick with hardwoods and all manner of wild game, and the endless sparkling rivers that teemed with fish. After hardship, deprivation, and numberless tests of their faith, the Pilgrims had somehow begun to carve a new home and a good life out of an untamed and sometimes hostile wilderness. They were grateful to be fed and sheltered, thankful simply to be alive. And when they counted their blessings of thanksgiving, they were wise enough to be thankful for one more thing: none of them worked in radio. Because if they did, instead of feasting on maize pudding, fresh trout, and smoked venison, they'd have bitten into a cold Jumbo Jack with cheese and a bag of greasy curly fries while huddling together for warmth backstage at the local TV station's annual Christmas extravaganza. And verily, though they would be subjected to numerous mortifying and sadistic torments at the hands of the local TV weatherman, they would be neither paid for their labor nor given so much as a fruit basket for their trouble. The poor Pilgrims would even be made to buy their own cold Jumbo Jacks—and that's assuming they could find a drive-thru pathetic enough to be open on the one major holiday devoted entirely to cooking and eating at home. Welcome to Thanksgiving in the glamorous world of media.

Here's the deal: when you're a kid, growing up in front of a television set, you get the idea in your head that being on TV is a cushy, dazzling job. And it probably is—if your name is Katie Couric, Diane Sawyer, or Oprah Winfrey. Admittedly, Katie and Diane are forced to wake up insanely early for hair and makeup. But unlike the rest of us, they can doze off in a chair as a professional makeup artist transforms them into goddesses. (Think of that the next time you nearly blind yourself with a mascara wand trying to put on makeup in rush-hour traffic.) TV on the local level is another thing altogether. It's a pretty low-budget game.

My first "real" (i.e., poorly paid and vaguely related to my major) job out of college was operating a camera and helping out with the 11:00 P.M. news at a small TV station in a city I'd better not name. In addition to doing the news, we also produced commercials, including a weekly spot for a regional family-owned supermarket chain. The "advertising director" for the stores was a towering bottle-redhead given to copious amounts of big jewelry, cosmetics, and Estée Lauder's White Linen perfume. She was also the owner's daughter. She reveled in the creative authority she exercised over us, the oppressed hourly workers of a TV station roughly the size of your bathroom. To an auteur like her, we were but the crude tools provided to realize her artistic vision, and she made sure we knew it.

In she'd cruise to the studio, bearing shopping bags full of raw meat or cantaloupes or boxes of Duncan Hines cake mix—whatever happened to be on sale that week. We'd then toil for hours, trying to get the lighting just right on the 93 percent lean ground beef, or the pimpled yellow flesh of a bone-in chicken breast. Did I mention that she was also the star of these minimasterpieces? Oh, it was Method acting at its finest! Over and over we'd reset the TelePrompTer, and over and over this manicured gargoyle would deliver her lines in a simpering twang that practically screamed, *Rich-bitch phony!*

At the end of each shoot, once she was completely satisfied that we'd successfully translated her vision of discount meat and produce to the small screen, she'd pack the props back into the shopping bags and enlist one of the crew to haul them out to her Mercedes sedan. The raw meat, though, that was for us. "On me!" she'd trill. "You kids enjoy a little treat!" Take it from me: there's nothing like a slab of raw pork that's been smoldering under blistering television lights for three or more hours to stimulate the appetite. You could practically see the bacteria colonizing on its greasy, grayish-pink surface. Between perks like that and the four dollars an hour they were paying me, when I was offered the chance to jump to radio, I took the leap and never looked back.

So why, then, were my precious little girls standing backstage at a local TV show eating Thanksgiving dinner out of a Jack in the Box bag? Why were we shivering outside on this cold November night when other families were just pushing back from their second piece of pumpkin pie? And how had I, a woman on a mission to build and maintain the ultimate happy family, ended up here? I was supposed to be home, presiding over an orgy of holiday memory making, yet instead I was waiting in the wings to deliver such deeply meaningful lines as "Isn't that a beautiful Christmas tree?" and "Is everyone having a good time?" and "Don't worry, kids! Santa will get here tonight to light that tree; I just know he will!" Meanwhile, just out of sight and only a few feet away, my own children were sobbing and screaming my name. They didn't care one bit whether or not Santa came to light the mall's giant Christmas tree. They didn't want to hear about the show having to go on, or about Mommy's silly job. They didn't give a damn that the whole thing was being televised to a home audience of, well, who, exactly? Who, on Thanksgiving night, given hundreds of channels to browse, would pause in their surfing long enough to watch me, my partner, Bob, and two embarrassed TV meteorologists stumble through a full hour of Christmas-themed time-travel skits? Inmates, I thought bitterly. Travelers stranded at bus stations. People who'd lost their remotes. By this point in my musing, a producer appeared to lead me to my first camera position. My youngest wept in panic as her father pried her from my arms. With her little arms outstretched and tears streaking down her frozen cheeks, Caramia hollered, "Mama! Mama!" Her precious, grief-stricken face was the last thing I saw before the spotlights blinded me to her suffering. Showtime.

It would be far too painful to recount each and every moment of my time onstage. Let's just say that Meryl Streep couldn't have pulled any of it off, either, and leave it at that. Some things are too horrible to relive. And now, thanks to my status as a cheesy local celebrity, our family Thanksgiving was a total loss. Walking back to our car, Olivia chattered on and on, a running monologue of maternal abandonment. "I wanted you, Mommy. But you couldn't hear me. I said, 'Mommy!' but you didn't come. I was very sad. You were far away, Mommy. Why were you far away? Why, Mommy?" Caramia was in my arms, still hiccupping a bit from so much crying, and clinging to my neck for dear life like a baby possum. Mark didn't say much—he didn't need to. Beyond observing that at least we hadn't traded precious family time for cash, since no cash had actually changed hands, he limited himself to eye rolls, heavy sighs, and an extra-solicitous approach toward the children. This deceptively calm and rational strategy was even more diabolical than his customary foaming and ranting. Clearly, he'd picked up a few new tricks over the last eleven months. This was far more valuable than any of the Smug Points he'd managed to rack up. This looked dangerously like the dreaded high road we were always supposed to be taking. God knows I couldn't let him conquer *that* peak. He'd be insufferable. What to do? Desperate, I went for the unexpected move, the surprise attack—an apology.

"I am really, *really* sorry about this. This is the last year that we'll spend our Thanksgiving eating fast food and shivering, I promise. I'm done. No, this time I mean it."

He sighed again. "It's not that *I* mind standing around backstage while you do the twist for no money with some nimrod dressed up as an elf, but the girls, well, that's just sad. They cried the whole time you were up there. It was awful. And Caramia's teeth started chattering, it was so cold down there on the ground. We should have stayed home, but . . ."

He left it unsaid. They came because I wanted us all to be together. I had thought that any outing, no matter how stupid or how grim, might become a wonderful adventure as long as we were all in it as a family. I was wrong about that. Pointless suffering does not a bonding experience make. Especially when the people shouldering the brunt of the suffering are too small to have had a proper say in the matter.

"Never again. I swear it. You've been a really good sport about it for a long time. I'm not going to ask you to suck this up ever again. And tomorrow, you know that I'm going to cook a turkey. The kids will never know the difference, and we'll have a really nice late Thanksgiving. When next year rolls around, I'll just have to blackmail someone else into taking my place. Okay?"

Glancing back at the girls, dreamy in their car seats, lulled by what surely had to be the mind-destroying three thousand and ninth spin of *Meet the Wiggles*, he muttered, "Yeah, okay. You know it's nothing but a giant clusterfuck anyway, year after year."

He had a point. The best thing about local television is probably the incredible volume of ridiculous experiences you'll have while making it. Of course, these same ridiculous experiences—things the viewer almost never sees—are also the worst thing about local television. Over the decade or so that Bob and I had been involved in this Thanksgiving night holiday extravaganza, we'd come across a drunken Santa; a Santa with a hillbilly accent so thick that even the well-behaved live audience was driven to heckling; a Santa so plump and jolly that he couldn't fit inside the TV weather helicopter for the obligatory aerial shots; fireworks that didn't go off; weather that didn't cooperate; and a girl in a teddy bear costume who, unable to see while wearing the gigantic bear head, tumbled off the stage and was roughed up by a band of rotten kids who couldn't resist the opportunity to take a cheap shot at a giant stuffed animal.

Bob and I had been required to wear costumes, too—everything from elf suits to wrapped packages complete with enormous bows clamped to our heads. When his three kids were small, he thought it was playful and charming for them to see their dad wearing rouge and big, pointy shoes. By the time I got around to having babies, Bob's children were teenagers and understandably mortified to be seen with him in public if he insisted on being tricked out in antlers and a cape. As a result, Bob had begun to lose his enthusiasm for making a costumed ass of himself. Also, we were usually forced to make oceans of unscripted onstage chitchat—desperately buying time for whatever was going wrong at the moment (and something is *always* going wrong, believe me). We had to soldier along with this charade while trying to ignore the impatient glares of people in the crowd, some of whom were loudly and belligerently demanding that we just shut up and start the fireworks before their kids froze to death. You can't tell the audience the truth about the delay—imagine saying, "Folks, Santa's got a buzz on, so it's gonna take a little extra time to haul him up here for you. While we're waiting, let's all call Rudolph as loud as we can! On the count of three . . ." No, that can't happen. The only thing to do is prattle on like big, silly, gift-wrapped windbags who love the limelight and just can't bear to leave the stage.

"Not only am I totally finished with this gig," I announced, "I'm telling you here and now that we're not going to go all psycho for Christmas. We're going to keep it small and reasonable. We won't get more than just a few gifts for the kids, and that's it. Let's make a pact right now and really stick to it, okay?"

Mark pointed out, "You're the one who thinks she lives in a cooking magazine or something, not me. We could go ahead and skip Christmas and I'd be fine. Just skip it. Go skiing instead of buying a bunch of crap that nobody wants for a bunch of people that we hardly ever see."

"Hon, come on," I replied in my most reasonable and soothing tone.

"I'm serious. Let's go skiing. The girls won't even know the difference. Eric won't care—he'll be with his mother. Skip it, that's what I say."

I smiled a big, warm, understanding smile. A wifely sort of a smile. The kind of smile you don't even know you possess in your arsenal until about six months after the honeymoon. "You know you really don't mean that. Our kids are going to have Christmas. We're not going to skip it. You know that. And you're going to love every second of it, because I've already gone around one time with a holiday-hating lunatic named Dad, and I will slowly poison you to death before I do it again. This year, we *will* have a beautiful, calm, completely sane, loving-family Christmas. It'll be perfect. You'll see. I promise."

The next morning, as I set about preparing our day-late-and-a-dollar-short Thanksgiving feast, I began making plans. I had twenty-seven days to work with, just shy of four weeks in which to shop, wrap, ship, decorate, and bake, not to mention stuff my children's heads with yuletide mythology, from the Grinch to the Burgermeister Meisterburger. Because when I promised we'd have a sane Christmas, by *sane* I didn't mean stripped-down. I just wanted to move the center of the action away from the cash register and back into the spiritual arena, where it belonged.

Step one: Replace the wind-up musical bullfrog dressed as Mrs. Claus that occupied the place of honor on the table behind the couch with my late aunt's crystal Nativity scene. "A glass zoo! A glass zoo!" shrieked Olivia. Within half an hour, she'd carted Joseph and three of the animals off to set sail in a ship made of LEGO blocks.

"No, no, honey," I said, carefully prying a crystal sheep out of her hands. "These aren't toys to play with. These are just to look at. This is a very special decoration. Here is the Baby Jesus, see, and these are the animals in the stable, all gathered around him. And look, this is Mary, his mommy, and Joseph, his daddy. This is the true meaning of Christmas, honey. You have to be very careful with this."

"Yes! It is the Christmas zoo and I will be careful with this glass zoo, Mommy. Okay, Mommy? I will just play with it for one minute." She swiped at the manger.

"Olivia, this Baby Jesus is very fragile. We don't play with him. You can't put the Baby Jesus in with your LEGOs, sweetie. He might break, and we would be very sad. We don't want to break little Baby Jesus, do we?"

"Who is Baby Jesus, Mommy?"

"Baby Jesus is the Son of God. And Christmas is his birthday. That's what we celebrate when we celebrate Christmas. What do you think about that?"

"Is Baby Jesus having cake?" she inquired.

"Oh, punkin," I answered. "Aren't you precious to ask? But only God knows whether or not Baby Jesus gets to have birthday cake. I bet he probably does, though. Because everyone likes cake, right?" All those years of parochial school, hours of religion classes, and countless yanks on my hair by irritable nuns, and *this* is the best answer I can come up with for my toddler? "Everyone likes cake"?

As her little hand again stole toward the Nativity, Olivia sweetly asked, "Who is God, Mommy?"

I immediately dialed Marsha. "I'm really failing over here as a mother. Olivia has no idea who God is, she's asking for some of the Baby Jesus' birthday cake, and right now, she's got the Virgin Mary out of the Nativity set and wants to take her into the bathtub. This is hard. How on earth do people teach their kids about religion?"

"Hmmm. I hear good things about church. They have programs for this sort of thing, don't they?"

A trustworthy friend is a prize; a trustworthy, sarcastic friend with an evil sense of humor is a treasure.

"You know that the last time we took them to Mass, the baby screamed the whole time like Linda Blair and Olivia made dinosaur roars during Communion. Remember? I'm afraid to go back. What did you do? Did yours just get it by osmosis, or what?"

Marsha thought for a few seconds. "I don't really remember—it's been so long now. Plus, I'm not Catholic, so it's all probably a little bit different anyway. I think they probably picked up most of the key points in Sunday school. Something you might want to take a look at. How did your parents teach you?"

"By rubbing cigarette ashes on our foreheads on Ash Wednesday so that they could skip going to church while still looking righteous to the neighbors. Oh yeah, and my father spent a lot of time yelling, 'God damn you kids!' anytime one of us asked him for something frivolous, like food or shelter. I was thinking, though, that we might go with a slightly softer approach for Olivia and Caramia."

"Maybe you could get one of those Bible storybooks written for kids? Read to them from that?" she suggested.

"We already have one. There are just so many *words* in it. I'm fried at the end of the day. I can hardly get through *Go, Dog. Go!*—now I have to take on the barely illustrated '*Samson and Delilah*'? I thought you were supposed to be my friend. Where's the love here?"

She snorted. "Listen, one heathen tramp to another? Dump this on Mark. He's the one with a minister for a mother, right? He'll know what to do. We're just white trash that married up. Tell him that he gets to explain God to Olivia and, when the time comes, you'll explain to her how to post bail. You guys need to go with your strengths. That's what a partnership is."

"This is exactly the kind of sensible advice I come to you for."

"You're welcome. Better go fish the Blessed Mother out of the tub now before she sinks. And call me if Olivia starts asking about the Devil. I used to live with him."

With that Marsha hung up. Staring at the ransacked Nativity, I had to admit that we weren't off to a very promising start. But the girls were young. Caramia couldn't even talk yet. How much theology could they really be expected to grasp at such tender ages? Granted, they'd have no trouble explaining Mickey Mouse, Shrek, or SpongeBob SquarePants to anyone who asked, but, like most parents, I knew perfectly well who to blame for that outrage: the media. Having even a temporary scapegoat for my parental inadequacies was such a relief that I pretended not to notice as Olivia crept stealthily into the room and hauled one of the Three Wise Men off to her bedroom for a sleepover.

Step two: Resist the call to spend every last dollar we have on a pile of toys that our children will barely acknowledge, much less play with. We asked Eric and Olivia to each prepare a Christmas wish list. To our surprise, both lists were very short.

Eric's Christmas List

A Sting-Ray bike

Sony PlayStation 2

A broadsword from *The Lord of the Rings*

A hatchet

Throwing knives

Olivia's Christmas List

A magic wand that shoots pink fire to make dinosaurs real

A mermaid tail with a real fin

A snorkel

The items on Eric's list were either incredibly expensive, incredibly deadly, or both. However, everything he asked for was at least for sale, somewhere. Not that he'd be getting most of it. Throwing knives? A hatchet? Whether he was planning to work up a circus act or launch an insurgency, I didn't love the idea of a pack of uncoordinated twelve-year-old boys flinging knives around our backyard and accidentally cutting off each other's fingers.

Olivia's list, on the other hand, presented a challenge. Not even The Sharper Image sold a gadget to reverse extinction. As for a mermaid tail, our choices were seemingly limited to a disappointingly anemic Ariel costume from the Disney store or an array of sleazy seashell bras and glittery sheer skirts that would have looked right at home in a dockside strip club. A Web search turned up a handful of merchants trading in outrageously priced mermaid tails that were obviously produced for the Hollywood market—or the serious mer-fetishist with cash to burn. These were amazing, elaborate creations that appeared totally authentic, right down to the fins. There were only two problems. One, these particular tails didn't come in a size 4T. Two, their unbelievable cost—the better tails ran a thousand dollars or more. Ignoring the fact that Mark and I were neither filthy rich nor wildly indulgent, I had to question the wisdom of such an investment. The average small child might not enjoy being strapped into a polyurethane fish tail that left her legs and feet completely immobilized. I could only guess that the novelty of being left to flop helplessly about on the living room floor would wear off pretty quickly, not to mention that it seemed a cruel thing to do to a kid.

The only thing left on her wish list was a snorkel. A snorkel is easy enough to come by, but even in a festive shade of fluorescent orange, I feared that it would look a bit meager, sitting all alone beneath our Christmas tree. Plus, it would be a real pain to wrap.

I tried to negotiate. "Olivia, Santa might have a very tough time finding a magic wand that shoots pink fire to make the dinosaurs real again or a real mermaid tail in his workshop. What if he brought you a singing Elmo instead? Hmmm? Wouldn't that be awesome? How would you like that?"

"I don't want a singing Elmo, Mommy. I want a magic wand that shoots pink fire to make the dinosaurs real. Not a toy one, okay, Mommy? A *real* magic wand. Santa will build one just right for me in his magical workshop. And after I make the dinosaurs real again, they will come to my home and babysit me and sleep in my room. Right, Mommy?"

Her passion for the dinosaurs, her unwavering faith in the possibility of magic, the trusting way she gazed at me, her eyes saying, *You have never, ever disappointed me, not even once,* was too much to bear. I took the cowardly way out. "We'll see," I said weakly, and slunk off to Google magic wands, pink fire, and giant robotic dinosaurs. Surely there was someplace one could purchase a life-size animatronic *Tyrannosaurus rex.* Tokyo, perhaps?

Christmas morning drew closer. So far, I'd managed to stick to my promise of a non-psycho holiday. This year, there would be no whirlwind of delusional cookie baking. Delusional because the cookies that came out of my kitchen always wound up looking like the handiwork of the criminally insane. My gingerbread men wore the leering grimaces of serial killers, and my frosted Christmas trees looked as though they'd been harvested downriver from Three Mile Island. And sadly, in the case of my baking, appearances *weren't* deceiving—my cookies didn't taste any better than they looked. As if being an incompetent baker wasn't bad enough, I was also a luckless and clumsy one.

Before giving up on homemade Christmas treats completely, I bought a package of ready-made chocolate chip cookie dough at the supermarket. After all, the expression *nothing says lovin' like something from the oven* doesn't say anything about actually blending or mixing, right? Feeling at least halfway wholesome, I slid a sheet of frozen chocolate chip cookie lumps into the oven and set the timer. As I did, I must have bumped one of the range control knobs, accidentally turning a burner on. A short while later, a foul, acrid stench began to fill the kitchen. Weird, I thought. Something must be seriously wrong with that dough to make it smell like that. As it happened, something *was* wrong, and it took a billow of gray smoke for me to figure out what. It wasn't the cookies that smelled so rank; it was my Christmas present to myself, a new Michael Kors handbag, which was sizzling away on the back burner. Why did I put a Michael Kors bag on the range? Because I am an idiot, that's why. And because every other available surface was covered with crap.

So, having learned the hard way that baking is hazardous to pricey designer accessories, I bought a few cans of red and green icing, and a couple of jars of candy sprinkles, and turned the girls loose on the box of homemade cookies that had been sent to us by their grandma Jacque. In the grip of her own holiday dementia, Jacque, Mark's stepmother and a living saint, had shipped us a box containing approximately eight hundred of her famous *Lebkuchen*. *Lebkuchen* dough is as stiff as hardened cement and so unyielding that Jacque wound up injuring her hand trying to mix it. This, however, did not stop her from producing enough cookies to stretch from Wisconsin to New York. I saluted this noble sacrifice of her very tendons with a jumbo glass of red wine and fresh batteries in the digital camera. "Who wants to decorate cookies with Mommy?" I yelled. Olivia and Caramia tumbled into the kitchen, hooting with delight. They didn't give a flip whose oven those cookies came out of. My little co-conspirators smeared icing and sprinkles and agreed that yes, we were having the most fun ever. With the help of Christmas carols pealing out of the CD player, matching aprons on the girls, and a cinnamon-scented candle, I even fooled myself into thinking that we had covered the basics of holiday baking.

Surprisingly enough, Mark and I had also held the line on gifts. That turned out to be easier than I expected, as each day brought a UPS truck weighed down by a fresh load of cardboard boxes from my cousin Renee. A self-admitted crazy woman and godmother to our two daughters, Renee wanted her goddaughters to have the world's best-equipped dollhouse, by God, complete with dolls, furniture, and about a million accessories. These ranged from plates tiny enough to qualify for angels-dancing status and an entire multigenerational family of bendable, manically grinning Caucasoids to a menagerie of miniature cats, dogs, and parrots and a dining room table with an embedded computer chip that played a loud and shrill rendition of "The Tarantella" at the push of a button. And all of that was crammed into just *one* package. Box after box piled up in our living room, each bulging with untold microscopic plastic parts. It was a show of generosity that bordered on the sadistic. Heaving yet another shipment onto the rapidly growing heap, I wondered darkly if this might be payback for that awful thing I did to Renee's bangs with a pair of cuticle scissors back when we were kids.

"Call Renee and ask her why she hates us so much," Mark suggested. "And then apologize for whatever we did before she has a chance to send another damn box."

Our own shopping was intensely focused on finding an authentic *Lord of the Rings* sword for Eric that (a) didn't cost as much as my first car and (b) was dull enough to make it impossible for Eric to kill us in our sleep for not getting him PlayStation 2. Olivia steadfastly refused to consider any item that wasn't a living dinosaur, although she did allow that she might be open to a playhouse for the backyard. Caramia babbled and pointed, which we took to mean "Don't worry about me. I'd rather play with the wrapping paper anyway."

In between bouts of Web shopping and signing for more shipments of dollhouse accessories, I cruised Target for stocking stuffers and grilled Olivia on the true meaning of Christmas. By Christmas Eve, it seemed like she was beginning to really get it. "Tomorrow is the Baby Jesus' birthday party!" she warbled as we prepared for our annual Christmas Eve tradition of leaving carrots on the porch for Santa's reindeer. Every year, on his way around the world, Santa always managed to drop off brand-new holiday pajamas right before bedtime, guaranteeing extra-adorable Christmas morning photos. It was a lovely idea, invented by my sister-in-law Nancy, the ultimate bakes-from-scratch mother of five. Naturally, I'd stolen it the first chance I got.

We waited inside, listening for the sleigh bells that signaled the annual pajama drop. There they were! Giving the bell shaker, our teenage neighbor, a few seconds to make her getaway, Mark and I led the girls to the front door.

"Look!" Olivia squealed, yanking the baby forward by one arm. "Rudolph ate the carrots, Tiny! He ate them!"

Mark and I wrestled the girls into their new stocking-and-snowmen-festooned pajamas and, after much chasing and giggling, finally got their teeth brushed and their faces washed. With hours of dollhouse assembly, a playhouse to build, courtesy of my mom and stepdad, and all sorts of other critical Christmas Eve projects ahead of us, we hustled the kids off to their rooms, making dire threats about Santa not coming if they didn't get to bed right this minute.

As soon as their doors were closed, Mark and I flew into action. It was such fun! Consider: I didn't figure out until adulthood that the song about Mommy kissing Santa Claus was really about a kid seeing his or her own parents making out, and not about Mommy having an adulterous fling with jolly Saint Nick. That's how novel the idea of a happy couple making Christmas magic for their children was to me. As Mark and I tackled the task of setting up the dollhouse of a thousand pieces, and piled stacks of wrapped packages around it, I felt as normal and as wholesome as one of the Waltons. We crammed the kids' stockings full of bubble bath, Hello Kitty toothbrushes, and boxes of washable crayons. Eric got slightly more manly toiletries, in keeping with his older and more sophisticated tastes. As Mark and I worked, we heard a strange chirping sound. It was loud and piercing and sounded something like *Chirr-ippp! Chirr-ippp!* "What the hell was that?" Mark asked.

"What was what?" I replied.

"That noise. Something's making a noise. Did you wrap up another alarm clock?"

Two years ago, we'd purchased a rock-and-roll robot alarm clock for the son of a friend. Before wrapping it, I helpfully installed fresh batteries. Unfortunately, I neglected to check whether or not the alarm switch was in the "on" position. It was. At about one forty-five Christmas morning, we were catapulted out of bed by what sounded like a bad Anthrax cover band warming up in the living room.

"No, I did not wrap up another alarm clock. Maybe it's the dog you're hearing."

Chirr-ippp!

"There it goes again! Sshh. Be quiet for a minute."

We sat there in silence, waiting. *Chirr-ippp!* "I think it's coming from the dollhouse!" Mark whispered. He crawled toward it, pushing aside empty cardboard boxes and piles of wadded-up newspaper. We both stared at the dollhouse intently, as though it might turn out to be the Amityville Horror of plastic cottages. *Chirr-ippp!*

He sat back on his heels. "I don't believe it. Where are the instructions?"

"To the dollhouse? You said you didn't need the instructions."

"I don't, but I want to see them. They're over by you somewhere."

I fished around in the mounting piles of paper. "Got it!"

He studied the sheet for about ten seconds and then turned to me. "Your cousin bought the girls a *talking* dollhouse. It talks. Look, the pet parrot chirps. The TV comes on. One of these pictures says something. See? When one of those pieces gets close enough to the house—"

Chirr-ippp!

"—it goes off. Only Renee could find a talking frigging dollhouse. And it's *loud*. I should have known when we opened up that singing dining room table. . . . Seriously, did you give her kids a drum set or something when they were little? Is she trying to get you back?"

Chirr-ippp!

He sighed. "Here—hide the damn bird or it'll drive us crazy all night. And let's get to bed. They're going to destroy this place tomorrow morning."

But they didn't. The kids actually slept in, something they almost never do for fear that Mark and I might either attempt a quickie or try to sneak a little extra rest. We finally had to go and wake them up, which gave us plenty of time to set up the video camera and adjust the lighting.

Olivia paused at the top of the stairs, her eyes wide in surprise as she took it all in. The baby scooted under the tree, grabbed for the nearest package, and took an experimental bite out of the corner. They both fell upon the dollhouse, elbowing each other aside and grabbing for tiny chairs, bathtubs, dishes, and dogs. Even with just a few gifts, it took hours for them to open and play with each one. We drank hot chocolate, and ate waffles, and listened to Christmas music on the stereo. Caramia hugged her new Cabbage Patch doll with alarming ferocity and, every now and again, clamped her teeth down on its wee button nose and bit it for all she was worth. Olivia was so enchanted by the mermaid flippers and snorkel from Aunt Nancy and Uncle Mark that she nearly forgot about bringing the dinosaurs back to life. When she finally asked about her much-anticipated magic wand, Mark and I handed her the last unopened package from beneath the tree. She quickly tore the tissue paper off of a silver wand, a handful of mysterious-looking capsules, and a piece of parchment, rolled up and tied with a gleaming blue ribbon.

Carefully slipping off the ribbon and unrolling the paper, I said, "Look, Olivia! It's a letter addressed to you! Shall I read it?"

She nodded and clutched her wand in excitement.

"'Dear Olivia,'" I began.

I know how much you hoped for a magic wand that shoots pink fire to make the dinosaurs real again. That is a beautiful wish! But I must explain to you that God has His reasons for all things, and a time for all things. The time of the dinosaurs is over. Even Santa Claus cannot change that.

("Nice choice of font," Mark whispered. "Did you have to download that?")

But Olivia, because you love the dinosaurs so much, they are **already** real to you. That is better magic than any I could make! So, I am leaving a different magic wand for you, along with these magic dinosaur eggs. I hope that you will have fun making these dinosaurs appear. And I hope that you will always keep a place in your heart big enough for the dinosaurs.
Love,
Santa

I held my breath and stared at my daughter. Would she take this development in stride—or throw an unholy screaming tantrum? Or worse, would she cut loose with one of her patented wails of theatrical grief? It felt like a true test of our parental imagination—we didn't want to disappoint her or crush her budding imagination. She'd asked for the impossible, and we, of course, had failed to deliver. But what else could we have done? Granted, we could have bought her a reptile of some sort, like the horned mountain dragon, for example, to keep as a pet. Those things look enough like dinosaurs to fool the average preschooler. With our luck, though, Olivia would lose interest in the creature within a week, leaving her father and me saddled with feeding, sheltering, and paying exorbitant vet bills for some ill-tempered lizard that gave us both the creeps. Plus, the information we'd been able to find regarding the life span of the horned mountain dragon was just vague enough to make us worry that the beast not only would end up being a burden during our golden years but also might actually outlive us. That was a risk we dared not take, even if it meant sacrificing our shot at being The Greatest Parents Ever. So we got Santa to write a letter instead. Would this desperate gambit work?

Olivia stared at the capsules in her hand. "Magic dinosaur eggs! Santa Claus gave me magic dinosaur eggs! Daddy, can I make a dinosaur next day? I will do that next day, okay?" And dropping the capsules and wand into my lap, she scampered off to play with something else.

Mark and I glanced at each other. He raised an eyebrow. No tears, no yowling, not so much as a question. Unbelievable. We'd gotten away with it—for now, anyway.

Later that day, after a lunch consisting mostly of champagne, Fig Newtons, and Hershey Kisses, I flopped down on the couch and gathered both girls close. "Have you two had a fun Christmas so far?" I asked.

Caramia clapped her hands and nodded. Olivia, with great enthusiasm, proceeded to rattle off a list of all the things she'd liked best. Naturally, the gifts she'd received far outranked any sentimental notions of family togetherness.

"That's great!" I said the second she paused for a breath. "It's fun to get presents, isn't it?"

"I like presents, Mommy!" Olivia concurred. Caramia nodded in agreement.

"Well, Christmas is about *much* more than presents. I have a book here that Grandma Anne sent to us. Look—it's called *Someone's Coming to Our House*. Shall we read it now? It's a wonderful story about the true meaning of Christmas—"

"I know! I know!" interrupted Olivia. "It is about the Baby Jesus, who is made of fragile, and lives at the North Pole! He didn't bring me a magic wand that shoots pink fire to make the dinosaurs real again because he wrote me a letter instead. Isn't that the wonderful story, Mommy? Isn't it? I love the Baby Jesus! He's so . . . shiny!"

Maybe it was too much champagne. Or too many days of twinkling lights and syrupy music finally corroding my sanity. Or maybe
it was the look of pure, unbridled joy on the faces of my children as
they clapped their hands and bounced on my lap. I was certain that
one of them, at least, had at last figured out what Christmas was
truly all about. Whatever the answer, it seemed that I'd finally
learned to take my happiness anywhere and any way I could find it.

Our house wasn't overflowing with the latest and coolest and
most popular toys. There wasn't a new sports car wrapped in a giant
red bow out in the driveway. I hadn't baked a single cookie, made a
single wreath, or even gotten the Christmas cards all mailed out on
time. The only holiday portrait we'd managed to get was a shot of
Caramia on the mall Santa's lap. Mark had taken her one morning
while I was at work, and the result was a disturbing photograph of a
red-faced, howling baby caught in an existential nightmare—the infant version of Munch's *The Scream*. Dressed by Daddy in head-to-
toe black, right down to her black Converse high-tops, Caramia
looked like a miniature gangster locked in a wrestling death clinch
with some grinning, elderly, red-suited nut. Just the kind of charming keepsake every mother yearns to paste into a baby book.

Yet I was having the best Christmas of my entire life, and I
knew it. What was different? Was it having a family of my own, a
little nest of warmth and normalcy in a life that had always sorely
lacked for both? We were making our own traditions now, and I
liked that, liked the predictability of it and the control I had over it.
I thought back to certain Christmases in my past, remembered the
year that one of my father's criminal cronies showed up at the door
with a box of frozen jumbo shrimp, and bottles of designer perfume for the women—all stolen, of course, though we preferred to
describe our gifts as having "fallen off the truck." He passed
around the goodies, demanding from each of us "one little kiss for
Santa Claus." I don't know which was more disgusting: his boozy
breath, his leering face, or the covert ass-grab that he managed to

pull off despite being weighed down by ten pounds of slowly thawing crustaceans. Just knowing that my daughters would be spared having to endure the kind of sleaze that resembled outtakes from *The Sopranos* cheered me. That life was behind me now, gone forever. Had it taken me this long to finally see that?

I'd spent nearly an entire year cajoling my family from one adventure to the next. Things had gone surprisingly well, and surely this quiet, cozy, low-key, nearly perfect Christmas was proof of how far we'd come. But I wanted more, a bigger finish, a grand climax to all of our efforts. I felt vaguely unsatisfied. Was I too much of an overachiever to ever truly relax? Was I too nuts to ever be normal? Whatever the answer, and I was willing to admit that it might be a whole lot of both, I couldn't shake the feeling that my work wasn't quite finished, that there was more, much more yet to be done. I knew in my heart that this little experiment was meant to end not on a drowsy December afternoon, with Bing Crosby crooning on the stereo, but in a blaze of glory. Or if not glory, at least melodrama. I was convinced that my full-scale yearlong assault on domestic happiness had to have a big finish; it just had to.

Turns out, I was right.

13

Gross!

If anyone ever establishes a support group for crazy dictators, please call me. I should be a charter member. All of us deposed tyrants could gather together in a church basement somewhere in the heartland and share the grim stories of our doomed reigns while sipping watery coffee from Styrofoam cups. There, amid the warmth and fellowship of the equally misguided and insane, a tyrant might confess to her crimes, saying, "I did it all for their own good!" and "I was only trying to be a strong leader!" and "I just wanted them to love me for it!" There, among her own kind, she would *not* be labeled a Type A perfectionist wacko but a misunderstood visionary. Too bad all of this ego-boosting approval would be coming from a band of dangerous lunatics.

I didn't mean to turn into a fascist. Who does? I just wanted everyone to be happy. I wanted my family to achieve our fullest potential. Fueled by my mad vision of suburban utopia, I vowed to let nothing stand in the way of glory. Nothing! And I succeeded, beyond my most wildly optimistic expectations. My entire family

gamely went along with whatever I proposed, with minimal grumbling. Even my husband, who grumbles constantly just to keep his
grumbling skills sharp, fell into line. Forced marches, sleepless
nights, craft shows—nothing was beyond them. I should have been
ecstatic—and I *was* happier, make no mistake—but something was
wrong or missing, something critically important. I felt like Mus-
solini after he'd finally gotten the trains to run on time: *Okay, that's
done. So now what?*

I was suffering from tyranny burnout. Bending others to my will
just wasn't satisfying anymore. I still longed for all of the same
things, but it wasn't good enough to merely drag my spouse and kids
along for the ride; I wanted them to want all of those same things for
themselves. I wanted them to be just like me. Obvious as that seems,
it had taken me a whole year to figure it out. Now that I finally had, it
was time to face reality. Namely, that other people, including the
ones I'd married and given birth to, might not share my passion for
all things nuclear family. Even a million picnics, firework shows, or
neighborhood hootenannies probably wouldn't persuade them to
see things my way. The last thing I wanted to be was a bully—June
Cleaver with a bullwhip and a martini: "You damn kids better smile
or Mommy will start screaming! Everyone be happy—or else!"

So we wouldn't be perfect and glossy like those families I grew
up watching on TV. We wouldn't move through the world as a single
grinning unit, leaving smiles and frame-worthy photos in our wake.
Eric would continue to prefer PlayStation to a family picnic, or pretty
much any other activity on offer. Mark would continue to choose a
solo ride on his mountain bike over an afternoon at the local Frontier
Days Festival. My daughters would be forced to hang out with me
until they started getting better offers, which, if the lives of my
neighbors' kids were any indication, should start rolling in at about
age six. Hell, by then my kids would be embarrassed to be seen with
me, much less march by my side in the neighborhood parade. Best

to start facing facts now. No matter how good your intentions, you can lead your family to the Kool-Aid, but you can't make them drink.

I coped with this bracing realization by throwing myself an existential pity party: I took to the couch in a pair of ratty pajama bottoms and immersed myself in a marathon of crime documentaries on cable. One dreary night in late January, my husband came looking for me.

"You've got some time off from work coming up," he remarked.

"Yeah, I guess. A week in mid-March," I answered.

"Well, did you want to do something?" he asked.

"What do you mean?" I yawned.

"Did you want to go somewhere? What's your big idea? I know you've got a plan. You might as well tell me now what you've been thinking about."

"Nah. I just thought we'd hang out here. Do nothing. The kids are so young, and traveling with them is such a hassle right now, don't you think? Let's not do anything."

"You don't want to go *anywhere*?" He sounded incredulous.

"Not really."

"Not even for a few days?"

"Just seems like a lot of work, doesn't it?"

"Since when?"

"I don't know. Since now. Why don't we just hang out at home? We can go out to dinner, maybe. Or for a little hike. Or not. Whatever." I turned my attention back to *Forensic Files* on A&E. It was obvious that the wife was guilty. Didn't she know how tricky murder is when you're married? The spouse is *always* the first one they suspect. And no matter how well you think you plan, the forensic evidence will trip you up every time. Just lose a single eyelash at the scene of the crime and *bam!* Your own DNA sends you straight to death row. Tonight's hapless killer had clearly never watched a single episode of the show that was now coldly dissecting her crime. She'd made some really amateur mistakes. Hiding the poison in her makeup bag? Come on, lady! Like your purse isn't one of the first places they're going to search?

Mark stood by the couch for a few minutes longer, a look of disbelief on his face. "All right, then," he said, mostly to himself. "I guess we don't *have* to go anywhere. If you don't want to."

Three days later. Saturday morning. While Olivia munched on a frozen waffle—being sure to drag as much of her hair as possible through the pool of maple syrup on her plate—and Caramia finger-painted on the table using smeared banana, Mark casually asked me about our weekend plans.

"Um, I thought I might take the girls to Costco for some diapers," I respond.

"That's it?" he replied, a bit suspiciously.

"Well, we need juice, too, I guess. And some paper towels. I should make a list. Didn't some coupons just come in the mail?"

He pushed aside a box of Frosted Cheerios and stared at me. "We don't have anything else to do, all weekend long? We don't have any plans? There's not someplace that we have to be?"

I watched as the dog reared up onto his hind legs, cranked his head almost completely sideways, and curled out his lower lip, delicately snagging the single sticky chunk of waffle that Olivia had dropped onto her chair.

"Complain about Champ all you want," I remarked, "but this place is going straight to hell when he dies. He cleans up around here a lot more than you think. Good boy, Champ. Way to help out, buddy."

Mark glared at the dog, then stood up and began clearing the table. "All right. You go to Costco. I don't know what you're trying to prove; I really don't."

"Why are you so weird?" I asked. "I don't know what you're talking about."

Truth was, I *wasn't* trying to prove anything. I liked warehouse shopping, liked the satisfying heft of a five-pound jar of peanut butter or a twenty-pound box of laundry detergent. Just knowing that we had two dozen or more individual servings of cling peaches in our possession at any given time made me feel ready for anything. Hurricanes, power outages, terrorism—we'd be serving fruit cup while the bombs dropped, thanks to buying in bulk. Plus, the warehouse had shopping carts shaped like race cars, and free treats in the bakery section. I could trick the kids into thinking they were having a good time, while simultaneously loading up on three months' worth of toilet paper. Throw in a few free balloons and it was like a day at Disneyland minus the lines. I fished a baby wipe out of the diaper bag and pawed unsuccessfully at Olivia's syrup-matted hair while she squealed and squirmed.

"You go for a bike ride. You're always complaining that you never get to ride your bike. Stand still, Olivia!"

"Mommy! You're hurting me!" Olivia wailed.

"Cut the drama, honey. I'm barely touching you." I turned back to Mark. "Now's your chance to ride. We're going to Costco. Come on, girls, let's go find your shoes."

As I hauled the girls up the stairs, Mark called after me, "Well, do you want to do something later? Go to the park?" His voice sounded almost forlorn.

Much later that night, after we'd tucked the girls in and wedged seventy-five rolls of Charmin, a gross of yogurt-covered raisins, and an industrial-size barrel of hickory-smoke-flavored barbeque sauce into the pantry, Mark again brought up the subject of taking a trip.

"That week in March," he began. "I have an idea."

"I told you, I'm cool with doing nothing."

He pressed on. "What's the one kind of vacation you've always said that you wanted to do?" He paused, then added, "Hit the open road?"

"Do you mean an RV trip?" I asked.

"An RV!" he said triumphantly. "I found a place where we can rent an RV. We could do an RV vacation. What do you think about that?"

"Rent an RV. How much does it cost? It's probably outrageous, isn't it?"

"Less than you think! A lot less. And think of all the money we'll save on hotels!"

"Yeah, but won't the gas kill us? What kind of mileage does it get? Is it big enough for all of us? Do you know how to drive one of those things? And where would we go?"

"We can go anywhere you want. How about Florida? Take the kids to the beach. The gas mileage isn't all that bad. It's like an SUV. You want to do it? Rent an RV?"

It was true: I'd always wanted to take an RV across America. The idea of traveling with my house on my back like a turtle was an appealing one. I figured that in an RV I'd never again have to hold it in for miles while begging the bladder-punishing sadist I'd married to stop for yet another bathroom break. And, since traveling anywhere with small kids meant being loaded down with tons of gear, including books, crayons, assorted toys, snacks, movies, car seats, and possibly two types of strollers (collapsible and jogger), an RV seemed like the perfect solution to the problem of hauling all of the crap that we could no longer survive without. My inner suburban drill sergeant, the one that had been lying dormant for three bleary weeks while I stared morosely at Court TV, stirred back to life. An RV trip—it offered just the right mix of challenging logistics and potential disaster. Suddenly, I was up off the couch and shuffling toward the computer. Standing over Mark's shoulder, I gazed for the first time upon our future vacation home on wheels.

It was thirty feet long, a number that meant almost nothing to me. So dim and weak is my grasp of spatial reality that given any measurement in feet or inches, I immediately use my own height to convert that number into an equivalent number of mes, standing end on end. Neanderthals in their primitive caves worked with tools less crude than this. Using the "height of me" method of calculation, a thirty-foot RV was roughly six of me, minus one set of legs. That certainly seemed big enough. It had one bedroom with a queen-size bed, one bunk over the cab, and two additional beds that converted to a dinette. It had a full bathroom, including a shower, and even a few amenities that our real house lacked, like a convection oven. This beauty was ours for about a thousand dollars a week. Not cheap, but considering how much we'd be saving on airfares, hotel rooms, and rental cars, it was a bargain. Amazingly, the unit that we selected was not only available; it was, according to the Web site, virtually brand-new. How lucky were we? Soon we'd be tooling around the Sunshine State in an almost-new RV, with every necessity and convenience at our fingertips, laughing at those poor suckers who could only dream of being able to make microwave popcorn while blasting down the interstate at 60 mph. Ha-ha! And fetch me a cold drink out of that refrigerator while you're at it!

And the best part? It was all Mark's idea. That meant I was off the hook if anything went wrong. It wouldn't be another case of I-told-you-so and this-was-all-your-doing. No matter what happened, he couldn't complain or whine or act like a big martyr. Those were the rules. For what could be the very first time in our entire relationship, I wasn't the one selling some wacky, complicated, half-baked, potentially ruinous idea. I felt strangely powerful—like a buyer, for a change. It was *his* job to persuade *me* to do something risky or stupid. Having spent years coaxing him from one stunt to the next, I knew only how to answer objections, not create them. But I'd learned from watching that it was critical to play it cool, to make him earn it. It was all I could do to keep the smug grin off my face as I cleared my throat and said, "Hmmm. That's an interesting idea. Rent an RV. Well, we might have some trouble getting the girls to sleep at night. . . ."

"Nah. They'll be great," he assured me.

"And you might get tired of having to drive so much. I don't think that I'll be able to handle one of those things. . . ."

He snorted. "Not a problem. It'll be fun."

I paused and pretended to mull it over, just long enough to make him sweat a little bit. See how he liked playing crazy Lucy to my buzzkill Ricky.

When I answered, it was with the kind of line I'd been handed so many times. Not a roaring "yes!" and not an emphatic "no!" but an answer that clearly registered an inner conviction that the idea being proposed was flawed, if not completely idiotic. Before speaking, I gave the mandatory heavy sigh, the sigh of one too weary and put-upon to mount any further resistance. "Oh, all right. Let's do it. And if it's really horrible, we can just turn that RV around and come home."

He beamed. "I'll go make the reservation!" He marched happily out of the room as I snickered to myself.

With only six weeks to plan every aspect of our dream vacation, naturally Mark did nothing, not even pick up a map. It wasn't laziness; the poor thing had been rendered virtually helpless by marriage to a borderline psychotic event planner. I fought the nearly overwhelming urge to rush out and buy three guidebooks and a map of every RV-friendly location in Florida, knowing that if I did, we'd be right back to our old pattern. As a recovering fascist, I knew that would be disastrous. But it was tough. Sometimes I'd say, "Hey, hon? How're you coming on planning our RV trip?" He'd reply, "That's on my list for tomorrow." When tomorrow came, he'd forget to check his list. Before we knew it, the trip loomed a mere five, then four, then three weeks away. Mark eventually dug out the atlas, opened it up to Florida, and then left it on the kitchen counter to gather dust. Daytona, the Keys, Miami, Sanibel Island—all were soon buried under a gentle drift of junk mail and scribbled pictures that we fully intended to stick in a baby book or a storage bin or something, one of these days, as soon as we got a spare minute.

Two weeks prior to our scheduled departure, we were crawling through afternoon traffic, running more of the endlessly irritating errands that now filled our days. (Attention, all childless professionals: If you hate the thought of constantly driving around to buy, repair, replace, retrieve, and otherwise manage a mountain of stuff that you didn't even know you needed until you had it and it started malfunctioning—like, for example, a pet, a car, a house, or another human being—then DO NOT get married, have kids, and move to the 'burbs. Just don't. Even if you think that it will be different for you. We *all* thought that. We were wrong. You will be, too.) The girls caterwauled in the backseat like a pair of petulant Pomeranians, and it was obvious that if we didn't feed them soon, they'd attack. Wedged between them was Alex, a thirteen-year-old neighborhood kid who hung out with Eric when Eric was around, and practically lived with us when he wasn't. Alex was such a fixture that Olivia was three and a half before she figured out that he wasn't even related to us, much less her other brother. Eric was at his mom's house, which didn't stop Alex from coming over after school to play Mark's guitar and mooch some dinner.

Bored, hungry, restless, Olivia was poking Alex in the side of his head and cackling like a demon baby. "Ow! Knock it off, Olivia!" he yelped.

"Milk! Milk!" sobbed Caramia.

Spotting a strip mall just up ahead, I hissed, "There's a Chili's. Pull over. Let's just get dinner right now before they kill each other."

We straggled into the restaurant, sulking teenage boy, hyper toddler, whimpering baby, aggrieved husband, and me, a woman in serious need of a margarita or three.

Mark and I spent the next forty-five minutes trying to distract the kids while waiting for our food to arrive. We played the coaster game, which involves spinning, twirling, and flipping the cardboard drink coasters, an activity guaranteed to amuse small children for at least ninety seconds. We played peekaboo with the napkins. We made the cutlery sing and dance. Our waiter, who had apparently just arrived on Earth and was confused by both what a restaurant was and what exactly all of the humans clustered around the tables were hoping for, periodically glided by and pretended not to see us. By the time he finally dumped our food in front of us, everyone but Alex was either in tears or close to it. Olivia pounced on her cheeseburger. Alex buried his face in a plate of ribs. Mark reached for the salt. I picked up my fork.

Caramia, however, took one look at her plate of plain pasta and then turned to me. Leaning close, a puzzled look on her face, she croaked, "Mama?" and as she did, a spew of vomit shot out of her mouth, soaking the shoulder and back of my T-shirt.

"Gross!" Alex yelled.

"Mommy, Tiny threw up," Olivia announced, reaching for a french fry. Olivia had a gift for stating the obvious, usually at precisely the most annoying moment. She added, "There is throw-up on you, Mommy." Another bite of cheeseburger. "Tiny threw up, Daddy."

"I can see that, Olivia," Mark growled. "Where is the damn waiter?" He called out to the horrified hostess who had witnessed the whole event, "Can you please get our waiter? And tell him we need all of this to go." Mark scooped up Caramia and began blotting at her clothes as she wept.

I closed my eyes and counted to five. Drenched in warm, sticky, curdled-milk barf, I paused to meditate on what a long, miserable night no doubt stretched out before me. Eating was now out of the question. Sleeping looked like a long shot. It was likely that there would be a great deal more vomiting yet to come. And the preferred target was always me, the human vomit-seeking sponge. My youngest would wait all day, if need be, and then crawl across broken glass before she'd miss a chance to retch on my head. I opened my eyes and met those of a woman one table over. She was about twenty-five, stylishly dressed, her fork hovering in mid-air over a salad. She was gape-mouthed. Who wouldn't be? We were a revolting spectacle: the puke, the crying baby, the aggravated parents, the two older kids alternately wolfing their food and complaining about how disgusting the whole scene was. The table alone looked like a scene out of a nightmare, with vomit slowly dripping onto the floor, wadded-up napkins everywhere. It was official: we were *those people*, the ones who give child rearing a bad name.

As we stood to leave, gathering our hastily boxed meal, I apologized for the mess to the hostess, the extraterrestrial waiter, and the still-staring woman at the next table. "I bet you'll never want to have kids now, and it'll be all our fault," I said, lamely trying for a bit of humor.

She shook her head and whispered, "Oh my God, I'm pregnant right now. I'm only three months, though, so you can't tell. It's my first. But,"—she waved her hand at the slimy chaos we'd left in our wake— "it's not always like this, right? This doesn't happen all the time, right? This isn't typical, I'm sure."

I could have lied to her, could have told her what she wanted to hear, but that would have been mean. So I didn't. I looked her right in the eye and spoke the truth. "Actually, it *is* like this all the time. Good luck to you." With that, I shuffled off into the night, holding my wet shirt away from my skin and trying hard not to breathe through my nose.

Vacation planning tip number one: Do not allow your entire family to be infected by a raging gastrointestinal virus less than ten days before departure. Caramia barfing on me in Chili's triggered a five-day sick fest at our house. Olivia was next. She crawled into our bed at one o'clock the next morning and threw up eight times in the next six hours. By 9:00 A.M., Mark was facedown in one bathroom, while I commandeered another. All we could do was turn the TV on to the Noggin channel ("It's like preschool on TV!"), dump a box of saltine crackers onto the coffee table, pour Gatorade into the sippy cups, and then hug our respective toilets while praying not to die. It was days before any of us could bear to nibble on something other than a cracker, a banana, or a spoonful of rice. I couldn't go to work; Olivia couldn't go to school—a place we soon learned was all but decimated by whatever foul bug this was. Olivia had picked it up from a schoolmate, but no one was talking. Which was a good thing: If I could have found Patient Zero, I think I would have clocked them with a juice box.

One week away from departing on our dream RV vacation, we were all still a bit weak, still barely able to eat. That's when the next wave hit. Olivia came home from school hot, with a hacking cough. I came home from work with a fever, aching all over. Within hours, I couldn't get out of bed. With no one able or willing to enter the hot zone to stay with our kids, Mark forced me to drive myself to an urgent care center late one Saturday night, where they confirmed the worst: flu. The whole family was advised to start on something called Tamiflu immediately. Snuffling, miserable, and awash in self-pity, I drove to four different drugstores trying to fill the prescription. Every pharmacy was apparently out. After begging a softhearted Eckerd part-timer to make some calls, I eventually located the last four doses in town, and headed out, half-delirious, in my pajamas. As I wobbled to the counter to pay, the pharmacist said, "Hey! Love your show. I listen every morning. You look a lot different than I imagined." Since he'd probably imagined a person who wore actual pants, brushed her hair once in a while, and didn't have three-day-old mascara ringing her eyes, I wasn't offended. Based on the way I felt, I didn't expect to live much longer anyway. Who cared about appearances?

"Thanks. Appreciate that." I coughed. "How long does this stuff take to work?"

"You should start to feel a little better in a week at most. Why? In a hurry to get back to work?" He chuckled.

"No, it's not that. We're taking our kids on an RV trip next Friday."

He shook his head. "I don't know about that. Your kids are pretty small, right?"

"Yeah. And they're sick, too." I coughed.

He nodded. "Six days . . . well, maybe you'll all be okay by then." He didn't look like he believed that for a minute. "Here you go. Take it as soon as you get home. Feel better. And good luck with that trip!"

Tamiflu or not, Olivia and I stayed sick. The baby had been eligible for the flu shot that the rest of us were denied due to the so-called shortage. She got away with nothing more than a bad cold. Mark washed his hands till they were rough and bleeding in places and somehow managed to dodge the flu. Might have been the drug, might have been luck, but they were spared the worst of it. Not so for Olivia or me. While the two of us coughed and gagged and dragged ourselves listlessly from bed to couch, Caramia tore around the house with her usual energy. She poked and prodded Olivia, climbing on her and tugging her hair until Olivia cried for mercy. It was as though the baby knew that she had a brief window of opportunity to terrorize us all, to punish us for being so much bigger and stronger.

Lying in bed and listening as Caramia pulled open drawers in the bathroom and rummaged through their contents, I had dark thoughts of Benadryl-spiked sippy cups. Not that I had the energy to pull off anything so evil; I barely even moved when Caramia sailed past me with a fistful of tampons. Rolling over, I thought, Maybe she can do something artistic with them. That'll keep her busy for a while.

My fever didn't break until the night before our scheduled departure, and Olivia's didn't break at all. Still, we pressed forward. Friday morning, Mark and I showed up at the RV rental lot, signed the paperwork, paid our deposit, and collected the keys to our new temporary home.

The reality was somewhat shabbier than the Web site had led us to expect. *New* must be a relative term on the Internet, because our thirty-foot land yacht looked like it had seen some heavy use. The upholstery was a stained and dingy blue, and there was a certain smell in the air—the smell of hot vinyl, enclosed spaces, and public restrooms. It was also a good deal smaller than I imagined, back when I was figuring out how many of me it would take to equal thirty feet. Also, when we finally finished our orientation tour and had been shown the water and sewer hookups, and had signaled our comprehension of the need for special RV toilet paper, we learned that a thirty-foot recreational vehicle doesn't purr like a kitten when you fire it up. It rumbles like the big, gas-inhaling truck that it is. I had pictured a luxury condo on wheels; in reality, it was more like a covered wagon with a motor. Loud, echoey, taking every bump like an insult, it was a clumsy beast, pure and simple. I risked a glance at Mark as he eased the colossus into traffic.

"What do you think?" I cheerfully ventured, knowing that if this had been my idea, I'd be in for an earful.

"It's a little loud, but it's not that bad to drive. It's even kind of fun." He smiled in an encouraging sort of way. Was I in some fever-induced hallucination, or had my fun-grudging spouse somehow morphed into the good-to-go sitcom hubby of my dreams? I pinched myself and hoped I wouldn't wake up.

He leaned back in the seat and added, "Not being able to see out the back takes some getting used to. You've got to use the mirrors more than you're used to. You'll see for yourself when you drive it."

Not if I can help it, I thought. *Drive* this? I could feel the wind gusting around the cab, trying to tug us right off the road. Behind me, cupboard doors rattled and shook. Every time a tractor-trailer tore past us, our whole rig shuddered and swayed like a rickety metal shed in a storm. Was this even safe? What the hell were we thinking, strapping our babies into this thing? I surreptitiously tightened my seat belt, smiled back at my husband, and said nothing. This might have been his idea, but it was my dream, and he was only trying to please me. Either that or punish me. It was too soon to tell which.

We parked the monster—which was emblazoned on each side with a full-color photograph of the Grand Canyon and the words *RENT ME* in giant, screaming red letters—in front of our house and began the process of loading it up for our trip. While neighborhood kids clambered in and out of it, awestruck by the overcab bunk—all kids are impressed by bunk beds, God only knows why—Mark and I ferried pile after pile of stuff from our front door to the RV. Sheets, pillows, blankets, towels, dishes, cups, forks, spoons, cooking equipment, DVDs, toys, books, games, toiletries, clothes, stuffed animals, groceries, a small TV, beach supplies, Mark's mountain bike, my laptop, a soccer ball, an umbrella, a portable gazebo, and four bottles of wine later, we'd managed to transfer most of the contents of our home to our vacation vehicle. It took us about three and a half hours to get the job done. Flu, fever, and days without food had left me weak and dizzy; the only thing that kept me awake was the too-low door frame of the RV. Every third entrance or so, I slammed my forehead into it hard enough to leave a plum-sized bruise that took ten days to fade.

With their sharp instinct for parental suffering, my two little ones did everything they could to help out. Caramia crawled in and out of the driver's seat, laying on the horn and shouting, "Go! Go now!" Still feverish, Olivia sprawled in the overhead bunk and occasionally peered over the edge, her face a pitiful little moon. "Now is it time to leave in the house on wheels? Is it time now, Mommy?" she'd rasp, over and over and over and over until I started aiming my head at the door frame in hopes of knocking myself out cold.

With every last one of our worldly possessions finally stowed away, we were ready to hit the road. As we made our final preparations, the ten-year-old boy who lived across the street took a last look around the cabin of the RV. "You guys are lucky," he said wistfully. "I wish I could go with you."

"That's sweet, Andrew," I replied. "But I think I'd go nuts if we had to pack one more kid into this thing. Besides, you're going somewhere with your mom and dad this week, aren't you?"

He sighed. "We hafta go to Palm Springs for my dad's work." To hear Andrew say it, you'd have thought that Palm Springs was one of the world's biggest hellholes. He wandered back to his own driveway, staring at us with undisguised longing.

Mark fired up the engine as I buckled the girls into their car seats. We had a map, *Finding Nemo* playing on DVD, enough special RV toilet paper to last a week, and a full tank of gas. We were off.

14

Invisible Alligators

In a vehicle that gets eight miles to the gallon, you actually have the novel experience of watching the gas gauge drop as you drive. We weren't two hours into our inaugural RV trip when Mark announced, "We're going to have to stop for gas pretty soon."

"You're kidding me," I replied. "We just left. How can we already need gas?"

"Well, we do. Look." He pointed at the gauge. The needle hovered between the half- and the quarter-tank marks. I relaxed.

"We have plenty of gas," I said. "You make it sound like we're about to run out."

Mark made a point of always filling up at the quarter-tank mark; I made a point of pulling into a gas station only when the needle was pinned below E, the fuel light was on, and the car started gagging and sputtering. I suspected that he frequently tried to lecture me on this subject, but since I automatically tuned out and went to my happy place every time he brought it up, I couldn't be sure.

"We *are* about to run out," he insisted. "You're not supposed to wait until you're on fumes. How many times have I told you that? Start looking for that El Cheapo place. How many miles did it say on the billboard?"

"El Cheapo is two exits up," I announced, after studying the map. Having learned fairly recently that highway exit numbers correlate to mile markers, a discovery as profound for me as the realization at age seven that pickles start out life as cucumbers, I felt downright cocky about my new navigational skills. Unfortunately, my husband was less than sympathetic when he discovered that I was clueless about this painfully obvious feature of America's roadways.

"You really didn't know that? How could you not know that?"

"Oh, please." I tried to defend myself. "Like that's something that everyone knows? What class did they teach that in?"

"Try driver's ed!" he hooted. "I can't believe you don't know that!"

"Yeah, well, how many Shakespearean sonnets do you know, Mr. Highway Trivia Genius?"

"Shakespeare won't get your ass to the beach, Miss Poetry. You're gonna need an interstate for that." He chuckled to himself, smug and superior, his peculiar engineering brain a humming vortex of numbers and logic. Like that spooky computer HAL in the movie *2001: A Space Odyssey,* except with chest hair. I almost invoked the Broken Home defense, but since Mark's parents divorced when he was six, I knew that wasn't going to save me.

"Look, there's El Cheapo! I told you it was two exits up! Who's got the map now, baby! Ha!" This giddy feeling of accomplishment lasted for the fifteen minutes it took to refuel our house on wheels. Cost? Eighty-six dollars. On the plus side, I didn't have to take the girls into a gas station bathroom and explain to Olivia that the coin-operated condom dispenser wasn't exactly a gumball machine. On the minus side, our fuel costs were threatening to make a week on the road cost as much as a trip to Paris.

Six hours, ten minutes, and close to two tanks of gas later, we rolled into America's Oldest City, Saint Augustine, Florida. Tasked with locating our berth for the night, a KOA Kampground "just minutes from the beach," I pored over the directions we'd printed out from the KOA Web site.

"Two miles after this light, you turn right and it's supposed to be there."

"Supposed to be where? Are we on the right road or not?"

There are still places in Florida so pitch-black after sundown that not even the glare from the floodlit outlet mall that's inevitably nearby can penetrate the darkness. We happened to be rolling through just such a place.

"Yes, we're on the right road." (I had no idea if this was true or not.) "I told you that I've got this map figured out now. How hard can this be to find? The ocean's straight ahead—we can't get that lost. There it is! Turn here!"

In a close call, the result of having failed to make a reservation, we barely snagged the last available campsite at the KOA/Saint Augustine Beach. The girls were exhausted but stir-crazy from having been locked into their seats all day. While Mark hooked our rig up for sewer, water, electricity, and cable TV, I took Olivia and Caramia out for a stroll. While they bounced along, careening from one side of the path to the other, I spied through the windows of our fellow campers. They appeared to be a diverse bunch. Huge luxury coaches with slide out compartments, awnings, and what looked like real granite countertops were parked right next to simple two-man tents. Many of the campsites were outlined with decorative lights draped in the trees and staked into the ground, festooned with garden gnomes, pink flamingos, and colorful flags reading, "The Parkers' Pad" or "The Thorvalds—Kent and Debbie." The whole scene was like some alternate reality, a compact, colorful, weird, strange, fun-house-mirror version of America, hidden in plain sight behind a frowsy strip mall.

We slowly looped back around to our own campsite, which

wasn't hard to find. Those huge images of the Grand Canyon really leapt out at you, even in the dark. Banging through the door—and narrowly dodging another wallop to my head—I said, "You've got to take a look at this place. I think some of these people must live here all the time. They're landscaping their campsites. They've got *gnomes*. Who takes a gnome on vacation? A gnome means you're here to stay, don't you think? I mean, you're not going to just keep packing and unpacking your gnomes, right? And they're heavy—"

"Go ahead and flush!" Mark interrupted, an enormous smile lighting up his face.

"What?" I asked.

"Flush! Flush all you want. And look, we've got running water!" He turned on the kitchen faucet to demonstrate. "You push this red button over here, wait a few minutes, and you've got hot water. Want to take a shower? You can. I've got us all hooked up for electricity, *and* we've got HBO. Go ahead; go use the bathroom! Check it out!" He glowed with pride, the human male at his most primal. From the unforgiving landscape of campsite seventy-four, relying on nothing but his wits, cunning, an extension cord, and a length of plastic tubing, he had fashioned a shelter for his mate and offspring.

I dutifully squeezed into the bathroom, flushed the toilet, and hollered, "It works!"

"Damn right it works! Who's the man! Come on—let's get these kids to bed!"

The upper bunk of an RV has got to rank in the claustrophobic top ten terrifying places. Lying up there in the dark, it takes very little imagination to feel like you are in a coffin about to be buried alive. Olivia climbed up all by herself, then insisted to the point of tears that I follow to give her a cuddle. Up I went. Lying down, with the ceiling mere inches from my face, I stroked my child's hair and tried to remember precisely what evil thing a hotel had ever done to me to make me so determined to sleep in a camper. Waiting for Olivia to drift off to sleep, I fought the panicky urge to pound on the ceiling and scream, "Open up! For God's sake, I'm not dead!"

Below me, Mark had a different sort of a fight on his hands. At home, Caramia slept in a crib. But there was no crib here, and no room for one, either. Despite the fact that we had surrounded her converted dinette bed with cushions, it took her about a minute to figure out that there were no bars holding her back. First she tried to climb up onto the stove. Then she barreled to the rear of the RV, clambered up onto our bed, and started to jump. Each time, Mark chased her and carried her back to the dinette. She'd be quiet for a moment and then *plop!* We'd hear the sound of her plump little feet hitting the floor and she was off again. It took a prolonged bear hug/wrestling hold before Mark managed to subdue her. With Olivia finally snoring and snuffling like a piglet with hay fever, and Caramia asleep at last, Mark and I tiptoed back to our relatively private, relatively jumbo-size sleeping quarters, and collapsed into bed.

There, in the darkness, snug in our cozy wheeled home, we each lay lost in thought. Mark was probably debating whether or not he was too tired to get his caveman groove on. I debated whether or not my fever had returned and, if it had, was it worth the effort to get back up and try to find the Tylenol. Just then, Olivia started coughing and hacking in her bunk. With each cough, the whole trailer shook, just a little. We'd already dosed her with Children's Motrin for her fever, Robitussin for her cough, and the antibiotic-of-the-week for whatever else the pediatrician thought was ailing her. We had nothing left to pour down her throat that might stop the hacking. After a few minutes of it, we did the only thing left to parents in our situation: we both started to giggle, and then to laugh. It was a good thing we were amused, because Olivia kept coughing and the trailer kept shaking for most of the night.

Come morning, I dished up scrambled eggs and frozen waffles and watched my husband for signs of aggrieved irritation. There were none. No complaints about not getting enough sleep, or about the girls waking up at six o'clock and demanding to be taken to the beach. Not a single "I told you so." In fact, he seemed almost jolly. Was this the same man who, only four months ago, suggested we cancel Christmas for being too much of a hassle? The same man who'd nearly detached a retina from excessively rolling his eyes at nearly every single thing I'd proposed our doing for the past twelve months? I was suspicious; I couldn't help it. Still, if this was some sort of psychological head game we were playing, I was up for it. I decided that the wisest strategy would be to accept his entirely new personality without question. Then, if it did turn out to be an act, I'd get to play the wide-eyed victim of his cruel manipulation, leaving him looking like a great, big, mean bully. I gave him my biggest "Donna Reed meets the Cheshire cat" smile and passed around paper cups full of orange juice. I just don't get why some people think marriage is dull. It's like a high-stakes game of Risk, but with sex, money, and appliances. How fun is that?

Confinement in an RV is one of the better litmus tests for the average happy family. There isn't any way to really escape each other. And unless you have the wisdom and foresight to tow a car behind your RV, there's no way to escape the RV, either. Once that thing is parked and hooked up, it's a hassle to unhook everything just to take it for a spin. Not to mention the fact that it's big, unwieldy, tricky to park, scary to reverse, and generally ill-suited for city driving. Which meant we'd be doing a lot of walking if we had any hopes of getting off the KOA reservation. It turned out that the writer of the campground brochure had a different idea than we did about what exactly constituted "minutes from the beach." A five-minute walk seemed about right to us. The reality proved to be more like twenty-five minutes. Not an unreasonable challenge for a healthy adult but a punishing marathon for a toddler. Good thing we'd packed our stroller. We strapped the girls in and then proceeded to nearly smother them under a mountain of towels, buckets, shovels, water bottles, sunscreen, and cameras. We headed out and, dodging traffic, made our way to the ocean.

The strip of beach we landed on was one of those rocky, picturesque expanses much favored by exuberant Labrador retrievers and their equally sporty owners. As owners of an aged French bulldog, a creature who even in his prime became breathless just rolling out of bed, we'd never known the joys of taking our dog to the beach. Instead, Champ was home, sleeping on the furniture and peeing on the carpets under the watchful eye of a professional pet-sitter. In Saint Augustine, we shared the beach with people who frolicked at the surf's edge with their handsome dogs—the type of people so obviously busy starring in their own private outdoor adventure movie that they didn't even see the posted signs reminding them to scoop after their pets. The occasional pile of fresh dog shit nestling in the sand offered a bracing contrast to the crisp blue sky and white-capped waves of the Atlantic. Naturally, our daughters couldn't stay away from the stuff. It was magnetic. The undertow should have taken lessons from Rover's beached droppings. We moved three times, and yet three times Caramia and Olivia were sucked inexorably right back to the few square inches of Florida coastline where we didn't want them to step.

Between chasing them away from the excrement, helping them hunt for shells, and keeping the baby from being carried out to sea, Mark and I spent a lively afternoon in the sun. The joy on Olivia's face as she watched a sand crab scuttle just past her foot, or Caramia's breathless surprise after a wave unexpectedly washed over her head, was everything any parent could have wished for. By the time we'd gotten them loaded back into the stroller for the walk home, they were dreamy-eyed and yawning. "Nap time!" Mark leered. While we walked, I envisioned a lazy afternoon of love there in our very own Geico Tiny House. Olivia's coughing wouldn't be the only thing to set the place swaying. We were on vacation; it was time to relax, toss inhibition to the wind, and go for a little

Kampground-style kinkiness. Totally cut loose, get wild, anything goes. Then reality rudely intruded on my extremely mild fantasy—our babies would be just a few feet away, doing their usual hair-trigger napping. Sex was a suckers' bet—and as always, Mark and I were the suckers.

By day three, we'd started to get the hang of life on the road. Mark did most of the driving. The few times I took the wheel, I couldn't help but grimace and let out muffled shrieks every time a big truck passed us on the highway. Not surprisingly, this sort of behavior made Mark extremely tense. It reminded him of when we were dating and took a weekend trip to Charleston, South Carolina. He'd had a long week of traveling for his job, so I offered to drive while he napped. As he was settling in, he said, "Don't you want to listen to music?"

"No, I'm just thinking," I replied.

"Thinking about what?" he asked, yawning.

"About the voices you hear in your head sometimes, that tell you to just drive the car straight into one of these embankments. Or if you're on a bridge, to just drive right off the edge. You know what I mean, right? About the voices?"

He sat bolt upright. "Not tired anymore. Why don't you pull over up at that next exit and I'll take over? Okay? Just pull the car over, nice and steady. There you go."

So now my job was to read the map and keep the girls entertained. The latter was easy; Mark and I were so gung ho at home about restricting their television viewing that an Elmo DVD easily hypnotized them into submission. We'd driven halfway across Florida before they looked up and realized that the vehicle was moving. The map was another story. I'd turn it this way and that and squint hard at the numbers, trying to guess at distances and exits. Mark would ask me trick questions, like "Should we take 4 through Orlando or not?"

With or without a map, I couldn't see why anyone would volun-

tarily drive through Orlando at rush hour, unless they were headed
for Disney World, which we most assuredly weren't. I was so early
into my recovery from fascism that I didn't feel strong enough to
tackle the temptations of the Magic Kingdom. Just thinking about it
made me break into a cold sweat. I had a chilling vision of myself
threatening my weeping, overexhausted kids: "What do you mean,
you're afraid of Mickey? All we've heard about for the past three
weeks is Mickey! Now get your butts over there and hug that damn
mouse so Mommy can take a picture! And you'd better act happy
about it, little miss, or I'll scream!" No, I wasn't strong enough for
Disney. Fearing its near-supernatural pull, I felt we should give the
Happiest Place on Earth a wide detour.

Unfortunately, my hopeful suggestion that we bypass Orlando
altogether and stick to secondary roads that would route us through
smaller towns was met with a derisive snort. "You only want to go
through Gator's Knuckle because you think that it's going to be
'charming.' In reality, the speed limit will be thirty-five, there'll be
traffic lights everywhere, and the most scenic thing we'll pass will
be a Burger King."

Seven hours later (ninety minutes of which we spent crawling
through the hopelessly snarled traffic on I-4 in Orlando), we pulled
into campsite number eighty-one at the Pine Island KOA. Not surprisingly, there were plenty of pine trees on Pine Island, each provid-
ing excellent cover for the indigenous hordes of starving, homicidal
mosquitoes. Pine Island also boasted eagles, ospreys, manatees, and
the kind of rugged old-Florida landscape that made you want to quit
your job, sell your house, bury your secrets, and start life over working on a dock in an out-of-the-way fishing village. What Pine Island
did *not* have was a beach. Which was a curious thing, what with it being an island and therefore surrounded by water.

"No beach at all? Not even a small one?" I interrogated Margie,
the helpful KOA employee who checked us in.

"No, sweetie. No beach anywhere on the island." She paused for a moment and pursed her lips, deep in thought. "Now, there *is* a place up the road just a bit where you might could wade a little. It's not a beach, but you can get your feet into the water."

"So there's no sand or anything? Just dirt or mud or whatever?"

"That's right! No sand," she replied brightly, as though sand were some sort of heinous nuisance that no right-minded person would want any part of, like nettles or chiggers.

"Well, okay, thank you anyway," I answered. "It's weird, no beach, don't you think? This *is* an island."

"It is that," she agreed. "It certainly is that. Enjoy your stay, honey."

Mark greeted the news that we'd plunked ourselves down on what might very well be America's only beach-free island with predictable disbelief.

"You're *sure* she said that there's no beach?"

"That's what she said. And I looked on the map, and there's no beach on that, either."

"Maybe you didn't ask the question the right way?" he suggested.

"How many ways are there to ask where the beach is? It's not the toughest concept in the world to grasp, is it? Sand, water, shells—where can we find them? You go ask her yourself if you don't believe me." I was defensive; who wouldn't be? "Look, we'll just take the kids to the pool, and then we'll get some dinner. The no-beach lady said that there's a little town about two miles up the road. We could walk—it'll be nice."

The little town turned out be a place called Saint James City. When we headed out, the sun was just starting to go down. The sidewalk was wide and smooth, with fields of scrubby pine and tropical-looking vegetation on both sides of the road. The occasional car or truck zoomed past, but for the most part, all was quiet and downright pastoral. This felt markedly different from the white-sand-and-orange-juice Florida of vacation brochures. This was a place where nature wasn't just another stage-managed tourist attraction; it was still boss. We saw no other people walking or jogging, and the few houses we passed looked faded and weary from fighting not to be engulfed by all of that hungry, creeping green. We were amazed to spot a bald eagle, enthroned in the topmost branches of a hurricane-battered tree not ten feet from the road.

A normal person, one suffering from no mental derangement, probably would have found the whole scene incredibly lovely and relaxing. I, on the other hand, could think of nothing but hungry alligators slithering out of the undergrowth to eat my babies. When the gators did come, as I was certain they would, I would have no one to blame but myself. I was the one who refused to be content with lying around watching television and eating junk food like normal families. No, I insisted on dragging my family into the Everglades—or something pretty close to the Everglades—and turning us all into gator bait.

"Hon," I said. "I think we should come up with a plan right now in case an alligator attacks us."

Mark looked at me, sighed, and shook his head. "An alligator isn't going to attack us."

"You don't know that. They snatch dogs right off of leashes. They're faster than you think."

"An alligator isn't going to attack us," he repeated.

"Fine. But if one does, I'll take the stroller and run while you distract it, okay? That's our plan."

"So I get eaten while you run away?" he asked.

"It's not going to eat you. You're too big. It'll try to drown you and stuff you under a log so that you can rot for a while. So you'll have a few minutes to outsmart it, right?"

"Oh yeah, right. So that's our plan, huh? You run off with the girls and I get drowned and stuffed under a log?"

Before we had a chance to finalize our alligator defense strategy, we arrived on the outskirts of Saint James City. It was a thumbnail of a place, hugging the very edge of the island so tightly that it nearly tipped into the water. Margie at the front desk was right; there was no beach to be seen, not even an ashtray's worth of sand to spread a towel on. The buildings were low-slung, beaten by salt and weather. It looked like a place where hardworking people lived, not a place where tourists came to buy shells or T-shirts. Just ahead was something that looked like it might be a restaurant. It was a narrow building, with a halfhearted porch tacked to the front and a few neon beer signs in the front windows. Drawing closer, we saw the marquee:

WELCOME
HEAVY SMOKERS AND HARD DRINKERS
NO FOOD

"I guess that place is out," said Mark, in the tone of a man slowly growing accustomed to misfortune and strife.

A little farther up, we spotted another establishment: the Ragged Ass Saloon. Scruffy and defiant, squatting right next to the water, it was one of those places that make a virtue out of not trying too hard to seduce or impress. There was a deck off one side, packed with people who appeared to be eating as well as drinking. Compared to the last place we'd passed, with its ominous warning of NO FOOD—as though the act of eating was somehow the sworn enemy of a truly good time—this was a beacon of hospitality. My hopes of finding incredible local seafood quickly evaporated, though, when I realized that *what* they were eating looked suspiciously like tortilla chips and deep-fried jalapeño poppers. It occurred to me that maybe the last thing people who fish for a living wanted to see staring up at them from their plates at the end of the day was fish. That was logical—more logical, for example, than our clueless hike into Saint James City at dinnertime. We couldn't escape the fact that the Ragged Ass Saloon wasn't the kind of place Mr. Rogers would have chosen to bring *his* family, but we were desperate and running out of options. Our girls were hungry. The Ragged Ass Saloon had food. And cold beer—a bonus after that nerve-racking trip through gator country. We nodded at each other and found a parking space for our stroller, close to the door and right next to a Harley.

Predictably enough, hungry, tired, hyperactive toddlers don't make up the usual clientele at ye olde Ragged Ass. As Caramia bolted for the deck and the waiting open water, Olivia zipped out the other door to play in traffic. Herding them back to our table with promises of lemonade, a shamefully meager bribe, Mark and I searched for something to entertain them. We'd forgotten to bring our own crayons and somehow knew better than to ask our waitress if there might be a box of Crayolas on the premises. The girls refused to be entranced by the old singing salt-and-pepper-shaker routine, and roared in protest when, out of desperation, Mark and I wrestled each of them into a loving headlock. Having had months and months of practice in ignoring the dirty looks of strangers when our children misbehaved, pretending to be invisible at our table by the window was no trouble at all. By the time our pizza arrived, we had our own ideas about why the place was called the Ragged Ass.

After a meal that rowdy and out of control, it was almost a relief to resume being stalked by invisible alligators and gobbled half to death by vampire mosquitoes on the walk back to the campground. Fed, tired, and secure in the knowledge that they'd come one step closer to giving both of their parents a bleeding ulcer, the girls were quiet in their stroller at last. Unperturbed by the murky darkness that had swallowed us whole, Mark pushed them with one hand, humming to himself in a satisfied Pooh Bear sort of way. And I kept a wary eye on the underbrush, ready to bolt at the first glimpse or any sign of a ravenous reptilian snout. Which explains why I stepped on a roadkill armadillo before I saw it. Never doubt that the cost of vigilance can be mighty stiff, as stiff as an old sunbaked, crunchy, leathery, dead armadillo.

My next encounter with Margie at the KOA front desk proved equally unsatisfying. I'd gotten it into my head that, despite our plentiful electricity, running water, and cable TV, we were roughing it, by golly, and needed to start building campfires to sing around and toast s'mores on. In the spirit of authentic outdoor adventure, I offered to make the lonesome twenty-yard trek to the campground store to buy a bundle of firewood.

"We don't sell firewood, dear. There are no fires allowed," Margie cheerfully informed me.

"We can't have a campfire? But this is a campground. Camping is done here. Campers have campfires," I politely protested. No point in attacking Margie. She seemed like an awfully nice lady who had somehow gotten stuck with sharing all of Pine Island's bad news.

"Mmm-hmm," she agreed sadly. "Fires *do* have a way of getting out of control, don't you know. You wouldn't want to burn everything up, would you? No fires. Fires are just not allowed."

Mark was incredulous when I reported this latest development. "Are you kidding me? We can't have a fire?"

"No. No fires."

"We're on an island without a beach, at a campground where you're not allowed to have a fire? Unbelievable."

Here we go, I thought. Here's the moment of truth. Here comes Mr. Cranky-'n'-Irritable with his favorite lecture: "*You and your crazy ideas and your Hallmark movie moments and look where it's gotten us and blah blah blah.*" There was a long pause during which neither of us said anything. Olivia absently scratched at her mosquito bites and picked dandelions in the weeds just beyond our door. Caramia had toddled one campsite over and was trying to steal seashells out of a neighbor's bucket. I was torn between stopping her and hoping she just wouldn't get caught. On beachless Pine Island, a seashell was a rare and valuable commodity. What kind of harsh campground justice would our darling baby face for filching a conch shell?

Mark rubbed his eyes. "All right, well, then I guess we can't have a fire. Maybe we can have one at the campground in Ocala. No big deal, right? Who wants to go to the pool?"

Later that night, as Olivia hacked and our trailer shook, I studied Mark as he slept and wondered, Who is this stranger in my bed? Had aliens seized the real Mark and left me with this Ray Romano–inspired imposter? It was as good an explanation as any. The real Mark wouldn't have a minute's patience for any of this nonsense, from living in the Geico Tiny House to being forced to spend hours rumbling along the interstate in what amounted to a clattering tin shack. He craved action, speed, danger. Instead, he was trapped in one of the slowest vehicles on the road by day, and surrounded on all sides by mellow retirees at night.

The closest Mark got to a surge of adrenaline was letting me drive long enough so that he could use the bathroom. There, swaying as I inevitably gave the wheel another panicky jerk, he took on the challenge of peeing without hitting himself or the floor. At those moments, he had the thrill of feeling as though his very life depended on zipping up and getting me out of the driver's seat. It was a poor man's extreme sport, but it was all Mark had.

If an alien personality transplant wasn't the reason for my husband's newly agreeable outlook, what was? An answer came to me the next morning as we made our slow way through Fort Myers and Punta Gorda, heading north toward Ocala and Gainesville. It was Stockholm syndrome. Like any hostage deprived of contact with the outside world, Mark had come to identify and sympathize with his captor: me. After a year of being hammered with my warped Hollywood-style approach to happiness and family togetherness, he now believed in it. He was in so deep that he even considered these ideas to be his own. In fact, this whole jaunt in the RV *was* his idea, wasn't it? Staring out the window at the rolling countryside bordering I-75, I pondered two things. First, was it morally wrong to take your own spouse hostage and ultimately brainwash them if the end result made the whole family happier? And second, who knew there were so many cows in the state of Florida?

Before making camp at our final destination, the Ocala KOA, we paid a visit to Silver Springs. Silver Springs is like an amusement park, but instead of gravity-defying rides, it offers sedate cruises on glass-bottomed boats, a zoo, and various animal shows, ranging from tropical birds to alligators. If the pace at a typical amusement park is crackhead meets espresso, then Silver Springs is more like Valium meets your mother after her knee replacement. It's a wonderful place, gentle and sweet, a fading old beauty in a part of the world better known for frenzied, wallet-grabbing, high-concept theme park entertainment. Because we arrived on an overcast weekday, Silver Springs was almost completely ours. We wasted no time making our presence felt.

Both of our girls tried to jump out of the glass-bottomed boat— at the same time. You'd be surprised at how little small children care for natural wonders. Pure water bubbling up from the mysterious depths of the earth is all well and good, but if Nemo isn't swimming in it, then forget it. No interest. They did enjoy the zoo, but many of the animals seemed to be sleeping, whereas Olivia apparently hoped they might break into song. We got lucky at the bear exhibit when two of the three bears waded into their boulder-strewn swimming hole and started bitch-slapping the daylights out of each other. There were seven or eight children gathered for this spectacle, and every last one of them burst into enthusiastic applause. And when one bear finally ran out of patience and began ferociously gnawing on the other bear's face, the preschool audience went totally wild. Kids are nothing but bloodthirsty little savages when you get right down to it.

Our last stop of the day was the petting zoo. I had high hopes for this, imagining the many endearing Kodak moments awaiting us in a pen full of sheep and baby goats. We paused at the giraffe enclosure when we learned that, for a dollar, you were allowed to feed the giraffe a big cracker. Olivia flatly refused to put her hand anywhere near the giraffe's mouth, so we gave the cracker to Caramia and hoisted her as high into the air as we could. The creature craned its neck and unfurled a garden hose of a tongue, gently lifting the cracker right out of the baby's fist. She shrank back in horror, although whether from the sight of the giraffe or from its extremely pungent smell I can't say. And neither could she, limited as she was by a vocabulary of about a dozen words.

A high wooden privacy fence surrounded the actual petting part of the petting zoo. As we approached, the gate flew open and two women and three kids rushed out. "I wouldn't go in there if I were you!" one of the women panted. "Those sheep are dangerous! They butted the children and chased them! They're not friendly. You'll be sorry when they scare your little girls."

We thanked them for the warning, but there was no turning back. If Olivia didn't get into that pen to pet a sheep, we'd hear about it for the next five hundred miles. Assault and battery at the hooves of an angry sheep would be less painful than that—and quicker, too. We pushed open the gate and entered a large ring, with a dusty bare earth floor and a few forlorn racks of hay scattered here and there. The animals looked at us curiously, and a few slowly began to approach. To our left was a roped-off area with a sign reading: "Animal Time-Out—Please do not enter this area or disturb the animals while they are resting in here." If they had a keeper, that person was nowhere to be seen. The place was silent. Our girls stared at the beasts, roughly a dozen sheep and a handful of goats, and the beasts stared back. It was like a barnyard version of *High Noon*. Then Olivia and Caramia took off running.

"Come here, you sheep, and let me pet you!" Olivia bellowed, thundering toward them in her flashing light-up Hello Kitty sandals.

"Baa baa!" Caramia hollered, stomping after her sister.

Going as pale as sheep can, the whole lot of them hesitated for a second and then bolted as one into animal time-out. Once in, they refused to budge, huddling together while the girls hung outside the ropes and babbled at them. They would not be cajoled or enticed into stepping forward. It was a standoff, us against them, humans versus sheep, and neither side wanted to blink first. After five minutes or so, even Olivia lost interest in begging, and we headed for the exit. Not two minutes after we'd left the enclosure, I peeked in. The fleecy cowards had slunk out of time-out and were milling about in a tight cluster, obviously waiting for their next victims. "Who's the big, brave killer sheep now?" I taunted them. "Yeah, that's right. I'm talking to you, Woolly! Ha-ha!" That I saw nothing wrong with picking a fight with a pack of farm animals was clearly a sign that we'd been on the road for too long. Time to make camp and call it a night.

Conveniently snuggled up right next to the interstate, the Ocala KOA didn't pussyfoot around with a bunch of silly rules. Fires weren't just permitted; they were encouraged. All you had to do was hand over seven bucks and within minutes a grinning silver-haired dude in a golf cart would appear at your campsite to deliver the wood. Not wanting to spoil the kids with too much luxury, however, Mark and I insisted that they join us to hunt for kindling. We prowled around under the trees, looking for twigs and pinecones. Our fellow campers were the usual suspects: a few tents, a couple of pricey, maxed-out rigs, and a scattering of homesteaders who'd made their patch of ground a little more permanent by laying stone walkways, hanging twinkling lights, and planting decorative flags. We waved to a family that had gathered around a big-screen TV perched on a picnic table, and smiled at a man taking a miniature poodle for a walk. In front of us, the girls bent to pick up sticks, their faces filthy, something gooey matted in their hair. Olivia's nose was runny; Caramia sported an overscratched, festering mosquito bite on one leg.

"We have grubby campground babies," I observed.

"They have grubby campground parents," Mark replied. "What do you want to do about dinner?"

The novelty of cooking in a space measuring approximately thirty-six square inches had rapidly worn off. Keeping the girls away from an open flame long enough to scramble an egg or whip up a batch of pancakes wasn't easy. They wanted to "help," and if they couldn't help, they wanted to cry, and when crying got boring, they wanted to stealthily open the door, bolt into the road, and get kidnapped. You'd think that two adults could wrangle two kids in a space no bigger than a minivan. We thought so, too. But our daughters were like mercury: beautiful, slippery, and deadly if mishandled. If breakfast was tricky to pull off, dinner was nearly impossible—especially given the limited number of foods both kids would reliably eat. Trying to boil water for pasta on a gas burner positioned only a few perilous inches above the baby's bed was such a heart-stopping ordeal that I'd sooner eat a bowl of twigs than repeat it. Mark and I had also experimented with grilling on a portable propane grill, impulsively purchased for forty bucks at the KOA store on Pine Island. This led to a tense hour spent laboring over a slab of beef that arrived at the table simultaneously burned *and* undercooked– and tasting weirdly of gas to boot. Worse, I managed to singe my eyelashes in the process, and probably got West Nile virus from the kamikaze mosquitoes.

"Look, there's no way we're pushing a baby stroller down the freeway and risking our lives for dinner at the Cracker Barrel," I said. "That leaves us with a menu of Cheerios, peanut butter, and sliced ham. Don't you wish we could just call and have a pizza delivered?"

"Maybe we can," Mark answered.

"Yeah, right. Who ever heard of delivering a pizza to a bunch of tents?"

"They delivered firewood," Mark reminded me.

"That was the old dude who runs this place. You think he's got a pizza oven in that golf cart, too?"

An hour later, as our campfire hissed and crackled, Mark uncorked a bottle of red and carefully filled a plastic tumbler for each of us. After spraying down the girls with enough insect repellent to possibly render them sterile later in life, I halfheartedly wiped the grime off of our campsite picnic table and laid it with our best paper plates and napkins. Golf Cart Man had nodded when we inquired about pizza, disappeared for a moment, and then returned with a phone number written on a napkin. Clearly, he was the guy to know at the Ocala KOA. Now a red Honda Accord chugged past us and then reversed to a halt. "Pizza for number thirty-eight?" The driver took in the wine and the fire, the flames casting a lurid glow on the shot of the Grand Canyon decorating our rented camper. "Nice setup you got here. That'll be eighteen sixty-four. Cash only, no checks."

Having blown most of our cash on trinkets at Silver Springs and firewood at the KOA, Mark and I had to scramble to come up with enough for a tip. Emptying my pockets of change, I thought fondly of the rows of suddenly useless credit cards tucked neatly in my wallet. In the cash-only campground economy, we were like shipwrecked sailors: water, water everywhere and nary a drop to drink. While I fished out quarters and dimes and Mark explained our plight to the pizza guy, he glanced doubtfully at our dirty kids and nearly empty wine bottle. "Yeah, well, thanks. You folks have a good night!" he said, and trotted back to his car.

It was there, in front of a smoky fire, in the shadow of a six-lane highway, beneath a canopy of scrubby Florida pines, that I finally understood the secret of happiness. All my life I thought that happiness was what arrived on your doorstep once you'd checked off every last item on your personal to-do list. I thought it was a reward, a destination that could be mapped, a transcendental state that could be achieved with hard work and a bit of good fortune. I took my cues about happiness directly from the Founding Fathers: I *pursued* it, like a hound pursues a fox. And like the hound, all I did was run myself into the ground, exhausted, while the fox always stayed ten paces ahead. What I didn't understand was that happiness isn't a target or a goal or a blissful state of being that magically descends when all of the right buttons are pushed. There are too many sorrowful things in a life, too many missed opportunities, too much lousy bad luck, for any of us to risk sitting around and waiting for a miracle to transform us. Happiness isn't a prize to be won. Happiness is a habit, plain and simple.

If my family had been plunked down into this very scene—camping trailer, interstate, bugs—one year earlier, we would have been *miserable*. Mark would have hated being made to live in what was essentially a moving van with a toilet. I would have hated being grimy and frazzled and sleep-deprived and unable to use my credit cards. We would have quarreled and blamed each other for every discomfort and inconvenience. A year earlier, we were both still jockeying for control and playing the resentment game when our wishes weren't fulfilled or our minds weren't instantly read. We had the rings and the family, but what we hadn't yet figured out was the marriage. How do two completely separate beings join their dreams and their days and their families without making a total mess of it? And who gets to decide whose way is right?

When I set out to transform our little band into the world's happiest sitcom family, I had no inkling of just how crazy that truly was, not to mention how selfish. Looking back, I can hardly believe I had the idea, much less the energy, to attempt something so quixotic and insane. Yet here Mark and I were, in a place we never knew existed, eating gritty pizza and watching our daughters lick bits of charred marshmallow off of foraged sticks. And after more than a year of seizing every possible moment, spending every last nickel, and schlepping from one silly spot to the next, we *weren't* beaten down and exhausted. We were happy. The *real* kind of happy, the happy that comes from appreciating what it is you've been given, for what little time it might be yours. The kind of happy that means no matter where in the world you happen to land, you're home.

When we began, I knew I was in it alone. My husband didn't share my vision—he thought I needed a shrink. If having such an idealized TV-type family was so important to me, then I had to be ready to put in the work and willing to make all of the first moves. No sulking or pouting when he didn't come along peacefully. No silent treatment when he opted to be less than a good sport. No martyr act when my efforts went unnoticed or unappreciated. If I wanted more romance, then I had to be more romantic. More family outings on the weekends? I scheduled them. From picnics to pony rides, I never waited for anyone else to deliver. I made it a point to act like a better wife, more affectionate and more interested in the baffling intricacies of my mate's beloved bicycles and motorcycles and cars. I worried less about how our house looked, less about what kind of meals we ate, and less—much less—about my career. Instead of fretting over all of the things I couldn't control, I focused on joy. And somehow, while I wasn't looking, and had no idea to expect it, it became a habit. For both of us.

Perhaps wiser folk could save themselves a lot of money and trouble by skipping the journey from city, to cornfield, to campground and figuring out in the comfort of their air-conditioned houses that happiness is a habit, like any other, and more addictive than most. Sadly, we weren't that wise. The hard way is the only way I've ever learned anything. It took me a year-plus, buckets of antibiotics, barrels of gasoline, hours of lost sleep, miles of trekking and trudging, and countless forced smiles to realize that the only way to get everything you want is to give everything you have. I had to learn how to give, and I had to learn how to let others give, too. It wasn't an original insight—more like Buddha crossed with Dr. Phil—but it changed my life and, ultimately, the life of my family.

I'm writing this in a kitchen that's still a cluttered-up disaster. Olivia just turned four and is celebrating with infected and inflamed adenoids that leave her congested, dripping, and snoring like a wino. She's scheduled for surgery in a week. Caramia not only has double conjunctivitis—that's oozing pinkeye times two—but is cutting her two-year molars with all of the good-natured grace of an angry grizzly bear. Eric, now twelve but not exactly a teenager, is already showing signs of barely tolerating our mortifying company; the next six years should be a rollicking good time for all. The dog, out of blindness or dementia or both, daily collides with the walls and wets his own bed. As a clan, we're still as loud and disorganized and buried beneath endless piles of bills and junk mail and dirty laundry as we ever were. In other words, nothing has changed—and yet everything has.

There's no such thing as a perfect family. They make it look easy on TV because they can always rewind the tape, erase their mistakes, and start over. They never have more than an hour to fill, and there are plenty of people waiting in the wings to clean up the mess. I used to think how great it would be if life worked that way. No hassles, no aggravation, no apologies. That was before I figured out that the real fun of real life isn't waiting to be found in the biggest or flashiest or most spectacular places but in the small, quiet, mundane moments that disappear when you're not looking. Those are the things that can't be scripted or bought. They can only be seen and felt and remembered. And, if you're lucky, shared.

That night in Ocala, after Mark and I had sponged the girls down as best we could with baby wipes and tucked them into their makeshift beds, we returned to the fire. Staring down at the ring of shimmering coals, neither of us spoke for a long time, just sat and listened to the whoosh of passing traffic on I-75.

"Well," Mark sighed, "might as well open another bottle and have a toast." He poured, and we clinked our plastic cups together. "Here's to us. We're still married after being locked up together in a camper. I think that counts as an accomplishment, don't you?"

"I'll drink to that," I replied.

Mark stirred the embers with a long stick. "We should have an agreement. About our marriage."

"An agreement? What do you mean by 'an agreement'?"

"Let's promise that, no matter how bad things get, instead of killing each other like those people on *Forensic Files*, we'll just split up. Okay? So if you ever think you want to murder me, just come tell me, and I'll leave peacefully. And I'll do the same for you. What do you think?"

My husband never looked more handsome than he did at that moment, the firelight flickering on his face, the skin beginning to peel off of his sunburned nose.

"That is the single most romantic thing you've ever said to me," I answered. "It's a deal. I promise not to kill you."

We snuggled by the fire for a while longer, eating raw marshmallows out of the bag and polishing off the last of the wine. Finally, Mark stood up and stretched. Gazing with satisfaction around our disheveled campsite, he began laughing. "I can't believe I'm about to say this, but this has actually been *fun*, hasn't it?"

"It really has," I agreed. "There was just one thing missing: Eric. He would have loved this. We should have pulled him out of school."

Mark answered like the true Mr. Agreeable he'd become.

"Next time. Definitely."

Perfect.